THE CACHE MEMORY BOOK

SECOND EDITION

THE CACHE MEMORY BOOK

SECOND EDITION

JIM HANDY

Academic Press
An Imprint of Elsevier
San Diego   New York   Boston
London   Sydney   Tokyo   Toronto

Permissions may be sought directly from Elsevier's Science and Technology Rights Department in
Oxford, UK. Phone: (44) 1865 843830. Fax: (44) 1865 853333. e-mail: permissions@elsevier.co.uk.
You may also complete your request on-line via the Elsevier homepage: http://www.elsevier.com by
selecting 'Customer Support" and then "Obtaining Permissions".

ACADEMIC PRESS, INC.
An Imprint of Elsevier
1250 Sixth Avenue, San Diego, CA 92101-4311

United Kingdom Edition published by
ACADEMIC PRESS LIMITED
An Imprint of Elsevier
24–28 Oval Road, London NW1 7DX

Library of Congress Cataloging-in-Publication Data

Handy, Jim.
    The cache memory book / Jim Handy.—2nd ed.
      p. cm.
    Includes index.
    ISBN-13: 978-0-12-322980-9 ISBN-10: 0-12-322980-4 (alk.paper)

    1. Cache memory. I. Title.
TK7895.M4H35   1998
004.5'3—dc21

97-35868
CIP

ISBN-13: 978-0-12-322980-9
ISBN-10: 0-12-322980-4
Transferred to Digital Printing 2007
    06 07 08 09 EB 9 8 7 6 5 4 3

Dedication to the First Edition
This book is dedicated to
my wife, Mary Pope-Handy, the love of my life,
who suffered arthritis, asthma, pneumonia, and two kids
in diapers to give me time to write.

Dedication to the Second Edition
I dedicate the second edition, again, to my wife, Mary,
and to my young son Brian, and to my even younger daughter
Clair, all of whom supported my efforts. No man could ask for a finer
and more loving family than ours.

CONTENTS

INTRODUCTION
TO THE SECOND EDITION

Although it's been four years since the publication of the first edition, it's somewhat surprising to see that the basics of cache design have remained largely intact. Although great strides have been made in the number of transistors on the processor chip itself, with the bulk of these going into the cache memory, we find that very small changes have been made to the policies used by the processors' on-chip caches. With the exception of some minor improvements in the complexity of the handling of write cycles, the structures have remained relatively straightforward. Nearly everything that is now being used was covered by the first edition in detail.

So then, why do a second edition? No matter how timelessly they are written, technology books constantly need to be revised, and this one is no exception. Many of the example processors used in the original text are now either obsolete, or promise to become obsolete in the very near future. The first edition contained a complete chapter demonstrating example cache designs which today's designers can implement more elegantly with far fewer chips than they could have at the time of the last publishing. In the introduction to the first edition I said that this chapter "will become outdated much sooner than the others" (and I was more correct than I expected). Furthermore, few of the processors in these examples are used any longer with external cache chips, since their higher speed successors are preferred now for use in high-performance systems. I have, however, elected to retain a single one of these caches, the oldest, incidentally, to illustrate in

Chapter 1 that the gate count for a true-to-life cache design is not all that high, and that cache designs need not be shied away from.

I have also added a new Chapter 5 showing how others have approached certain difficulties they have encountered. It is fun to see how others have found their way around particularly thorny problems, ones you might even encounter yourself. None of these solutions is overly complex, but they show great amounts of ingenuity.

I have added words to the glossary and the text; however, the discipline seems to be moving more and more toward uniformity, probably owing to the greater amount of communications that now are happening between cache designers. As fields become broader, and communications between companies become more frequent and open, company-specific buzzwords give way to more standard ones, and people discover others' buzzwords before deciding that they need to invent a new one of their own.

Finally, as opposed to the cacheless system I used to create the first edition, the second edition is being crafted on a Windows 95 machine using a 133 MHz Pentium with an 8KB primary cache and a 256KB secondary cache. Surprisingly enough, the newer versions of the software I am using to create the revised text and graphics slow things down to the point that there is not all that much difference in speed at the user interface between the new machine and the old.

INTRODUCTION
TO THE FIRST EDITION

Disraeli is said to have observed that "There are three kinds of lies: Lies, damned lies, and statistics!" Readers of this text will have the dubious honor of becoming intimate with the last category, since cache design is an imprecise art, based upon incompletely measured statistical premises which work well with certain software performance benchmarks, and fail for others. Throughout the text, we will try to reassert the dependence of cache performance upon code structure.

This book is directed toward the practicing system design engineer, not the college student. There are no problems at the end of each chapter. The intent is that this book will be used for self-guided study and as a reference source. If you want to learn a particular side of the subject, you can look either in the table of contents or the glossary to the page where that subject is discussed. The book is more a practical "how to" guide than an academic tome in that it takes more of a qualitative than a quantitative approach, an approach which can be justified by the fact that cache performance is highly dependent upon the code and hardware used in the particular system being designed. Most often, I'll assume that the reader is challenged with designing a cache to optimize performance of a system using an existing CPU, and probably an existing bus and existing code. Several unique money-saving and time-saving approaches can be used if the software, the bus, and especially the CPU can be designed for optimal performance with the cache and memory subsystems, but most systems don't fit within this category.

An intuitive, rather than an analytical, approach has been taken, as there is a wide array of papers and theses supporting arguments in favor of almost any cache architecture which may be referred to in addition to this text. The style here is informal, technically detailed, and, hopefully, *readable!* The *last* thing I want to drive you to do is to look something up in your dictionary! You won't find words like "infrastructure" or "paradigm" in this book, and chapter names do not start with words like "On" (i.e., "On Computationally Derived Isoplanar Wavefront Boundary Effects at Material Interfaces").*

Caches are not really all that difficult to understand. Engineers who were required to apply Smith charts in school know how arcane design can be. (From my college days, I have mistrusted all the Smiths I have happened upon.) Cache design, on the other hand, is very straightforward, however obscured it may be with buzzwords. The fundamental principle is that you are required to cheat wherever possible.

I have taught courses which present cache as some new language to be learned. The rationale behind this is that cache designers tend to use a terminology which is unique to their field. You will need to learn this lingo in order to discuss your design philosophy with anybody outside of your design group. Over two hundred fifty buzzwords unique to cache design appear in the glossary at the back of the book. The glossary is cross-referenced to the chapter and section which first defines the word. I have taken pains to assure that every buzzword I know has been clearly discussed. After reading this book, you should be able to understand clearly the difference between a "fully associative write-through primary logical cache" and a "direct-mapped sectored snooping copy-back secondary cache with allocated writes, concurrent line write-back and primary invalidation by inclusion."

A serious disadvantage to both the uniqueness of the cache language and the newness of the technology is that the terminology is in flux, and you will often see the words in the text being used in a completely different sense, or worse yet, a different word being used to describe the same function! Some design communities (i.e., IBM and DEC) tend to employ different buzzwords than most other cache designers. The author was seriously considering naming this book *Buzzwords: A Book of Cache Design.* Cache is not the only field to which this is happening. Several of the author's software-

---

*My wife, a student of theology, recently brought home a paper whose opening sentence reads: "Hermeneutics is sufficiently well-established for the principle of the empty head to be a dead letter." Given that "hermeneutics" is the only buzzword used in this sentence, and all the other words are supposed to be intelligible to all readers, you can understand why I happen to think that some people write with the apparent intent of confusing their audience. I honestly believe that the writer of this offensive prose sweated over the sentence for about the same amount of time as it took me to write this entire book, with the intent of making his work look more impressive.

inclined friends used to refer happily to themselves as "hackers" and to system saboteurs as "pirates" until the press got confused and widely associated the word "hackers" with perpetrators of notorious software crimes. The English language is dynamic, and those at the forefront of technology are doomed to suffer the consequences.

This book pertains only to CPU caches and not to disk caches. The operation principles of either device are similar, but disk caches are often implemented in dynamic RAM (DRAM) using software control, whereas CPU caches operate at such a high speed that hardware control must be used, and the cache itself must be implemented in static RAM. The statistics supporting CPU caches are well developed and pertain to the way code is written. The statistics for disk caches are entirely different, depending on the operating system calls caused by the particular software being run upon the system, and cannot be derived directly from anything presented within this text.

Likewise, most of the mapping algorithms presented within the text are also used within memory-mapping units (MMUs), which, thank goodness, are incorporated within most modern CPUs. If they were not, most system designers would be forced to confront the same problems twice, in two different lights. Some readers may desire to look once again at the specifications for the MMU in their system after having read and understood this text.

NOTE: SOME ASSEMBLY REQUIRED

The cache designer is advised that a good understanding of the code being executed in the system is key to a good cache design. Code will be used in this book to illustrate the underlying phenomena which allow caches to operate. This does not imply any depth to the algorithms being used, but I do assume that the reader will not be baffled by extremely simple assembly code examples used in the text. Wherever possible, designers are encouraged to discuss their designs not only with the other members of their hardware design teams, but with the software designers whose code's performance depends on the performance of the cache design. Those software designers might also be challenged to write code which will cause the cache to operate poorly, not only in the spirit of friendly competition, but also to familiarize themselves with code structures which should be avoided to maximize system performance.

Likewise, I assume the reader to be intimately familiar with the basics of processor interfaces and system buses (at least for one CPU, direct memory access [DMA] devices in general, and one general-purpose backplane). Should this be a problem, there are zillions of publications available from processor manufacturers, system manufacturers, and educational and technical publishers, most of which do an excellent job of curing this disorder.

This book is laid out in five chapters. Chapter 1 is an introduction to cache theory, followed by Chapter 2's overview of cache architecture. Chapter 3 reviews cache needs for RISC CPUs, while Chapter 4 focuses on the problem of coherency and shows tricks which have been used in commercially available machines. The author has taken pains to define succinctly all the terminology which is peculiar to caches today.

The last chapter of the book, which will become outdated much sooner than the others, describes a few real-life examples of discrete cache designs which support commercially available microprocessors. These designs are offered in a very deep level of detail so that they can be picked over, and so that designers might be able to borrow from the examples to design caches of their own.

According to MicroPatent, a New Haven, Connecticut, patent database firm, 96 patents covering cache design were granted in the United States alone during the one-year span from September 1991 to September 1992. Clearly, cache design is a rapidly evolving technology, and, although I have done my level best to be current, this book cannot hope to keep abreast of all new advances. Please overlook any omissions. I hope to have the opportunity to include them in a future edition. Feel free to contact me through the publisher with any criticism or comment which might help amplify or clarify any future version of this book.

A word about the conventions followed in this book is in order. The first incidence of a buzzword is shown in boldface type, and the glossary reference will be to that single use of the word. I have taken pains to assure that the first incidence of any word is accompanied by its definition. Numbers are specified in one of three formats: decimal, hexadecimal, and binary. Decimal numbers are the default, and any decimal number with more than three places of accuracy is separated, using the American convention, with commas (i.e., 1,000). Hexadecimal numbers are used for addresses and are separated into groups of four digits by spaces (i.e., 9ABC DEF0). In the rare instances where binary notation is used, it will be formatted the same as hexadecimal numbers, and the text will explain that binary notation is being used. For the sake of clarity, no other representations will be used (i.e., octal). Abbreviations like 8K and 1 Meg represent the common usage that $8K = 2^{13}$, and 1 Meg = 2^{20}.

A final note of irony: All of the text and graphics of this book were created by the author on Macintosh Plus and Macintosh SE computers, neither of which have cache memories, and neither of which could make good use of caches since they are based around 16 MHz 68000 microprocessors. Yes, some operations, especially the creation of some of the more complex graphics and the repagination of the text, would have been much less frustratingly slow on a machine with a better, faster CPU and a cache.

ACKNOWLEDGMENTS

The author would like to thank all those who gave their own time and effort to the making of this book. This includes the several cache designers who took the time to explain their own work to me during my marketing work at Integrated Device Technology. Thanks also go to Bob Cushman, who saw to it that I was able to spend my time in this pursuit; Dave Wyland, a superb engineer whose desk analogy I have stolen; and Frank Creede, of Logic Innovations in San Diego, a methodological designer who taught me that logic design isn't even half of getting a cache to work reliably. Of course, I owe a debt of great gratitude to the many pioneers of cache design who have documented their work through the academic papers, trade press articles, and patents which I scoured in preparing this book.

Thanks also must go to the readers of my manuscript, who have pointed out both errors and sections which needed clarification. These include Sandeep Agarwal of Sun Microsystems, Inc., Mountain View, CA; Neil Birns of Signetics, Sunnyvale, CA; Ross Harvey of Avalon Computer Systems, Santa Barbara, CA; Kelly Maas of Integrated Device Technology, Santa Clara, CA; Satya Simha of mips Computers (a division of Silicon Graphics, Inc.), Mountain View, CA; Tony Matt of Quickware Engineering and Design, Waltham, MA; and Lisa Thorell of Dataquest, San José, CA.

Thanks also go to those companies who have supported my work through the contribution of useful data. These were Integrated Device Technology, Inc., of Santa Clara, CA; Chips and Technologies, Incorporated, of San José,

CA; Corollary, Inc., of Irvine, CA; and the VME International Trade Association (VITA) of Scottsdale, AZ.

As all authors of technical books say, all errors or omissions are solely my own. If you spot anything which you find erroneous, difficult, or lacking, please let me know through the publisher.

CHAPTER **1**

WHAT IS A CACHE MEMORY?

1.1 CPU SPEED VS. SYSTEM SPEED

The problem is simple. Designers are constantly trying to get the most out of their designs in the most cost-effective means. As faster versions of a particular CPU become available, the designer will often try to improve the throughput of an existing design by simply increasing the CPU clock frequency.

After a certain point, the speed of the system's main memory (sometimes called a **backing store**) becomes the limiting factor in the throughput of the system. This is illustrated in Figure 1.1. The X-axis represents CPU clock frequency, and the Y-axis the overall throughput of the system. For this example, we will maintain that the system is compute-bound; that is, the performance of the system is constrained by the performance of the CPU, rather than by the speed of an input/output (I/O) device (i.e., a disk drive). CPU caches are most important in compute-bound systems, since they serve solely to increase the efficiency of CPU-related operations.

We will also assume that the performance of the system's main memory as seen by the CPU is the same across the range of CPU clock frequencies.

1

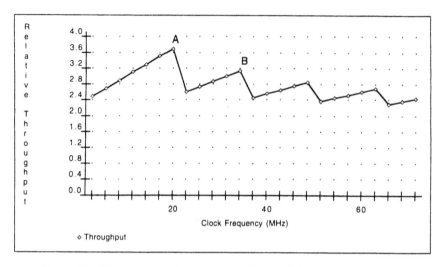

Figure 1.1   Throughput vs. clock frequency of a typical single-processor system.

In other words, if the main memory has an average access time of 60ns, this access time will be the same despite the CPU speed. (The 60ns figure is not a particularly fast speed even at the writing of this text, much less a few years from now. The author asks the reader to insert any appropriate number when the text is read, and anticipates that the problem will remain the same.) The value of the constant main memory access time assumption will be defended in Section 1.2 of this chapter.

At the early part of the chart, throughput increases linearly in proportion to the CPU clock speed, up to the peak at the point labeled A. This is intuitive. Suddenly, there is a drop to a lower level. Why is this? At clock frequencies up to about 20 MHz, the processor is free to run as fast as it can, without wait states from a 60ns main memory. Once the processor requires an access time of less than 60ns, a wait state must be inserted to account for the difference. A single wait state will suffice until the clock frequency requires an access time of less than 60ns, even with the single wait state. This is labeled point B. Once again, the throughput of the system suddenly drops, as it did with the addition of the first wait state. As the graph shows, increases in clock frequency merely take the throughput of the system through a narrow band, indicated by the sawtooth pattern in Figure 1.1, without any hope of improving performance beyond a certain limit set by the memory access time. Even worse is the trend of both the peaks and valleys of the sawtooth graph to decrease as the system clock frequency increases, a phenomenon I'm not sure I can fully explain.

Of course, this problem can be fixed through the use of fast main memory. The only question remaining is what speed of main memory must be used to support the fastest possible operation?

1.2   THE COST OF FAST MAIN MEMORY

Fast main memory is not inexpensive. As a general rule, the difference between the price of a fast memory chip and the next fastest speed grade can range up to 50% or 100%! All this to gain an extra 20% in speed!

If the world were a fair place, a 20% increase in speed on a dynamic RAM (which I'll call a DRAM for the remainder of this book) would support a 20% increase in speed in the CPU. Unfortunately, this is far from what really happens.

Most systems insert some sort of buffer or two between the CPU and the DRAM, and another buffer or two between the DRAM data output and the CPU data input pins (Figure 1.2). These buffers serve not only to increase the small current available from the CPU to drive the address inputs of the many DRAMs in the system, but also to isolate the CPU from the memory during those times when another device must have control of the main memory. Examples of such devices include DRAM refresh circuitry and DMA devices such as small computer system interface (SCSI) ports and disk I/O. The buffers have a fixed propagation delay, that is, the propagation delay of these devices does not decrease with advances in semiconductor processing anywhere near as drastically as does the access time of DRAMs and static RAMs (which we'll call SRAMs from now on), or as fast as microprocessor clock speeds increase.

Other static times are write cycle data and address set-up and hold times (with respect to write pulse edges), which are usually the same for any speed grade of DRAM or SRAM. A typical SRAM might have a write data set-up time of around 5ns, with a hold time of 0ns. The problem here is that, although manufacturers try to reduce these figures in the specifications of their faster parts, the improvements are far from proportional to any improvements in read access time. As a result, a larger and larger proportion of the overall CPU clock cycle time gets consumed by these static times. In a shrinking clock period, once these static set-up and hold times are removed, the time left for a memory access must shrink far faster than the clock period in order to satisfy the needs of the CPU.

Figure 1.3 shows the relationship between the clock frequency of an uncached processor system and the access time required of a memory subsystem in order to support zero-wait read cycles on that system. For this example, the system of Figure 1.2 was used, based on a 386 processor since this

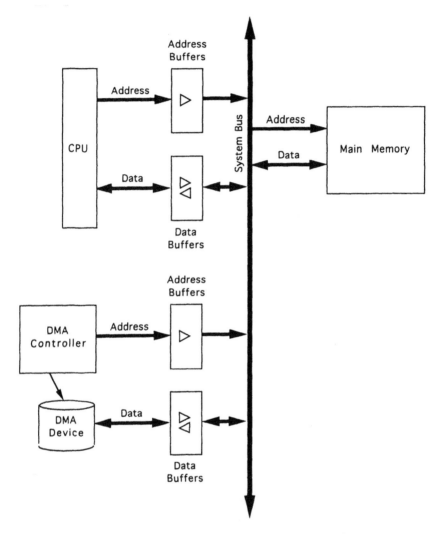

Figure 1.2. A typical processor system, with processor, main memory, a direct memory access (DMA) device, and the buffers required to allow the DMA and processor to gain alternate access to the main memory.

processor does not have an internal cache, with all buffers offering a 5ns propagation delay, and no other delays in the system such as those caused by pin capacitance or PC board loading (these will be spelled out in detail in Chapter 2, Section 2.5). To be fair, I've included both modes of operation for the 386, pipelined and nonpipelined. For either case, the trend

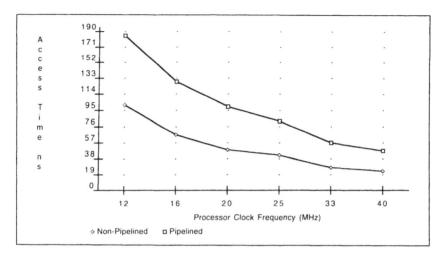

Figure 1.3.   This graph shows the access time of a zero-wait-state main memory plotted as a function of the clock cycle time of the CPU for the system of Figure 1.2. The slope of the curve is very steep, showing how the speed of the main memory required in order to support increases in processor speed outpaces the speed increases of dynamic RAMs brought about by advancing both the CPU and the DRAM to the same process technology.

asymptotically approaches a 0ns access time, but the timing for pipelined operation reaches zero at a higher clock frequency.

1.3   THE CONCEPT OF LOCALITY

We are all very practical designers. When asked to design a system which performs to a certain target specification, we try to achieve the specification for the lowest reasonable cost. The arguments presented in the preceding two sections would seem to indicate that it would become prohibitively expensive to design a system which took advantage of the fastest CPU speeds available today.

This is where statistics come to the rescue. Back in the 1960s, researchers at IBM discovered that nearly all code was extremely repetitive in nature, a fact which can be used to the advantage of computer throughput. If anything repetitive can be stored in a small, very high-speed memory, then the effect of wait states can be limited only to the less repetitive portions of the program which can be stored in slower, less expensive memory.

What portion of a program is repetitive? This question is answered by the principle of **locality,** both spatial (locality in space) and temporal (locality in time).

1.3.1   Locality in Space

Locality in space, spatial locality, or **locality of reference** are terms for the phenomenon that most computer code executes out of a small area repetitively. This space is not necessarily in a single address range of main memory, but may be spread around quite significantly.

For the sake of illustration, an assembly code program is shown in Figure 1.4. This program is not written in any sort of rigorous manner, but should be adequate to show the general idea of locality in space. The program is a much simplified version of the kind of code which is found in all comput-

```
ADDRESS      LABEL     INSTRUCTION           COMMENT

0000 1000    START:    LOAD   SP,#F000 0007  ;Load stack pointer with a value
                                             ;which will assure a stack thrash.

0000 1004              LOAD   R1,#0000 0063  ;Set up loop counter to loop 99 times
                                             ;(63 hexadecimal).

0000 1008    LOOP:     JSR    SUB1           ;Jump to a subroutine with a
                                             ;thrashable address.

0000 100C              DJNZ   R1,LOOP        ;Repeat the above process 99 times
                                             ;before proceeding.

0000 1010              BLAH                  ;Continue this program

0000 1014              BLAH

0000 1018              BLAH
;********************************************************************
;*                                                                 *
;* The following is the subroutine called by the main program shown above  *
;*                                                                 *
;********************************************************************

0001 1008    SUB1:     LOAD   R2,(R1+#1000)  ;Get a character pointed to by
                                             ;R1+1000 hex

0001 100C              CMP    R2,"A"         ;Is the character an upper-case A?

0001 1010              JNZ    SKIP           ;No. Leave the character as-is

0001 1014              LOAD   R2,"z"         ;Yes. Change it to a lower-case z.

0001 1018              STORE  (R1+#1000),R2

0001 101C    SKIP:     RETURN               ;Return to calling routine.
```

Figure 1.4. An example piece of assembly code to demonstrate locality.

ers. First, a loop is used to look through a 99-character string stored in memory. Second, a subroutine contains a piece of code which might be useful to other parts of the main program. During the entry and exit of the subroutine, the stack is used to temporarily store and retrieve the calling routine's program counter. The function of this piece of code is to scan a string for an uppercase letter "A" and to change all such occurrences within that string into a lowercase "z."

The first perfectly obvious fact is that the code is written so that the same set of instructions, mostly those within the subroutine, is used repeatedly while the processor is running through the loop. The principle of spatial locality refers to the fact that the calling routine, the subroutine, and the stack space all exist in three very narrow areas starting at the three addresses 0000 0008, 0000 1000, and 0001 1008.

1.3.2   Locality in Time

The second principle of locality, **locality in time, temporal locality,** or **time of reference,** refers simply to the fact that the instructions in this example execute in close sequence with each other, rather than being spread through time. A processor is much more likely to need to access a memory location which it accessed ten cycles ago than one which it accessed ten thousand cycles ago (which is only 0.12 milliseconds on a 166 MHz Pentium). This appears awfully obvious, but without locality in time and in space, caches would not be able to work.

Combining both spatial and temporal locality, it is simple to state that the program in the example will spend a while executing the same few instructions 99 times before moving to another piece of code which will probably also be repeated. If the reader were to look at a real program, a much longer one than the example used here, repetitive sequences of a similar size to this would be found to lie within repetitive loops which were much larger, which in turn would lie within even larger loops, ad infinitum.

It would be a good idea to take advantage of both temporal and spatial locality by assuring that the repetitive portion of the program executes from a very fast memory while it is being used and resides in slower, less expensive memory when it is waiting to be used. At first glance, the most obvious way to achieve this is to divide the memory space into both faster and slower sections and have the operating system copy portions of code from the slower portions into the faster portion as required. This is exactly how a virtual memory system works, with the slower memory being the mass (magnetic) media and the faster portion being the main memory or DRAM. An alternative is to have a small, fast memory in addition to a full complement of slower main memory and to use specialized hardware to assure that the currently useful parts of main memory are copied into the small, fast memory. This is what we call a **cache memory.**

The software-based technique is excellent, inexpensive, and works well for memory mapping, but it is not used for cache management for two good reasons. First, cost considerations usually force caches to be very small, and mapping memory spaces into and out of the cache via software would consume too much time at frequent intervals, thus offsetting the speed gain of the cache. (Typically, a piece of software at least the size of our example loop in Figure 1.4 would be needed to move the example loop into the fast memory, and a small, fast memory would need to have its contents replaced relatively often.) Second, most caches are designed to accelerate already existing systems where the operating system and other software cannot be reconfigured to support a memory which is split into faster and slower portions. Software in such systems must be kept unaware that the cache even exists. All existing programs must run similarly, although faster, on cached systems. A cache which achieves this end is called a **software transparent** cache.

1.4   FOOLING THE CPU

What seems to make sense, then, is to design a memory controller which will move data back and forth between slow and fast memory in hardware, leading the CPU to believe that the same address is being accessed at any time, only sometimes that location accesses faster than other times. Although fooling the CPU like this sounds tricky, it is not. Once the reader gets over the basic concept, simple cache designs become almost trivial.

I like to use an analogy which a colleague once made to me, of a clerk's desk next to a phenomenal number of filing cabinets, possibly at an uncomputerized credit bureau (see Figure 1.5). The clerk's mundane job is to answer the telephone and read items from a credit applicant's file in response to the caller's queries. The files are stored by the applicant's telephone number (we'll use the U.S. style of a seven-digit number for the sake of this argument). In a typical day, the clerk will answer 50 to 100 calls and will get up from the desk and search the files 50 to 100 times. However, since the same credit applicant may have applied for a loan on the same day or two at five or ten banks, several of these calls will be for the same data as was requested in a prior call either that day or a few days before. (Astute readers will note that this analogy uses temporal locality, but ignores spatial locality.)

Now let's assume that the clerk is very clever and sees that there is an unused file drawer in the kneehole of the desk. Why not keep copies in the desk's file drawer of those files which are currently in high demand? The photocopy machine is close to the filing cabinets, so making an extra copy to take back to the desk is no problem. But who knows which files will be requested repeatedly and which will be requested only once? Being unable to predict the future, the clerk will simply make a copy of every document which is pulled from the file.

This starts off very easily. When a file is requested, the clerk puts a copy of it into the desk's file drawer and makes a note of the fact that it is in the drawer on a sheet of paper hung upon the wall. This sheet of paper is the directory to the desk's file drawer. When answering the phone, the clerk first looks at the directory to determine whether or not a copy of the requested file resides in the desk's file drawer. If it does, the clerk need not get up, but can save time and effort simply by pulling that file from the drawer. The directory also lists where a certain piece of information may be found within the file drawer. On those occasions when a copy of the file is not in the file drawer, the clerk will get up, copy the file from the filing cabinet bank, and add it to the drawer, making a note to that effect on the directory.

Everything works very well until the file drawer gets full. What then? Being very practical, the clerk decides to put the date and time of the last access to a directory entry alongside of that entry. When a new file is put into the desk's file drawer, the directory entry with the oldest date and time will be erased, the file will be discarded, and the new file and directory entry will be put in its place. (In another interesting analogy, Intel once likened the same problem to that of a shopper who went to the supermarket for some items, but preferred to store often-used items in the refrigerator at home.)

This is the concept behind cache memory design. The massive bank of filing cabinets represents the system's main memory, and the clerk is the CPU. The desk's file drawer is called the **cache data memory** or **data RAM,** and the directory is aptly called the **cache directory.** The exact implementation just described is rarely used, since the hardware requirements are more expensive than some very good alternatives. Several tricks are used in exact cache implementations, and a considerable amount of this book will be devoted to those tricks.

There are four fundamental parts of a cache memory, all shown in Figure 1.6. The cache data memory is the small, fast memory which is used to store replicas of instructions and data which could be accessed more slowly from main memory. When the size of the cache is discussed, the **cache size** is equal to the number of bytes in the cache data memory alone. The directory is not included in this number. The cache directory is a list of the main memory addresses of the data stored in corresponding locations of the cache data memory (i.e., if data in a certain cache data location comes from main memory address 0000 0000, then the cache directory would contain a representation of 0000 0000). So with each cache location, not only is data

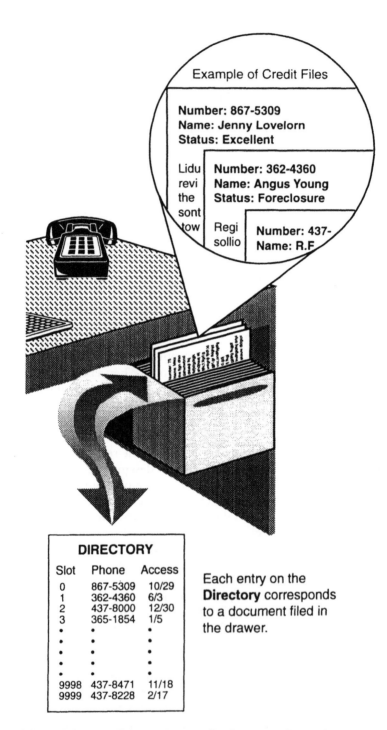

Example of Credit Files

Number: 867-5309
Name: Jenny Lovelorn
Status: Excellent

Number: 362-4360
Name: Angus Young
Status: Foreclosure

Number: 437-
Name: R.F

DIRECTORY

Slot	Phone	Access
0	867-5309	10/29
1	362-4360	6/3
2	437-8000	12/30
3	365-1854	1/5
•	•	•
•	•	•
•	•	•
•	•	•
•	•	•
9998	437-8471	11/18
9999	437-8228	2/17

Each entry on the **Directory** corresponds to a document filed in the drawer.

Figure 1.5. A clerk at a credit bureau is responsible for giving callers credit reports from a bank of 250 filing cabinets, representing the entire set of telephone numbers within an area code.

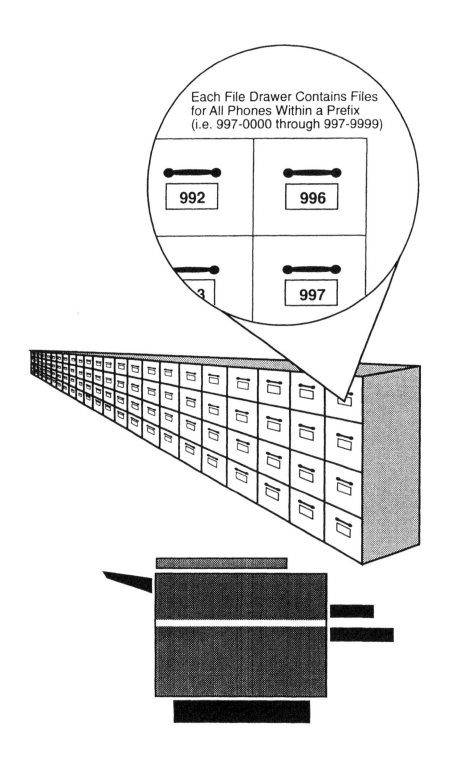

Each File Drawer Contains Files for All Phones Within a Prefix (i.e. 997-0000 through 997-9999)

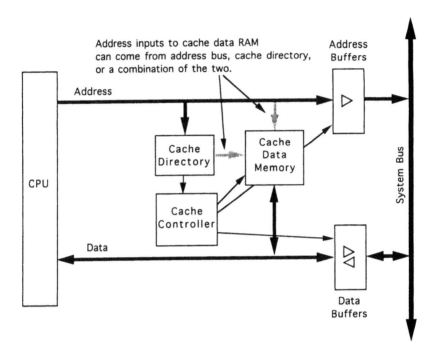

Figure 1.6. The cache memory consists of a directory, a cache data memory, buffers (to isolate the cache subsystem from the system bus), and the cache controller.

stored, but so is an address, making the combined directory and data RAMs behave like a single, very wide memory.

The bus buffers serve a very important function, even though they are basically the same chips which would have been used in the noncached system shown in Figure 1.2. These buffers are now controlled in such a way that if the cache can supply a copy of a main memory location (this is called a **cache hit**), then the main memory is not allowed to put its data onto the CPU's data pins. In many cache designs, the address is never even sent to the main memory unless the cache has indicated that it does not contain a replica of the data requested by the CPU (a **cache miss** or sometimes **fault**). So during all cache hit cycles, the CPU converses with the cache, and in all cache misses, the CPU converses with main memory. The data bus between the CPU, the cache data RAM, and the system bus buffers is sometimes referred to as the cache's **data path.**

Tying the whole system together is the cache's control logic, which is called the **cache controller** or **cache management logic.** It is this logic which implements the algorithm which moves data into and out of the cache data memory and the cache directory. This is the crux of cache designs, and the cache logic embodies the implementation of some hotly debated decisions called the cache **strategy**. When a strategy is decided upon and implemented, it becomes the cache's **policies**. Policies will be evaluated in some detail in Chapter 2. The control logic also determines when to turn the buss buffers on and off and when to read from and write to the cache data RAM. In some systems, the system bus interface is sufficiently complex that the system bus side of the cache controller is subdivided into its own portion of the cache control logic, in which case it may be called the **storage control element (SCE)**.

Cache size and policies both affect the **hit rate** of the cache (the percent of CPU cycles which are cache hits). The **miss rate,** conversely, is the remaining percentage of CPU cycles. Throughput of a cached system can be computed based upon the average number of wait states per bus transaction. This number equals the miss rate times the average number of wait states on the system bus (plus the hit rate times the cache latency, if the cache requires the use of wait states).

As an example, let us assume that all system bus accesses take three wait states, and the cache responds in zero wait states. With a cache memory offering a 90% hit rate (an easily achieved number), the average number of wait states for the cached system would be $10\% \cdot 3 = 0.3$ wait states per memory cycle. Fractional wait states are perfectly valid in this sort of calculation, since this is an average between wait state and zero-wait cycles. The same system with a much smaller cache might exhibit a typical hit rate of only 80%, and the average number of wait states would be double that of the larger cache, or 0.6 wait states. The jump in throughput is even more pronounced if DRAMs with slower cycle times are used, requiring even more wait states per bus cycle. An interesting way of looking at this is to expand the problem to see where all the system clock cycles are consumed. Let's say we have a processor whose average zero-wait instruction execution time is two cycles, and cache misses execute with three wait states for a total of $3 + 2 = 5$ cycles. Ten instructions in the system with an 80% hit rate cache would consume $10 \cdot 0.8 \cdot 2 + 10 \cdot (1 - 0.8) \cdot (2 + 3) = 26$ cycles, only 16 of which would execute from the cache. In other words, $10/26$ or almost 40% of the time the CPU would be attempting to get through 20% of the instructions. This also means that the bus will be in use 40% of the time, the implications of which we will examine in Section 1.8.

The process of cacheing follows a certain pattern. At power-on, the cache contains random data and is disallowed from responding to a request from the CPU. When the processor reads data from a main memory location, the cache data RAM is ordered to copy that location's contents, while the corresponding cache directory location is told to copy the address requested by the CPU. This same sequence would occur for any further cycles until a loop was encountered. Once the processor reached the end of the loop, it would again output the address of the first location, which in all probability would still be in the cache data memory. This time, however, the data from that location would be supplied to the processor from the cache, rather than from the main memory, as would the rest of the instructions in the loop. It becomes pretty obvious how much of a help this would be. In our example program, the instructions in the loop would operate at main memory speeds only during the first go-round, then would subsequently execute much faster from cache for the next 98 times through the loop/

This covers cached read cycles. What happens during write cycles depends greatly upon the cache policies chosen, and will be examined in depth in Chapter 2.

From the CPU's perspective, the data always comes from main memory, although at some times it arrives faster than at other times.

1.5   CACHE DATA AND CACHE-TAG MEMORIES

So we now know how simple it is to reroute the CPU's main memory request to be satisfied by the cache, but the design of the cache directory and cache data memories has yet to be explained. These might be pretty intimidating to the first-timer. The choice of directory architecture has a strong impact upon the design of the cache data memory, so the directory will be investigated first.

Certain college-level courses explain that the cache directory consists of a content addressable memory of **CAM.** This is a directory type which corresponds well to our example of the clerk in the credit bureau. A CAM is a backwards memory which outputs an address when data is presented to certain inputs. The address shows where a matching entry has been found within the CAM. All CAM locations are examined simultaneously for matching data, and if a match is found, its address is placed upon the address output pins. This is particularly useful when a 32-bit processor address needs to be converted to a much smaller cache address. The 32-bit processor address is presented to the data input pins of the CAM, and a shorter address pops out of the address output pins. In truth, CAMs are almost never used to implement cache designs, but they facilitate the explanation of a cache directory, so we'll examine CAMs here first, then see what the alternatives are.

One big question that comes out of this is "what is a CAM?" A CAM is made of a series of address registers, each of which contains a comparator which compares the address contained within the register to the address currently on the compare address bus (see Figure 1.7). This is achieved by

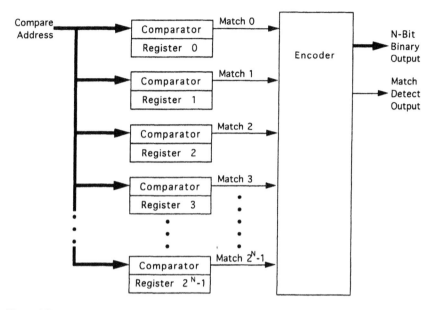

Figure 1.7.   In a content addressable memory (CAM), an address presented to the compare address bus is compared simultaneously with the contents of every memory location. If there is a match at any location, the address of that location is sent to the N-bit binary output pins.

having a separate comparator attached to each and every address register. Although this sounds like a lot of hardware, it can actually be manufactured relatively easily in silicon by using a specialized, seven-transistor, static RAM cell which is less than twice as complex as the industry's standard four-transistor cell. The comparator outputs are encoded by a simple priority encoder into a binary representation of the address of the matching entry. During a write cycle, both an address and data are presented to the CAM, and a write pulse is generated. During a read cycle, however, data is input to the CAM, and an address is output. The output address is the address of the CAM location which contains matching data. If no data match is found, a no-match signal is output from the CAM.

The reader might ask "Why aren't CAMs widely available?" The simple reason is that much simpler schemes perform nearly as well as the CAM approach, yet can be constructed from standard static RAMs and allow the use of less expensive cache data RAMs. These alternate approaches will be discussed here briefly and in depth in Chapter 2. Cache designers are not ready to pay as much for CAMs as CAMs would have to cost to attract the interest of semiconductor manufacturers. The author knows of only two kinds of CAMs available on the market today. The first is a mature product, an ECL

4×4 bit device which would have been designed into mainframe caches before faster (70ns) static RAMs became available. The other is a device designed specifically for LAN address filters, which requires a 48-bit compare
address to be input in three multiplexed chunks over a relatively long period of time (i.e., 100ns).

Back to the example: Let's assume that the system has just been initialized
and that no cache locations contain valid copies of main memory locations.
Where in the cache should we put the first location accessed by the processor? Some processors seek their first instruction after a reset from the first
main memory address, or address zero. Other processors start off at the top
of the memory space (FFFF FFFF). Yet others seek a vector at one of these
two addresses, then jump to the address pointed to by that vector.

If the cache directory is a CAM, then *any* main memory address can be
mapped into *any* directory location. This approach is called **fully associative,**
a term which simply means that any main memory address has the full freedom to be replicated anywhere within the cache. The method employed to
determine which cache location should be used to store a copy of a main
memory address is referred to as **mapping,** or **hashing.** (A fully associative
approach is just one of many hashing algorithms which we will examine in
this book.) An appropriate (hopefully unused) directory location would
have to be assigned whenever something was to be put into the cache. The
cache controller does this by assigning an address representing the directory
location to be used to store the incoming data. This address is fed into both
the CAM and the cache data memory while the main memory is being accessed. The data contained at the address of the main memory access
(which is a completely independent value from the directory address just
mentioned) is then written as data into the directory while the main memory data is both fed into the CPU and written into the cache data RAM (see
Figure 1.8). Later, when the processor's address again matches the address
stored in the CAM, the CAM outputs the address of the cache data RAM location which contains matching data. This address is fed into the cache data
RAM, which consists of a standard static RAM, and the data from that addressed location becomes available to the CPU.

Partly due to the lack of availability of large CAMs, several ingenious alternatives to the CAM approach have been devised. These alternatives also
tend to be significantly less complex than the CAM approach. Returning to
the file clerk analogy, let's put together an organizing system which will take
advantage of the fact that the desk drawer is the same size as any of the drawers in any of the filing cabinets. The phone numbers used are all seven digits long and follow the format 867-5309. Furthermore, let's say that the filing cabinets are arranged so that each drawer represents a prefix (the first
three digits of the telephone number), and each is capable of carrying the

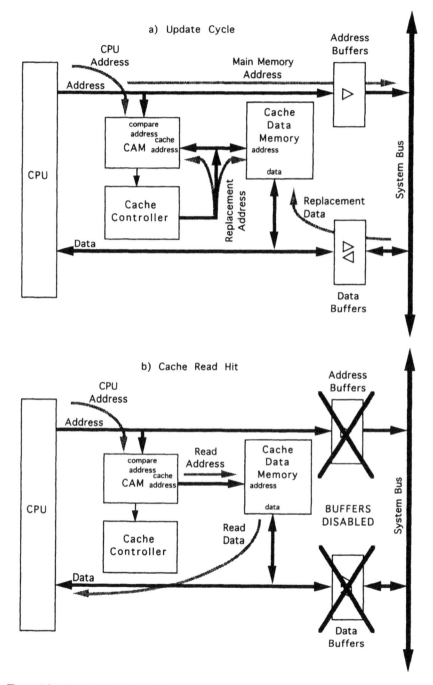

Figure 1.8. During the update of an entry in a fully associative cache (a), the cache controller feeds the address which is to be replaced into both the CAM and the cache data memory. When there is a cache hit (b), the CAM outputs this address to the cache data memory, causing its data to be fed into the CPU.

files for all 10,000 numbers or credit applicants within that prefix (from -0000 to -9999). So the first drawer would have numbers 000-0000 through 000-9999 and so forth. The clerk could also arrange the desk drawer into 10,000 slots, so that each slot would only be allowed to contain a file whose suffix (last four digits) matched the slot number; in other words, the number 867-5309 would only be allowed to be placed within desk drawer slot 5309. The directory would still be a paper on the wall containing 10,000 entries describing the phone numbers of the data stored in each of the desk drawer slots; however, each entry would be at a location which matched the suffix of the phone number, so only the prefix would need to be written into the directory (so for the number 867-5309, the prefix 867 would be written onto line 5309). Furthermore, the clerk would no longer have to choose where to put a new cache entry, so the directory entries would no longer need to contain the time of their last access. This is the most popular hashing algorithm in today's cache designs and is called **set associative,** since, for the sake of clarity, the last four digits of the telephone number have been named the cache's set address, and within any set the entry is associative (can have any prefix).

With this new method, the clerk can begin to look into the desk drawer while at the same time looking up the entry in the directory. There is no longer a need to cross-reference the directory to determine which desk drawer location contains the file. If the prefix (867) at the correct set address (5309) matches the one being requested by the caller, then the clerk will pull the file from desk drawer slot 5309 almost instantly. In a set-associative design, the address which is output from the processor is split into the equivalent of a prefix and a suffix at a location determined by the size and architecture of the cache. The lower address bits, those corresponding to the suffix or last four digits of the telephone number in the example, are called the **set** bits since they contain the set address. Some call these the **index** bits, but this terminology is in direct conflict with the terminology used in virtual memory translation, so, in the interests of clarity, it will not be used in this text. The remaining (upper) bits are compared against the directory entry for the selected set and are referred to as the **tag** bits.

You may recall a statement I made when first describing the clerk analogy, that this analogy does not account for spatial locality. This is easy to see, because the clerk might at any time receive calls for absolutely any file, representing any telephone number, in any order. Computer code never runs in such a random fashion, but tends to be full of loops and repetition, and whenever the program counter is not jumping around on a loop or a subroutine call, code will execute sequentially. The set-associative approach takes advantage of this spatial locality by placing sequential instructions not at entirely random cache locations, but at sequential locations. As just illustrated, the set-associative cache does not allow a main memory location to be mapped into any cache address, but instead the cache is constrained so that the lower address bits of the cache location must match the lower address bits of the matching main memory address. Since the processor will be running through a small group of sequential addresses, this looks as if it should pose no problem, and the set-associative cache should run every bit as efficiently as the more complex fully associative design. We will see otherwise in Section 1.6.

An earlier paragraph stated that a fully associative cache (one with a CAM) would require the use of more expensive cache data RAMs than a set-associative cache. Why? In a fully associative cache, all address bits are filtered through the directory before being fed to the cache data RAM. This means that during the cached CPU's fastest cycle, a cache read hit, the processor address must first travel through the directory CAM and be translated into a cache address, then that address must be passed through the cache data RAM before the read data can be made available to the CPU (see Figure 1.9a). This means that the delay between the processor's address output and the data returning from the cache is at least equal to the combined propagation delays of the CAM and the RAM. Thus, if data needs to be returned to the processor within, say, 30ns, then that 30ns must be divided between the CAM and the RAM. Today's 150 MHz microprocessors require this transaction to occur in less than 20ns. A system with an 8ns CAM (good luck!) and an 8ns cache data RAM would be hard-pressed to use any logic in this critical path.

The set-associative cache reduces this CAM plus RAM delay into a single RAM access. In Figure 1.9b, the CPU address is shown to run directly to both the cache directory and to the cache data RAM. For the sake of simplicity, the design shown uses a cache directory which is made of the same depth of standard static RAM as is the cache data RAM. (Alternatives to this will be explained in painful depth in Chapter 2.) Let's assume that the cache is 8,128 (8K) locations deep, requiring 13 address bits to be fully accessed. The lower 13 CPU address bits are then routed to both the cache directory and the cache data RAMs simultaneously. While the cache data RAM finds its replica of the data stored at a main memory location with matching lower address bits (but goodness knows which upper address bits), the directory looks at a replica of the upper address bits stored at the location with the same lower address bits. This is pretty confusing, but, based on the desk analogy, just remember that the last four digits of the telephone number 867-5309 are 5309, so slot 5309 is accessed in the file drawer. The directory then must tell us whether there is a match between the stored prefix (867) or whether some other prefix's number (984-5309) is being accessed. To settle the delay issue, though, notice that during the processor cycle time, the

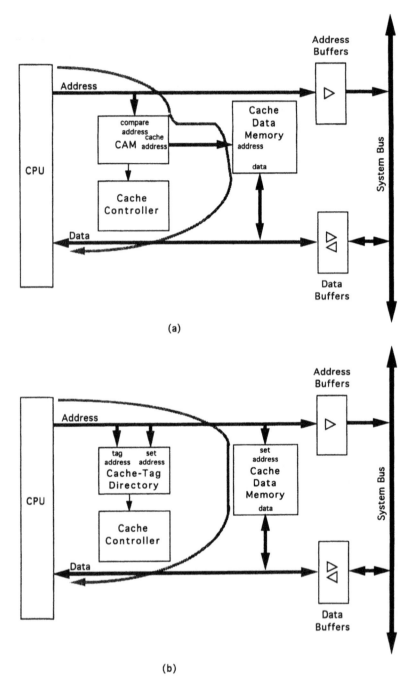

Figure 1.9. The critical speed path, from CPU address out to data in, runs through both the CAM and the cache data memory in fully associative cache designs (a). Set-associative caches (b) allow the CPU address to be fed directly to the cache data memory without going through any other devices.

cache directory and the cache data RAM are being examined *simultaneously*, with the output of the cache directory being used simply to tell the CPU whether to proceed at full speed (a hit) or to wait while a main memory access is used to fetch the data which was requested by the CPU but did not reside within the cache.

The directory in a set-associative cache is considerably simpler than that of a fully associative cache. The fully associative cache's directory not only had to keep track of whether or not there was a valid entry for a main memory location contained within the cache (a fact which has not yet been described, but will be in Chapter 2), but also had to track where that entry resides in the cache data RAM, while the set-associative directory must only look to see whether the cache entry with the same set bits as the CPU's output address came from the location which has the same tag bits, and whether that location is valid. This is a simple comparison. Does or does not the tag at location 5309 match 867 for the phone number 867-5309, and is the location valid? Obviously, the tag comparison can be performed using exclusive ORs feeding into an AND gate, the function of a simple address comparator chip (Figure 1.10). Validity is equally as simple and will also be described in depth in Chapter 2. Set-associative caches assume (until told otherwise) during a processor read cycle that the data in the cache is what the processor is requesting. The cache data RAM starts the read cycle with its data outputs turned on, and its address pins will be tied directly to the processor's less significant address output pins (see Figure 1.9b). The cache-tag RAM, meanwhile, is looking up the address' more significant bits to see if the cache entry is from the correct address. If there is a match between the requested address and the address of the cached copy of the main memory data, then the cache controller gives the processor a Ready signal to accept the data from the cache data RAM and allows things to continue as they are. If the cache contains data at the same set address which is from a different part of main memory (i.e., the tag bits don't match), then the cache controller declares to the processor that a cache miss occurred by not asserting the Ready input, then reads main memory data into the cache, allowing the CPU to continue as the main memory data and address are being written into the CPU. The cache data RAM in a set-associative cache need only have an access time of slightly less than the processor's minimum address to data cycle. The cache-tag RAM would have a similarly slow access time, less the delays needed for the comparator and the downstream logic. Slower static RAMs are usually much less expensive than faster ones, so the designer can save a lot of money by going with a set-associative design. Some static RAM manufacturers provide products which have a comparator contained within a standard SRAM. This provides the same function at a certain advantage in speed, component count, and complexity of the downstream logic. Whether

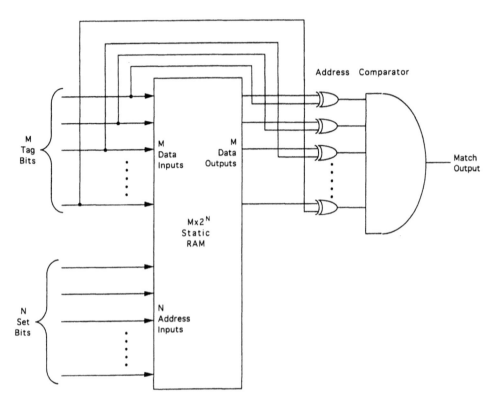

Figure 1.10. In a cache-tag RAM, the stored data at a certain RAM address (addressed by the set bits of the address bus) is compared against the upper address bits, or tag bits of the address bus. This comparison is performed with a simple address comparator consisting of exclusive OR gates feeding into an AND.

the directory is made from a simple RAM with a separate comparator or with a chip which includes both, the directory in a set-associative cache is called the **cache-tag** memory simply because it is where the address tags are stored. There are a few other terms for a cache-tag RAM, notably **tag RAM,** and **cache address comparator, address comparator, cache comparator,** or simply **comparator.**

1.6   THRASHING: GETTING THE MOST OUT OF THE CACHE

The entire argument in the preceding section ignored a phenomenon called **thrashing.** When a cache thrashes, a commonly used location is displaced by another commonly used location. Every time the CPU can't find what it needs within the cache, it must perform a main memory access at the slower speed of main memory. This makes these accesses at least as slow as they would have been had there been no cache.

Say the processor must examine two addresses in close sequence which contain the same set bits. How can this happen? There are several ways. First, most code is constructed out of calling routines and subroutines. There is a reasonable possibility that some of the code in the subroutine will have the same set bits as the code in the calling routine, since the calling routine may be nowhere near the subroutine. This is especially true for small caches which have fewer set bits, which makes the odds of a conflict higher. Next, consider what happens when a subroutine is called. The program counter and possibly lots of other registers are pushed onto the stack. Where is the stack? What are the possibilities that the stack's set bits match the set bits of some of the code in the calling routine and the subroutine? Another place where the set bits might get confused is when the program uses a pointer, say, to move a block of values or to examine a text string. Last, think of what happens when an interrupt is serviced. Will the interrupt's service routine (or some subroutine called by that service routine) have set bits which match the set bits of a calling routine address? Any of these scenarios can cause the cache to thrash.

For an example, let's reexamine the piece of code shown in Figure 1.4. Three addresses have the last three digits of 008 hexadecimal: the beginning of the loop in the calling routine, the stack pointer, and the beginning of the subroutine. If our cache uses these three last digits as a set address, or uses a subset of these three digits, then the cache will thrash. The next paragraph and the diagram in Figure 1.11 will illustrate this in detail. The stack pointer is a kind of "gotcha" in this instance, since it causes the CPU to overwrite other items in the cache. I'm pointing this out, because a lot of designers tend to forget that instructions which push and pop items perform reads and writes that you have to think about in order to remember. It is macho for a cache designer to always know where the stack pointer is, especially under a multitasking operating system.

First, the cache loads address 0000 1000, the "load stack pointer" instruction. This gets put into cache location 000, and at tag location 000 the tag address 0000 1 is written. All this happens at main memory cycle times, so the cache does not accelerate this particular cycle. Similarly, the next two instructions are loaded at main memory access times into cache addresses 004 and 008, and the tags for these two newly cached copies of these instructions are also filled with 0000 1 at tag addresses 004 and 008. The instruction at location 0000 1008 is a "jump to subroutine" (JSR), so the program counter is pushed onto the stack at stack location F000 0008, and, in

1) BEFORE OPERATION OF ROUTINE

Set Address	Cache Tag	Cache Data
000	?	?
004	?	?
008	?	?
00C	?	?
010	?	?
014	?	?

2) ADDRESS 0000 1000: LOAD STACK POINTER

Set Address	Cache Tag	Cache Data
000	0000 1	LOAD SP, #F000 0008
004	?	?
008	?	?
00C	?	?
010	?	?
014	?	?

3) ADDRESS 0000 1004: LOAD REGISTER 1

Set Address	Cache Tag	Cache Data
000	0000 1	LOAD SP, #F000 0008
004	0000 1	LOAD R1, #0000 0063
008	?	?
00C	?	?
010	?	?
014	?	?

Figure 1.11. The contents of a set-associative cache during execution of the code shown in Figure 1.4. Note that location 008 never retains the cache data long enough to offer any speed advantage.

this example cache design, will immediately overwrite the stored instruction from memory address 0000 1008 (the JSR instruction), once again at the slower speed of a main memory access. Upon entering the subroutine, the first instruction of the subroutine is fetched from address 0001 1008, once again at a main memory access time, and immediately replaces the newly cached copy of the program counter stored at cache location 008. When the return instruction is encountered, the pushed program counter is restored not from cache, but from main memory, since it was bounced out

4) ADDRESS 0000 1008: JUMP TO SUBROUTINE

Set Address	Cache Tag	Cache Data
000	0000 1	LOAD SP, #F000 0008
004	0000 1	LOAD R1, #0000 0063
008	0000 1	JSR SUB1
00C	?	?
010	?	?
014	?	?

5) CONTINUATION OF JUMP TO SUBROUTINE: PUSH PROGRAM COUNTER

Set Address	Cache Tag	Cache Data
000	0000 1	LOAD SP, #F000 0008
004	0000 1	LOAD R1, #0000 0063
008	F000 0	0000 100C (PC Value)
00C	?	?
010	?	?
014	?	?

6) FIRST SUBROUTINE INSTRUCTION, ADDRESS 0001 1008: LOAD REGISTER 2

Set Address	Cache Tag	Cache Data
000	0000 1	LOAD SP, #F000 0008
004	0000 1	LOAD R1, #0000 0063
008	0001 1	LOAD R2, (R1+#1000)
00C	?	?
010	?	?
014	?	?

Figure 1.11.   (*continued*)

of the cache by the first instruction of the subroutine. No cache speed advantage is realized for this stack address. Finally, the calling loop is reentered, and the JSR instruction from address 0000 1008 is again fetched from main memory, instead of cache, once again at a slower main memory cycle time. This whole process of the three items continually replacing each other in the cache is repeated 99 times. Obviously, locations with the lower address bits matching 008 have not benefited at all from the use of cache!

The main point of this illustration is to show that thrashing is commonplace in small caches, but fades in importance in larger caches, as the number of set bits increases, causing the likelihood of confusion between the set

7) AFTER LAST SUBROUTINE INSTRUCTION, POP PROGRAM COUNTER

Set Address	Cache Tag	Cache Data
000	0000 1	LOAD SP, #F000 0008
004	0000 1	LOAD R1, #0000 0063
008	**F000 0**	**0000 100C (PC Value)**
00C	0001 1	CMP R2, "A"
010	0001 1	JNZ SKIP
014	0001 1	LOAD R2, "z"

8) CALLING ROUTINE ADDRESS 0000 100C: LOOP BACK TO 0000 1008

Set Address	Cache Tag	Cache Data
000	0000 1	LOAD SP, #F000 0008
004	0000 1	LOAD R1, #0000 0063
008	F000 0	0000 100C (PC Value)
00C	**0000 1**	**DJNZ R1, LOOP**
010	0001 1	JNZ SKIP
014	0001 1	LOAD R2, "z"

9) REPEAT ADDRESS 0000 1008: JUMP TO SUBROUTINE

Set Address	Cache Tag	Cache Data
000	0000 1	LOAD SP, #F000 0008
004	0000 1	LOAD R1, #0000 0063
008	**0000 1**	**JSR SUB1**
00C	0000 1	DJNZ R1, LOOP
010	0001 1	JNZ SKIP
014	0001 1	LOAD R2, "z"

Figure 1.11. (*continued*)

bits of one address and another to decrease. You might want to consider the two extreme arguments to this. How likely is thrashing in a system with only a single set bit (the least significant bit of the address)? How likely would thrashing be in a system with as many set bits as the CPU had address outputs (the cache is as large as the largest possible main memory)? The second point is that thrashing is a phenomenon of set-associative caches, where cache lines are overwritten based on their set bits rather than on some more reasonable algorithm. A fully associative cache would have handled the problem just illustrated as easily as it would have conducted a transaction with no match between any address bits. In Chapter 2, we will examine cache architectures which fall between the set-associative and the fully associative models.

Another buzzword relating to thrashing is the **compulsory miss.** Some cache misses will occur no matter how good the cache design is, simply because the cache is being asked to provide data which it had no reason to have previously contained. Since there is no way to avoid such misses, they are called compulsory misses. Thrashing never causes compulsory misses. Just like most of the buzzwords in this book, though, there are some alternatives to the nomenclature compulsory miss, namely, **stationary miss** and **nonconflict miss.**

1.7 CACHES AND THE MEMORY HIERARCHY

Memory **hierarchy** or **storage hierarchy** refers to the distinct stages in the memory's price per bit, size, and performance. The most expensive memory in a computer consists of the registers within the processor itself. These devices are designed to perform extremely quickly, and their structure allows one register to be written to at the same time that one or more different registers is being read. That structure consumes several transistors per bit, and the cost as well as the speed are related to the number of transistors required by each bit. Access to the registers is via on-chip buses, so the access time for register data is not hampered by any requirements for the signals to go off chip. Most processors have only a few registers, or a few tens of registers, and these registers are the width of the data path within the chip. Register access times are usually under 2ns.

In most noncached systems, the next level of memory is the main memory. This is usually made out of dynamic RAMs (DRAMs) which have an access time several times as long as the access time of the registers. Dynamic RAMs are made using a single transistor per bit, with a small percentage of additional transistors required for the support circuits. The structure of a DRAM makes it the cheapest possible form of semiconductor memory. In contemporary microprocessor-based systems, a typical DRAM main memory might be somewhere between 16 and 512 megabytes. Access times to main memory today consume in the order of 70ns.

The next two levels are comprised of rotating media. Magnetic disk is usually used to store whatever is not capable of residing within main memory. Today's hard magnetic disks exhibit access times in the tens of milliseconds and contain from hundreds to thousands of megabytes. Hard disks are often backed up with removable media, which is often either tape or diskette. Either of these is significantly less expensive than hard disk, but both have access times of several seconds. Since this level is removable, the size is limited only by the user's desire to keep an inventory of tapes or diskettes.

Cache memory fits between the first and second levels of the description. Several microprocessors today contain an internal cache which is made of standard static RAM bits. Unlike registers, these locations cannot be written to and read from simultaneously, so certain operations will perform more slowly in on-chip cache than they would using internal registers. A register bit may require ten or more transistors to implement, whereas the SRAM cell used in the internal cache can be made of cells containing between four and six transistors per bit. Since the microprocessor is manufactured using the same chip, the on-chip cache is limited in size, mostly to keep the processor's cost from going through the roof. Die costs are not proportional to die size, but increase at more than a second-order rate. On-chip cache shares the advantage of not requiring an off-chip access at the expense of access time, so they are pretty fast. Today's microprocessors usually contain caches of between 8 and 64K bytes.

External caches are used both in systems which have and do not have on-chip caches. The external cache which is connected to an uncached processor serves to accelerate main memory accesses, as has just been explained. Such caches usually range from 256K bytes to 16M bytes and are made using economical SRAM chips constructed of four-transistor-per-bit memory cells. The cache's access time is around 3 to 15ns. If the processor has an on-chip cache, any external caches used will usually be implemented with architectures which differ considerably from the architecture of the on-chip cache, both to reduce costs and to make up for some of the deficiencies of the on-chip cache. These design issues will be examined in Chapter 2.

Table 1.1 shows in dollar magnitudes and bandwidth a typical memory hierarchy for a high-performance cached system, whose processor uses an on-chip cache.

Table 1.1. Memory hierarchy, and relative costs and typical sizes of each level.

Memory Type	Typical Size (bytes)	Cost per Megabyte ($)	Bandwidth (megabyte/sec)
Registers	10^1	10^5	500
On-chip cache	10^4	10^4	300
Off-chip cache	10^5	10^1	100
Main memory	10^7	10^0	50
Hard disk	10^8	10^{-1}	15
Magnetic tape	Infinite	10^{-2}	1

Source: Dataquest 1997.

1.8 REDUCING BUS TRAFFIC

One reason for adding a cache to a system has not yet been mentioned in this chapter: Multiprocessors can take advantage of cache memories to improve the effective **bus bandwidth** into their main memories. Bus bandwidth, also called **bus traffic** or simply **traffic,** is a measure in bytes per second of the maximum speed at which data can be moved around on the bus (bus transactions). For example, a bus with a word width of 16 data bits (2 bytes) which can transfer up to 8 million words per second would have a bandwidth of $2 \cdot 8 = 16$ megabytes per second. The percentage of the bus' bandwidth which is consumed by a processor is called **utilization.** (Similar to main memory bandwidth, the cache to CPU interface has its own bandwidth, which is called the **cache bandwidth.** If the cache bandwidth is lower than that needed by the CPU, the CPU must be slowed down, through either the use of a lower clock frequency or the addition of wait states.)

We will soon see that the use of cache memories to reduce a processor's main memory bandwidth needs is a very important benefit and should become much more important in the near future with the growing acceptance of multiprocessor architectures as a means of dramatically improving system performance. Multiple processors can get into trouble if their utilization approaches 100%, and perform worse than systems with fewer processors once the 100% limit is reached.

There are two kinds of multiprocessor systems, shown in Figure 1.12a and b. The top diagram shows what is called a **loosely coupled** multiprocessor system or a **distributed memory multiprocessor (DMM).** Loosely coupled systems are actually two or more distinct processors, each of which is capable of operating independently of the other(s). In the broadest terms, any two PCs connected via a modem or network could be called a loosely coupled multiprocessor system; however, the term is more often used for more intimately connected systems, perhaps connected via first-in/first-out buffers (FIFOs), dual-port RAMs, or dedicated serial buses. Most such systems have tasks divided well before run time to allow each processor to perform to its peak ability on a dedicated portion of the task. It is not unusual for the processors to be different types altogether (i.e., a digital signal processor and a general-purpose processor).

The type of multiprocessor system we will discuss in depth in this book is called the tightly coupled multiprocessor and is illustrated in Figure 1.12b. In a **tightly coupled** system or **shared memory machine (SMM),** a single main memory is accessed by two or more processors via the system bus. Task allocation is performed by software at run time, offering complete flexibility in the range of application programs which can be run on the machine. Currently, tightly coupled architectures tend to be used in file servers, su-

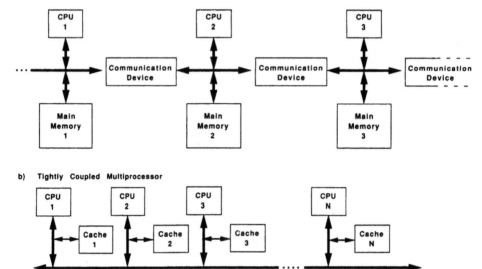

Figure 1.12. (a) A loosely coupled multiprocessing system. Each CPU has its own main memory and system bus. The processors communicate via the communication devices, which are usually accessed through each processor's system bus. (b) A tightly coupled multiprocessing system. All processors (or processor/cache complexes) communicate to a single main memory via a single system bus.

perminicomputers, and mainframes, but current trends indicate that they could become the prevalent architecture of the next century.

The reason that tightly coupled systems need cache is not hard to understand. In a tightly coupled system, each processor has its own cache (Figure 1.12b). The more often the cache is accessed, the less often the processor uses the bus to access main memory. This helps to keep the bus from saturating; that is, utilization is lowered to the point that the bus becomes more available in a timely manner to those processors that need it.

The amount of bus bandwidth required by a cached processor is proportional to the cache's miss rate, so it is not hard to see why designers of multiple-processor systems focus much more attention on miss rates than would the designers of single-processor systems. A designer of a single-processor system might hesitate to spend extra money to improve the hit rate of a cache design from 96% to 98%. The effect on benchmarks would be negligible. In a multiple-processor system, however, the difference between a hit rate of 96% and a hit rate of 98% translates to a difference in miss rates of 4% and 2%, or double. In other words, one design would require half the bandwidth of the other, so half the number of processors could be used in the system before the effects of saturation would be noticed.

Let's take a more graphic approach to examine what happens as processors are added in a multiple-processor system. Our ideal is to get an incremental performance increase proportional to the number of processors added to the system. A five-processor system should perform at or near five times the performance of a single-processor system. For the sake of this argument, let's assume that the processor used in the example uses two cycles per instruction, that all instructions require a single memory access (an unrealistically low number), and that main memory has zero-wait performance. With a single processor, half of the main memory's bandwidth is used, and we can achieve a normalized performance level of 100%. If we add another processor, and if the two processors are interleaved, they will consume the entire bus bandwidth and will perform at 200% of the level of the single-processor system. The addition of a third processor in such a system would add absolutely nothing, since it would not have an interleaf slot, and there is no memory bandwidth remaining to serve the third processor. The performance of this system versus the number of processors is shown in Figure 1.13.

This case is drastically oversimplified, but it serves to set the scene for more realistic problems. Typically, complex instruction-set computers' (CISC) instructions consume a variable number of cycles and use more than one main memory access per instruction. This immediately rules out the effectiveness of interleaving, which requires balance and predictability to be useful. In real-life systems, bus arbitration is used to allow all processors access to the bus as needed. The mere use of an arbitration mechanism slows things down, since the bus must be requested by a processor before it is assigned. This means that the main memory access cannot begin until one arbitration delay after the processor attempts to start the access. The effect of arbitration is that a single processor can no longer perform at the 100% level of the example above and that the addition of processors has a more graceful, if less helpful, effect on the system's overall performance. In Figure 1.14a, we see the operation of an arbitrated multiple-processor system as processors are added. The addition of processors increases the probability of simultaneous arbitration requests, so that the performance increase of added processors is not as dramatic as in the first example, and there is a more gradual rolloff when bus saturation is approached. In such a system, after saturation is reached, the addition of processors actually slows down

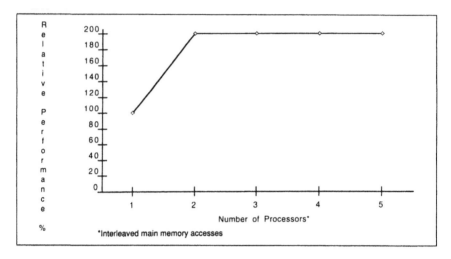

Figure 1.13. Performance vs. number of processors for the interleaved system described in the text. Each processor uses 50% of the available bus bandwidth, and no arbitration is required for either processor. Additional processors will be unable to access the bus, since it will be totally allocated to the two processors.

the entire system. One way of looking at this is that if each added processor requires exactly 20% of the available bus bandwidth (an unrealistically low level), then a six-processor system will require 120% of the available bandwidth and will perform at a 100%/120% level. High-performance processors actually require very close to 100% of the bus bandwidth, so the problem is much worse than this example shows.

We are still using a zero-wait main memory in our example. What happens when we add some realism to this dimension? It is easy to see that we can add a wait state to what is normally a single-cycle main memory access and halve the bus bandwidth, so the 100% number used in the preceding paragraph drops to 50%. Each processor can now operate at only 50%/120% of its potential. The normalized throughput of the six-processor system throughput drops to 6 · 50%/120% or 2.5 times the throughput of a single processor coupled with a zero-wait main memory system. If the per-processor bus utilization is bumped up to a more realistic 80% level, the six-processor system performs at 6 · 50%/480%, resulting in a combined system throughput of only 63% of that of a single, zero-wait processor!

So it appears that in the real world, uncached, tightly coupled multi-processors are not a cost-effective way to improve the throughput of a system. What happens when we add a cache (Figure 1.14b)? Let's go back to the interleaved example. Assume that we have the same zero-wait-state sys-

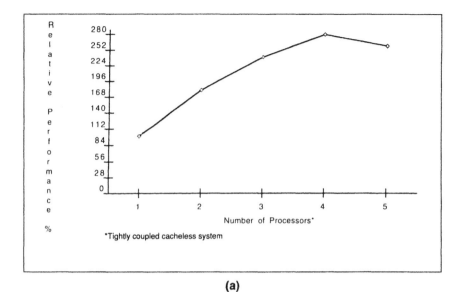

(a)

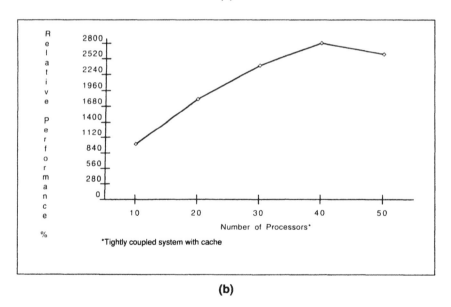

(b)

Figure 1.14.   (a) Performance vs. number of processors for the arbitrated system. As processors are added, the overall system performance increases with diminishing returns, until the system throughput actually begins to degrade with the addition of a CPU. The curve is based on actual performance data for National Semiconductor's 8060 CPU. (b) Performance of a similar system using cached processors. By reducing each processor's bus utilization to 10% of its uncached figure, ten times as many processors can be added before the bus saturates.

tem as in the first example and that each processor has a cache with a very modest 90% overall hit rate, or a miss rate of 10%. Suddenly, the 50% bus usage requirement drops to 10% of 50%, or 5%. This implies that the bus will not now saturate until 20 processors are installed! What a difference! Of course, this is all in a very ideal environment, where the processors only require 50% of the bus bandwidth, and the main memory has no wait states. We have just seen that wait states throw a whole new bent on the statistics, and most processors require their buses more than 80% of the time.

An unfortunate side effect of adding caches to multiple-processor systems is that the designer must now account for all sorts of potential new problems dictated by the possibility that two caches may contain copies of the same data, and these multiple copies don't automatically match each other. This is such a difficult problem that the whole of Chapter 4 is devoted to it! Suffice it to say that the benefits of adding caches to multiple-processor systems are strong enough to warrant the mind-numbing exercise of understanding multiprocessor cache protocols.

An odd twist that I have seen used to reduce bus traffic in multiple-processor systems involves slow caches built of dynamic RAMs. The larger the cache, the lower the miss rate. If traffic is your problem, then the miss rate is your solution. DRAMs give you four times as much memory per dollar as do SRAMs, but they are considerably slower. The designer of this cache was much, much more interested in bus traffic than in the performance of individual processors and thus chose to make a much larger, albeit slower DRAM cache rather than to make a faster SRAM cache.

1.9   REDUCING POWER CONSUMPTION

A new reason to use cache memories has recently surfaced and is the subject of some debate. Some folks contend that cache memories can be added to a low-power system (like a notebook computer), causing the overall power consumption to go down.

Opponents to this viewpoint immediately point out the high power consumption of the fast memories and logic usually used to implement cache designs. How can these be added to a system without increasing power consumption? In addition, they often quote statistics showing that the major power hogs of a notebook computer are the backlight on the flat-panel display and the hard disk drive, which together usually consume over two-thirds of the system's power.

Proponents argue that the cache cuts down on main memory cycles, often allowing them to be nearly equivalent in number to the minimum number of allowable refresh cycles. This in itself reduces the DRAMs' power consumption drastically in comparison to the power consumed when they are accessed for every memory cycle, nearly offsetting the power dissipation of an equal number of SRAMs. Further, if the number of DRAMs which are accessed at any one time is larger than the number of SRAMs which are turned on for the cache, the power consumed will necessarily be lower when the processor operates from cache than when it operates from main memory. Lastly, the fewer wait states incurred by the CPU between its shutdown periods, the lower the CPU's overall power consumption will be.

The jury is not yet in on this one. My own suspicion is that the advantage of a cache as a power-saving device is small if it even exists, and is highly software dependent. Imagine a system manufacturer boasting that the battery life of a certain model was typically three hours running Lotus 1-2-3 but up to five hours running Microsoft Word!

In certain hand-held systems, the processor's internal cache can be used in conjunction with hand-tailored software to reduce power consumption. First of all, software is chopped up to fit into the cache in modules, so that an entire module will reside in the cache when it is needed. When the module is being loaded into the cache, the main memory (sometimes a ROM or other nonvolatile memory) runs at normal power. When the module is being executed within the cache, the main memory need not be powered up, so it is either put into a reduced-power mode, or it is turned off completely. In this way, the power consumption can be reduced through the use of the cache, and if the software is properly tuned to minimize cache accesses, power consumption can be minimized.

1.10 AN EXAMPLE CACHE

Figure 1.15 shows an example cache just to assure you that cache designs are not that difficult. The cache is an old one designed for a 68020, a 32-bit Motorola processor with no on-board cache. The cache is designed using discrete logic rather than programmable logic, which is an advantage to us since it makes the design easy to understand.

Figure 1.15a shows two memory arrays, the cache-tag RAM at the left, and the cache data RAM on the right. With more modern parts the entire cache data RAM could be implemented using only one-quarter of a single 32K×32 SRAM chip. The cache-tag RAM has been implemented with integrated resettable cache-tag SRAM chips, devices which will be explained in detail in Chapter 2. Fundamentally there is little difference between these ICs and standard 8K×8s.

Moving to Figure 1.15b, we see all of the logic required to implement the entire cache. This amounts to six storage elements, 16 two-input gates, and

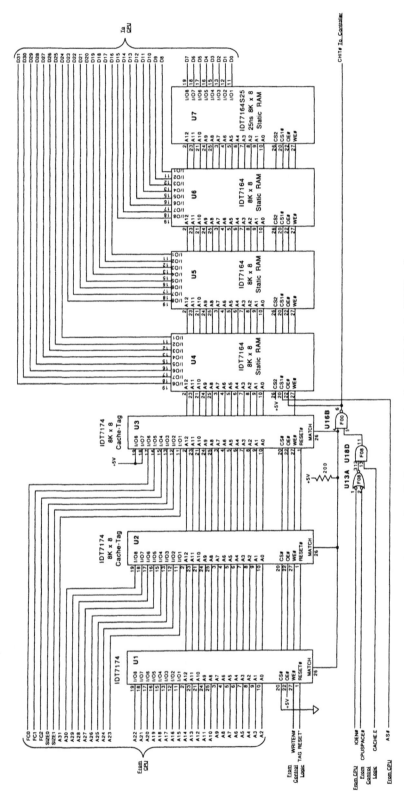

Figure 1.15a. Cache-tag and cache data RAMs for the 68020 cache.

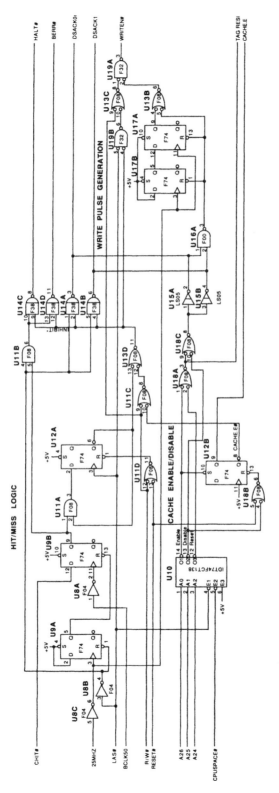

Figure 1.15b. Logic of cache controller for 68020 cache.

five inverters. The address decoder U10 is simply used to map addresses into software cache reset commands. The name of the cache's policies is actually far more intimidating than this handful of logic would lead you to believe. This cache is a direct-mapped write-through unified logical cache. As you can see, there is more to the name than there is to the logic.

Still, don't be led astray by the logic's simplicity! There are many approaches which at first seem quite simple, and require very little logic to implement, but they involve so many interdependencies with the rest of the system that the problem soon dissolves into a mind-numbing exercise, and many designers fail to get their cache designs right the first time. Chips & Technologies was hurt badly by delays in the M/PAX chipset stemming from cache policies, and Intel had shipped millions of Pentium processors before they had all the bugs worked out of their multiprocessing cache protocol.

CHAPTER 2

HOW ARE CACHES DESIGNED?

In this chapter we will examine some of the methodology or "tricks of the trade" used in cache design. Although no especially complex design techniques are used, a substantial amount of thought has been devoted to unmasking the obvious, and the typical designer will end up having to make mental notes about a lot of cache-specific rules of thumb in order to properly perform cache designs.

2.1 THE CPU-TO-MAIN-MEMORY INTERFACE

A CPU cache actually is inserted between the CPU and the system's main memory, as discussed in Chapter 1. Because of this, the interface between the CPU and main memory must be matched by the cache in order for the cache to deceive the CPU into believing that the cache access is actually a main memory access and nothing more.

2.1.1 Why Main Memory Is Too Slow for Modern CPUs

It seems that all portions of the computer system are speeding up simultaneously, so the system designer might very well come to the conclusion that

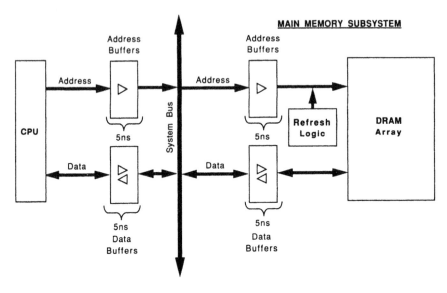

Figure 2.1.   A typical computing system, illustrating the delay paths between the CPU and main memory. In this example system, there is a backplane between the main memory and the CPU.

any increase in CPU clock speed will be matched by an increase in memory speed adequate enough that the system throughput can be increased by 50%, for example, simply by combining a 50% faster main memory and a 50% faster CPU. The same upgrades in semiconductor processing technology which made the processor capable of handling a 50% faster clock rate should be able to produce a like increase in memory speed, so there should be no problem.

The error in this line of thought is that it oversimplifies the problem. Quite obviously, from Figure 2.1, we can see that there are logic elements which isolate the CPU from main memory. Examples of such devices would be the buffers required to isolate the CPU from main memory during DMA accesses or DRAM refresh cycles. Buffers are also necessary in most systems simply because CPUs are not designed to support heavy loading on their output pins. Microprocessor timing and output current are usually specified into loads which are far smaller than the collective input capacitance of ten or more other ICs, so the address output buffers become a necessity.

Now each of these buffers adds a delay, which does not scale very well with the speed increases of the memories or CPUs of a similar semiconductor process technology. A 5ns gate in one technology would do well to lose 0.5 to 1ns by a change to the next generation process. Part of the reason for

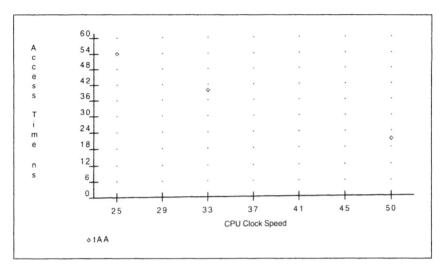

Figure 2.2.   Main memory address access times as a function of CPU clock frequency, as measured at the CPU's address and data pins. Data shown is for the 386 microprocessor.

this is that it takes a finite amount of time just to move an output pin up and down. This action takes around 3ns for TTL I/O levels. As the CPU gets faster, buffer delays consume a larger and larger percentage of the main memory's allowed cycle time.

Other timing which does not scale to process and further compounds the problem consists of specifications like data set-up time and data hold time. Although microprocessor manufacturers will often slightly reduce their products' set-up times for faster speed grades, the reduction is anything but proportional to the change in clock frequency and often runs into a brick wall at the faster CPU clock rates, showing no change between the fastest and the next lower speed grades.

Figure 2.2 illustrates the squeeze put onto main memory speeds by these less flexible parameters. Taken to the absurd, a fast enough processor would require a main memory with a negative access time in order for that processor to run at its fastest throughput. So far, dynamic RAMs have not shown any capability to predict the future.

2.1.2   How the CPU Handles System Bus Delays

Present-day microprocessors nearly all follow a similar bus protocol. **Split transactions** are only used in the most advanced processor interfaces. In a split transaction, the processor issues a command, then removes itself from the bus until a memory or I/O device issues a response. In systems not using a split-transaction protocol, once the address is issued, the processor stays in control of the bus and waits until the transaction is terminated. Should another bus master override this transaction, then the entire process is restarted once the processor regains control of the bus.

Microprocessors use an input signal to determine whether or not the data returned from main memory has settled and is valid. The microprocessor is then allowed to terminate the cycle. The name of this signal varies from processor to processor, but is generally referred to as a Ready signal. We will use the global term "Ready" in this book, even with processors which use a different naming convention.

The Ready input is generated by a device whose response time is set to match the access time of main memory or any other bus device over which the processor has control (i.e., I/O devices). In slower systems, the CPU allows ample time for all devices to respond. This would especially be true of processors running at clock frequencies of 1 to 10 MHz. In systems whose bus devices all respond as fast as the processor requires, the Ready input is often hard-wired to an asserted state, indicating that the data will always be ready in time for the CPU's request. Systems which require the CPU to pace itself to the memory or I/O devices might use monostable multivibrators (one-shots), short shift registers, or counters to generate varying length delays to account for different speed memory or I/O devices (see Figure 2.3). The delay times of these timing generators are triggered by the command from the processor to the memory or I/O device which tells that device to initiate a bus transaction. The timing generator is set to match or exceed the time required by the memory or I/O device to allow the bus transaction to be completed. Highly tuned systems will use one timing generator for each different delay in the system. Less speed-critical applications will use a single timing generator for all response times, and simply set the delay to match the slowest device on the bus.

Should the Ready input respond, when the CPU samples it, that the bus data is not ready, the CPU will wait for a clock cycle, then sample the signal again. All processor output signals are static from the time that the Ready input is expected until the time when it is asserted. Cache designers realize that their systems cannot realistically run without wait states, so they attempt to bring the number of wait states to an absolute minimum for a given processor clock frequency.

2.1.3   The Cache's Interface to the CPU

The cache has to be in control of the CPU. If the cache contains a valid copy of the data requested by the CPU during a CPU read cycle, then the cache

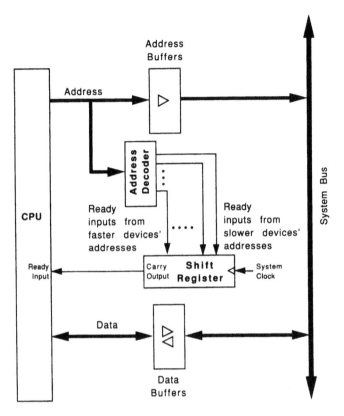

Figure 2.3.   Wait state generation in a typical microprocessor system. Decoded address outputs feed the parallel inputs of a shift register. A Ready signal appears at the CPU input pin after an appropriate number of cycles.

allows the CPU to progress at the cache's speed. If the cache does not contain a copy, then the cache initiates a main memory read cycle, copies the data supplied by the main memory (which the main memory has indicated is valid via a Ready output from the main memory to the CPU), and permits the CPU to continue. Data fed to the CPU is routed by the cache controller from either the cache, in the case of a cache hit, or the buffers which isolate the main memory from the cache/CPU bus, in the case of a cache miss.

The cache must intercept all of the CPU's signals, both inputs and outputs, and determine whether these signals are to be routed to/from main memory or whether they should stay local to the cache. In a way, the cache is an insulating layer between the CPU and the outside world.

There are four basic sorts of cache/CPU interaction, all of which are controlled by the cache controller: read hit, read miss, write hit, and write miss. These are illustrated in Figure 2.4. In a cache read hit, the buffers are turned off to isolate the CPU/cache subsystem from the rest of the computer, and the cache controller generates the Ready signal to the CPU. No interaction is required between the CPU/cache subsystem and the main memory bus, and certain systems take advantage of this by allowing DMA or other devices to control the main memory while the CPU operates out of the cache.

Occasionally, a designer will allow the CPU address to propagate through the address buffers to the bus at the beginning of every cycle, whether the cycle turns out to be a read hit or a read miss. The cache is designed in such a way as to initiate a main memory access at the same time as the cache access, rather than to wait for a cache miss before commencing the main memory access. This approach can shorten the main memory access time in the event of a cache miss and will serve to improve the operation of single-processor, single-tasking systems, but can work to the detriment of multi-tasking systems and multiprocessing systems, since the cache will allow the CPU to waste considerable amounts of main memory bus bandwidth. Such caches can be referred to as **look aside** designs. Since the processor has the option of going to either the cache or main memory at all times to request data, the look aside cache can be an add-on to the computer system.

Caches which place themselves right in the middle of things and intervene in all CPU to main memory transactions are called **look through** or **inline** caches. A look through cache first looks in the cache for the location to be accessed. Only after a miss is detected can the cache trigger the start of a main memory cycle. There is a plus and a minus to this. The plus is that a look through cache dramatically reduces main memory bus traffic. This is really important in systems where other processors must access the main memory bus. The minus is that all main memory accesses due to cache miss cycles are now lengthened by the time it takes to determine that a cache miss has occurred. Fortunately, this doesn't happen very often, and since the cache is designed to respond as quickly as possible, the delay is not large. Still, this is enough of a consideration to have earned its own buzzword, which is **lookup penalty.**

The read miss cycle, where the contents of the directory are found not to match the address being output by the CPU, is handled in just the opposite manner. The cache outputs are turned off, and the address and data buffers are turned on, allowing main memory data to be fed to the CPU. The cache controller's Ready signal is also turned off, and the system's Ready is directed to the CPU instead. As the CPU reads the main memory data, the cache controller commands the cache data RAM to grab a copy, and commands the cache-tag RAM to copy the tag bits of the CPU's address outputs,

thus overwriting any previously existing line of cache data and directory address which previously resided at the same set address. This "read from main
memory/write to cache" cycle is called a **line update, update, copy-in, fetch,
line fill,** or **line replacement** cycle. I'll try to stick with just "line fill" to keep
the confusion to a minimum. (Although we will not define the word "line"
in specific detail until Section 2.2.5, for now we will use the loose definition
that an entry in a cache corresponding to a single set address is a cache
line.) The new data is now available from the cache, where it most probably
will be accessed several more times during subsequent cache hit cycles before it, too, is overwritten. This paragraph describes the major, major concept behind cache memory design, so you don't want to skip ahead if you
feel like it didn't soak in.

Just as there are compulsory misses, as defined in Section 1.6, where
missed data could not have been expected to have previously resided within
the cache, a **compulsory line fill** is a line fill which could not have been
avoided by using a better cache strategy.

Write hit cycles are handled in either of two ways. These are complex
enough to warrant their own section, so a full explanation of these two
strategies is given in Section 2.2.4. In the example in Figure 2.4c, the matching cache line and main memory are both updated with the new data.

Write miss cycles are a free-for-all and are handled in any of a number of
different ways. In caches like the one in Figure 2.4d, write misses are ignored by the cache and are passed directly through to the main memory. In
others, the write data is used to overwrite a line in cache as it is written to
main memory. A third way of handling write misses is to overwrite a line in
cache and to disallow the write cycle from being copied into main memory.
In Section 2.2.4, I will try to justify these and other approaches and show
which fit into which write strategy.

Designers who have wrestled with problems of ill-defined restart sequences have probably already wondered how a cache comes up after a cold
start. Obviously, all the data in the cache data RAM, as well as all of the addresses in the cache's directory, are completely random. How do designers
avoid the possibility that this random data will be mistaken for good data
and will generate false cache hit cycles? There are actually two easy methods
of handling this situation. The least expensive method is to disallow the
cache from supplying data to the processor until a bootstrap routine (usually in programmable read-only memory [PROM]) has had an opportunity
to overwrite all cache data and tag addresses. A one-bit, hardware-resettable
flag feeds into the cache controller, signifying that the entire cache is to be
ignored. The bootstrap routine reads a memory block of a size equivalent
to the size of the cache, from the bootstrap PROM itself, and each of these
read cycles will be treated by the cache controller as a read miss cycle, so the

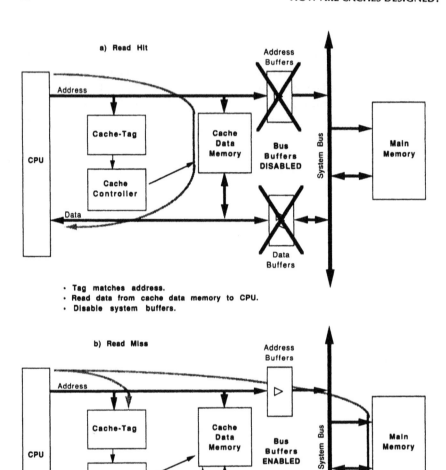

Figure 2.4.   Cache cycles: (a) Read hit. (b) Read miss. (c) Write hit. (d) Write miss.

cache controller will write a new copy of the bootstrap into the cache. Once the entire cache has been overwritten with this new data, the one-bit flag is set via software, and the cache controller now allows the cache to supply zero-wait data to the processor.

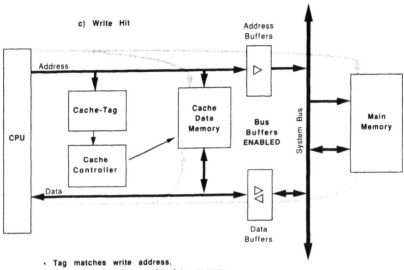

- Tag matches write address.
- Write new data into cache data memory.
- Write through buffers into main memory.

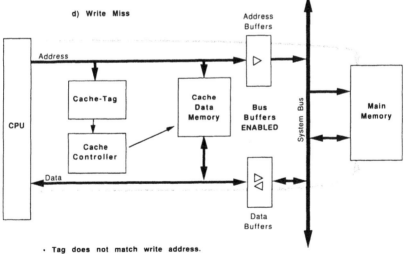

- Tag does not match write address.
- Write through buffers into main memory.
- Cache data memory undisturbed.

Figure 2.4. (*continued*)

A more common method of signifying the validity of the contents of the cache is to provide a **Valid** state indicator for every line in the cache. Although validity is usually indicated by a dedicated **Valid bit,** some of the more sophisticated coherency protocols detailed in Chapter 4 allow four or

SET ADDRESS	VALID BIT	CACHE-TAG RAM	CACHE DATA RAM
0	1	Address Tag 0	Valid Data
1	0	N/A	Garbage
2	1	Address Tag 2	Valid Data
3	1	Address Tag 3	Valid Data
4	1	Address Tag 4	Valid Data
5	0	N/A	Garbage
6	1	Address Tag 6	Valid Data
7	1	Address Tag 7	Valid Data

Figure 2.5. Typical contents of a cache data RAM and its matching cache-tag RAM and Valid bit RAMs.

five states to exist for every cache line, and the Valid state is one of many encoded onto two or three state bits. Figure 2.5 shows the memory organization of a cache-tag RAM and the corresponding cache data RAM in one type of system using Valid bits. Alternatives to this particular layout will be detailed in Section 2.2.5.

The problem still exists of how to assure that every line's Valid bit is reset to an Invalid state after a cold start. There are two easy answers to this problem. First, the cache with one Valid bit per line could replicate the cache Invalid flag just described, where the cache would be turned off until all Valid bits had an opportunity to be validated or invalidated. This may seem not to make sense, but we will see in Chapter 4 that such a scheme can prove beneficial if the Valid state is part of a more complex line status scheme. Second, all Valid bits can be reset after a cold start. There are three simple ways to perform this. One is to purchase specialty static RAMs which have a reset feature built in. The application in Figure 1.15 uses this method. Another method is to use a standard static RAM to hold the Valid bits and to use a small state machine to run through all addresses, writing an Invalid state to the Valid bits of all addresses after a system reset, while holding the processor in an idle state. This type of reset sequence is performed internally by certain CPUs. The last method is very similar to the method first described, where all cache locations are set to Valid states before the cache is enabled, but, with this last method, the entire cache is written to Invalid states during the cache's disabled state. The difference between this method and the one described at the beginning of this paragraph is negligible and would probably depend only on whether the bootstrap program was or was not cacheable.

There is an extremely simple method of generating Valid bits which is used in many commercially available cache designs. Cache-tag RAMs are constructed using a comparator and a standard static RAM. Certain inte-

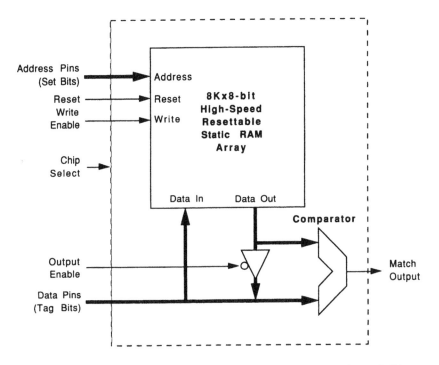

Figure 2.6. Block diagram of the internal workings of a typical cache-tag RAM.

grated cache-tag RAMs contain a comparator and a resettable static RAM (Figure 2.6). The reset pin on these RAMs clears every bit in the entire memory array to zeros. The trick is to tie any spare data bit inputs on these devices to a logic high level, so that, on a compare cycle, these inputs will either be compared to a zero, indicating that no tag address has been written into the RAM since it was reset, or a one, which means that a write cycle has indeed occurred, and the high level on these data inputs has been written into the selected RAM set address.

2.2 CHOOSING CACHE POLICIES

There are numerous cache policies, only the most common of which will be dealt with in this book. Cache policies are the rules of operation of the cache. Which cycles will be read from the cache instead of main memory? Where does the cache fit into the system? How associative is the cache? What happens during write cycles? All of these questions must be answered for all cases before the design is even started.

Cache policies are chosen for a single motive. The designer wants to get the most performance for the lowest cost. Two variables play into this equation: 1) Which is more important, to save engineering time or to save overall system parts cost? 2) Is the cache to be integrated or constructed from discrete components?

After reading this chapter, you should have gotten the impression that certain cache designs are pretty trivial and can be designed in little time. On the other hand, the last drop of performance can be eked out of a cache if the designer spends a near-infinite amount of time on its development. Another point I will be making where applicable is that certain architectures don't combine well with standard RAM organizations. In a few cases, this problem has been addressed by static RAM manufacturers, but, for the most part, more sophisticated architectures can best be handled in a dedicated single-chip cache design. This avenue has been explored by the designers of the internal caches on processor chips.

One problem in trying to produce the optimum cache design is the exercise of optimizing an equation which has about 20 variables. We will explore these variables in this chapter.

Cache policies may be chosen in a number of ways, depending on the generality of the system and the amount of resources available to improve the design. In the best case, the hardware and software of the system are being designed together, and the software contains few enough cases that the hardware can be optimized to a very good degree, based on a large amount of empirical research on the effects of different cache policies on the software's performance. In the worst case, the hardware designer is asked to design a cache without any knowledge of the software to run on the system, no empirical data, nor any chance to develop any, and with very little education about the trade-offs of various cache policies. Real-life scenarios tend to follow the financial strength of the company producing the system and the openness of the system. Closed systems designed within profitable firms will usually follow the best case scenario, while less profitable firms designing systems to compete in an open systems market will have to suffer with a scenario very similar to the worst case.

The following examples should help those designers who cannot afford much in the way of empirical studies and will serve to illustrate the trade-offs of various policies to those just learning the art of cache design.

2.2.1   Logical vs. Physical

In systems using virtual addressing, caches can reside either upstream (on the CPU side) or downstream (on the main memory side) of the processor's memory management unit (MMU). Both configurations are illustrated in Figure 2.7. The addresses upstream of the MMU are all logical or virtual addresses, and the addresses downstream are physical addresses. If the cache is placed upstream of the MMU, it is called a **logical cache** or **virtual cache,** and if the cache is downstream of the MMU, it is called a **physical cache.** Either placement has pros and cons.

Since the logical cache is upstream of a delay-causing device (the MMU), a logical design can run faster than a physical design. A logical cache for the Motorola 68020 CPU was shown in Figure 1.15. The 68020 used a separate chip for its MMU, and Figure 1.15's cache was placed on the processor side of the MMU chip.

Problems arise in logical caches with a phenomenon called **address aliasing,** simply **aliasing,** or **synonyms.** In virtual memory systems, the same physical address may be mapped to two or more completely different logical addresses. Say that both of these logical addresses were cached and that a write cycle occurred to one of them. The cache would update on cached copy of the physical address as well as the main memory itself (policies permitting), but the cached copy of the other logical address would remain unchanged and would subsequently contain erroneous data. Several solutions for this problem exist, and one will be documented thoroughly in Section 4.2.2, but these solutions are not trivial.

2.2.2 Associativity

In Section 1.5, we saw the difference between a set-associative and a fully associative cache. In a fully associative cache, there was one comparator per line in the directory, and all lines were examined at once for a match. In the set-associative cache, only one comparator was used, and the directory was divided into set bits and tag bits, the set bits determining exactly where within the cache a piece of data would reside. Since there was such a limitation, no two cache lines in the set-associative design could use the same lower address or set bits. This could lead to thrashing, a process where two addresses were continually displacing each other in the cache at the expense of throughput. You may recall that thrashing occurs not only because of instructions stepping on each other's toes, but also when something gets pushed into a stack location, or data is read or written, and the set bits happen to match the set bits of a valid cached location.

A middle ground lies between the two extremes of a fully associative design and a set-associative design. By adding comparators to a simple set-associative cache design, higher degrees of associativity can be achieved. By adding a single degree of **associativity** to the design of a cache, there will be

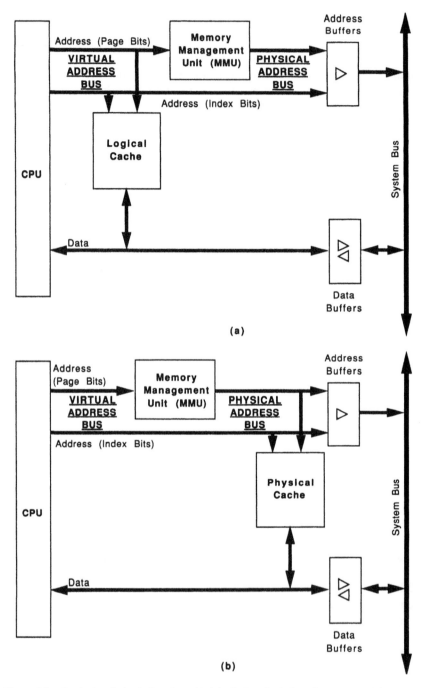

Figure 2.7. Logical and physical caches. (a) A logical cache is found upstream of the memory management unit. (b) Physical caches are on the physical address bus, downstream of the MMU.

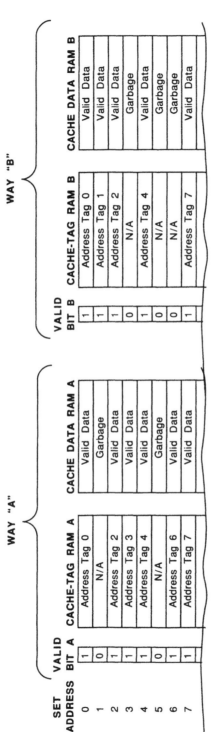

Figure 2.8. Contents of the cache-tag RAM and matching cache data entries in the two Ways of a two-Way set-associative cache. Note that these are simply two implementations of the simple direct-mapped cache of Figure 2.5.

another location into which main memory addresses with shared set bits can be mapped. If two locations would ordinarily thrash with each other in a single-comparator design, they will no longer need to thrash in a design with a second degree of associativity. The cache of Section 1.6 used a single comparator, a single cache-tag RAM, and a single cache data RAM, giving it a single degree of associativity. This is the simplest, most common way to design a cache and is called a **direct-mapped** implementation.

In smaller caches, a significant hit rate improvement can be realized through the implementation of greater degrees of associativity or more **Ways** (sometimes called **banks**) in the cache. Each Way in a cache is pretty much another cache which is a carbon copy of the others (Figure 2.8). Where a direct-mapped cache consists of a cache data RAM, a cache-tag RAM (built out of a RAM and a comparator), a cache controller, and isolation buffers, an **N-Way set-associative** cache uses N cache data RAMs and N cache-tag RAMs (built out of N RAMs and N comparators), a cache controller, and isolation buffers. In a set-associative cache, a main memory address can be mapped into as many different places in the cache as there are Ways. (One-Way caches are always called direct-mapped caches.)

Here's an example: A 16K-byte, direct-mapped cache for a 16-bit microprocessor could be designed using two 8K × 8 SRAMs for the cache data RAM, and possibly one more 8K × 8-bit SRAM and comparator for the cache-tag RAM (depending on the number of address bits used in the system, 20 for this example). To build a two-Way, 16K-byte cache for the same system, four 4K × 8-bit data RAMs would be needed, and two 4K × 9-bit RAMs and comparators would be required to implement the tag.

The reason that there are more tag bits in the two-Way design is that each cache acts independently, so they must each behave as if they were the only 8K-byte cache in the system. You can piece together a trend from this simple example. For a given cache size, increasing the associativity decreases the depth of the cache, thus decreasing the number of set bits. The displaced bits must in turn be made into new tag bits, so the cache-tag RAMs and comparators must be made wider. Given the number of address bits we have assumed (20), a 16K-byte cache would require the use of 13 set bits, seven tag bits, and a Valid bit, whereas an 8K-byte cache would need to have 12 set bits, eight tag bits, plus a Valid bit. In a similar manner, a four-Way, 16K-byte cache would require 11 set bits and nine tag bits. If you take this to the extreme, you come right back around to the content addressable memory of Figure 1.7. Each cache data RAM has been reduced down to a single location, and there are 2^N cache data RAMs in the fully associative cache. Likewise, there are 2^N separate cache-tag RAMs (and comparators), each of which stores only a single address. The number of set bits has been reduced to zero, and the address now consists entirely of tag bits. In a fully associative cache, every cache line is a different Way.

In an N-Way cache, all of the set bits are sent simultaneously to every Way's cache-tag RAMs and cache data RAMs, so the final decision of which Way to use comes down to enabling the appropriate Way's cache data RAM's data output pins when that Way's cache-tag RAM indicates that a hit has occurred.

One unfortunate casualty of the conflicts of terminology in this field is the word **page**. To an MMU, a page is the section of main memory referred to by the translated bits. This is the terminology we used in the preceding section. To certain cache designers, the word "page" refers to a Way in an associative cache, and to others, the word "page" means a single entry in the cache. In this book, page is only used in the MMU sense.

Back in Section 1.4, I briefly mentioned Intel's analogy that a cache was like a refrigerator which could be much more readily accessed from home than could a grocery store for a limited subset of the contents of the grocery store. In the same analogy, Intel cleverly likens associativity to shelves in the refrigerator, which neither increase nor decrease the space in the refrigerator itself, but reduce the competition for places to put the contents of the refrigerator, thus increasing the likelihood that you can get more inside. If we look back to the filing system analogy, higher associativity could be likened to adding file drawers to the desk.

As the cache's size increases, the hit rate improvement realized by increased associativity rapidly decreases (see Figure 2.9). In this example, once a cache transcends a certain size (around 4K bytes), doubling the size

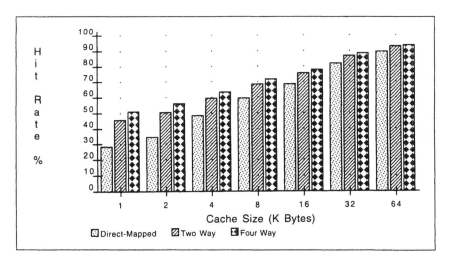

Figure 2.9. One set of statistics showing the relative performance of caches of varying sizes and associativities. Note that, for this example, the hit rate for a direct-mapped, 8K-byte cache is equivalent to that of a 4K-byte, two-Way cache. Above these sizes, a direct-mapped cache of twice the size outperforms all increased associativities.

of the cache improves the hit rate more than does increasing the associativity of a given size cache. Although a slightly better hit rate may be obtained for a 32K-byte cache through the use of higher degrees of associativity, the component count needed to implement such a cache would increase in proportion to the number of degrees of associativity and probably not be justifiable against going to a 64K-byte implementation. This is because each Way of a cache needs a separate cache-tag RAM as well as a separate cache data RAM. This is a key point in discrete cache designs, but is far less of an issue in integrated designs, since integrated caches aren't concerned with chip count, but are rather concerned with the maximum hit rate attainable within a certain die size.

You may want to keep in mind some commonly quoted statistics, however far they may actually be from the way your own system performs. The first is that a doubling in associativity decreases the miss rate by about 20%. This comes from research done by M. D. Hill in his thesis, "Aspects of Cache Memory and Instruction Buffer Performance," done in 1987 at the University of California, Berkeley. The second rule of thumb is that doubling the size of a cache decreases the miss rate by about 69%. This is from research done by Anant Agarwal at Stanford University. Looking at Figure 2.9, or at any similar chart, it is difficult to rationalize these numbers. Still, it does indeed appear that, above certain cache sizes, it is much better to increase the size of the cache rather than the associativity when the opportunity presents itself. As always, I will simply say that your cache must be designed for your system and your software. You just can't take advantage of anybody else's statistics for anything more than simple guidance.

There is another key difficulty in designing discrete multiway caches. Most caches are designed to support the highest possible processor clock rates, and consequently they tax the capabilities of even the fastest static RAMs and cache-tag RAMs. In a direct-mapped cache, the critical path for the cache-tag RAM runs through the static RAM and the address comparator, to the cache control logic, and eventually back to the processor's Ready input pin (Figure 2.10). The cache data RAM in direct-mapped designs is usually enabled onto the processor's data input pins as soon as the processor has indicated that a read cycle has begun, and is only disabled upon the detection of a cache miss, so the timing on the data RAM's output enable pin is not tight. In a discrete implementation of a multiway cache (Figure 2.11), neither (or none) of the different Ways' data RAM outputs can be enabled until *after* a cache hit has been detected. This means that the critical timing path now flows through the cache-tag RAM, then the comparator and cache controller, as before, and then through the cache data RAM's output enable pin, adding the "output enable to valid" data delay to the critical timing path. This is usually significant (around 5ns at the writing of

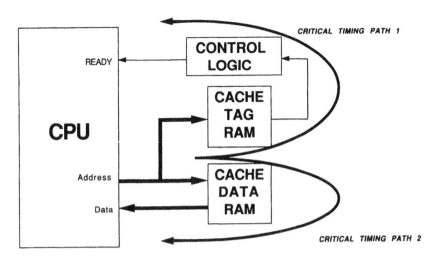

Figure 2.10.   The critical timing paths in a direct-mapped cache are from CPU address output to CPU data input, through the cache data RAM alone, and from CPU address out to CPU Ready in, which runs through the cache-tag RAM, the comparator, and the cache controller logic. The Ready path is usually the trickiest from a timing standpoint.

this book) and steers designers away from multiway implementations of discrete caches at the onset of the design.

Some mention needs to be made about the methods used to select which Way in a multiway cache should be replaced when a line needs to be updated. This policy is called the **replacement algorithm,** although some simply call it **placement.** A replacement algorithm selects which Way is to be updated when a new line is to be brought into the cache. (Recall that any main memory address can be put into as many locations as there are Ways in the cache.) Ideally, any stale piece of cached data which is no longer needed by the processor would be chosen to be overwritten. Some cache controllers watch over the accesses into the cache, and categorize the order in which each Way was accessed, making a note of which Way's line was accessed least recently. This is called a **least recently used (LRU)** algorithm. LRU statistics are maintained separately for each cache line.

In a two-Way system, a single bit per line can be used to implement an LRU (see Figure 2.12). When a cache hit occurs, the Way which was hit makes sure that the LRU bit is written to point to the other Way. When a line is to be replaced, that line's LRU pointer already points to the Way where the replacement should happen, and the pointer is rewritten to point at the other Way. The power-up state of these bits is insignificant, since everything in the cache is unusable.

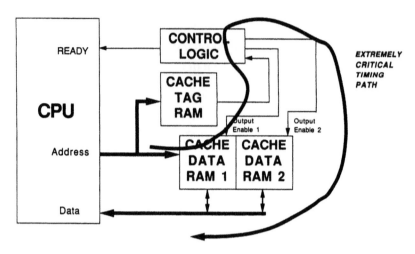

Figure 2.11. In a multiway cache, the outputs of all cache data RAMs are disabled until a hit has been detected. The most critical timing path then runs from the CPU, through the cache-tag RAM and controller logic, then through the output enable path of the cache data RAM before data can be returned to the CPU.

One interesting point is that true LRU replacement can quickly gobble up lots of bits of memory. It can be easily observed that there are $N!$ orders in which N letters of the alphabet can be ordered. A four-Way cache must have five LRU bits for each line to represent the 24 (4!) following possible states of use of the cache contents (order in which Ways A, B, C, and D were used):

ABCD	ABDC	ACBD	ADBC	ACDB	ADCB
BACD	BADC	CABD	DABC	CADB	DACB
BCAD	BDAC	CBAD	DBAC	CDAB	DCAB
BCDA	BDCA	CBDA	DBCA	CDBA	DCBA

since these 24 states require five bits ($2^5 = 32 > 24$) to encode.

Similarly, an eight-Way cache's LRU would require adequate bits to represent the 8! states of the use of the eight Ways of the cache. This amounts to 40,320 states, requiring 16 bits of LRU information per cache line. A 16-Way cache would require 45 bits per cache line, and a fully associative cache with 256 lines (which is essentially a 256-Way set-associative memory) would require more LRU bits than my pocket calculator is capable of representing!

Another problem facing designers of true LRU systems is that if the LRU algorithm is to be updated to show the order in which the four last Ways

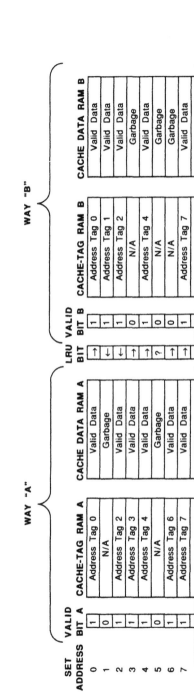

Figure 2.12. The two-Way cache of Figure 2.8 with an additional bit per line to mark which Way was least recently used for any particular line.

were accessed, then both a read cycle and a write cycle must be performed on the LRU bits during each processor cycle. Another way to see it is that if the LRU currently states the order as ABCD, and then D is accessed, the order must be changed to DABC. The ending order is inextricably tied to the initial order. The last sections of this chapter are devoted to timing problems in cache designs, and we will see that performing a simple read cycle is taxing enough in a cache, so a read/write pair could easily become impossible. Many alternatives to a true LRU algorithm have been tried, and the following paragraphs will briefly describe a few of them.

One alternative is that used by Intel in the company's IntelArchitecture microprocessors. Intel calls their method a "pseudo-LRU." Three bits are used per cache line, as shown in Figure 2.13. The top bit in the tree (AB/CD) is set when there is a hit in A or B, and is cleared upon a hit to C or D. Only one of the bits in the second level of the diagram will be set or cleared on a cache hit. If A is hit, the A/B bit will be set, and nothing will happen to the C/D bit. If B is hit, the A/B bit will be cleared, and once again nothing will happen to the C/D bit. The same scenario occurs for the C/D bit upon hits to the C or D Ways. The scheme can be implemented as write only; a simple write cycle can be used to update the pseudo-LRU bits during cache hits, instead of a time-consuming read/modify/write cycle. This can essentially double the speed with which the cache can be accessed over the speed of a true LRU algorithm. The only time that the pseudo-LRU bits must be read is during a line replacement, which will be a slower cycle simply since it involves an off-chip access.

The difference between this method and a true LRU is small and can be simply illustrated. Say that a certain line contains valid data in all Ways, A, B, C, and D. If the CPU executes a loop in which that line is continually ac-

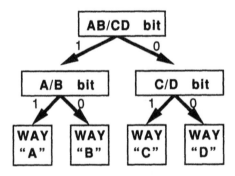

Figure 2.13. The pseudo-LRU scheme used in certain Intel processors to get away from timing and housekeeping difficulties posed by true LRU implementations for highly associative caches.

cessed in the order A, B, C, A, B, C, then the D Way would obviously be the least recently used. After the C access, though, the AB/CD bit would point to AB, and the A/B bit would point to A, forcing the update data to overwrite the A Way, rather than the D Way. The likelihood of this occurring is very software dependent, but is apt to be statistically small, and certainly fades in comparison to the possibility that the entire processor's clock speed might have to be slowed to accommodate a true LRU algorithm. Intel's pseudo-LRU also consumes half the memory bits, thus half the die space of a true LRU, die space which was probably devoted to issues more capable of improving the processor's overall throughput.

One interesting point is that Intel's embodiment of this three-bit scheme requires the use of a dual-port SRAM. No matter which Way is hit, two of the bits will be made to point away from the Way that was most recently used, and the third bit will stay where it was left by a prior operation. Intel's approach to keeping the third bit intact was to perform a read/modify/write on all three bits, which seems to bring the complexity back to near that of a more straightforward scheme. Rather than the write-per-bit memory that one would assume designers would have chosen, a technique which makes each bit behave as if it resides in a different memory chip, each with its own write control, Intel's PC processors read/modify/write the three LRU bits, causing the unmodified bit to get written back to the value it held at the start of the operation. The dual-port SRAM has one port dedicated to reading the LRU bits early in the cycle, and the other port dedicated to writing the modified LRU bits back into the SRAM late in the cycle.

An alternative, which is called the **least frequently used (FRQ)** method, is less often used in cache designs than in memory management units. This method is used to control replacement of the contents of the MMU's CAM. It is still useful in a cache architecture and should be illustrated here. Each cache line has its own pointer, which points to a random Way. In a four-Way cache, there would be a two-bit pointer at each line which would point to Way A, Way B, Way C, or Way D. When a line is accessed in this scheme, the pointer is also accessed. If the pointer is currently pointed at the Way which generates the cache hit, the cache controller would increment the pointer so it would finish by pointing to the next Way. On successive cache hit cycles to that line, the pointer is bumped every time it is found to be pointed at the Way being accessed, until it comes to rest upon a Way which no longer generates any cache hits. When this line is accessed during a cache miss cycle, the pointer will therefore be pointing to the most reasonable candidate Way for replacement. During the replacement cycle, the pointer is again bumped so that the most recently updated data is not immediately overwritten.

Although the least frequently used method is simple and elegant, it once again requires the use of both a read and a write cycle during every cache hit. This slows things down every bit as much as the true LRU. This means that the only advantage to using this method is that the overall number of bits required to implement it is significantly less than the number we worked out earlier for implementing a true LRU.

One of the most popular alternatives to a true LRU is the **random replacement** algorithm. It doesn't take any explaining for the reader to understand that the basis for this algorithm is that the Way to be replaced is chosen at random. Implementation is simple, especially if the designer is not worried about exactly how random the replacement really is. Somewhat random numbers can be drawn at almost no cost from a number of places. Naturally, in a four-Way random replacement cache, the cache controller runs a one-in-four chance of overwriting the most recently used Way, but this is still better than the 100% chance of overwriting a thrashed location in a direct-mapped cache. A big advantage to the random replacement algorithm is that, while true LRUs for a four-Way cache consume six bits per line, and Intel's method consumes three bits, and the pointer method consumes a mere two, random replacement requires no bits to implement.

Between the least frequently used method and random replacement lies a method called **not last used (NLU)**. Like FRQ, NLU also uses a pointer, but the pointer points at the most recently used Way and is simply a stored copy of the number of the Way which was last hit for any particular set address. The Match output of each cache-tag RAM is simply captured in a RAM which is as deep as the cache-tag RAMs. This can be done in a write-only cycle at a zero timing penalty. The idea behind the NLU replacement algorithm is that random replacement is fine, but it's a tad better if you can avoid the inherent possibility that you'll randomly step on the last-used Way for any set address. Since there is no penalty for using true LRU for a two-Way cache, this method would only be used for caches of more than two Ways, and then there would only be one chance out of $(N-1)$ (in an N-Way cache) of the random replacement algorithm stepping on the second more recently used Way of an address. NLU is probably a hair better than strict random replacement, but it's hard to imagine that it offers noteworthy improvement in cache performance.

There is nothing magic that requires a design to use a number of Ways which ends up being a power of two. Although the most common degrees of associativity are one (direct-mapped), two, and four, you can add or subtract associativity in the exact manner which best fits your system. Sun Microsystems has used a five-Way internal instruction cache plus a four-Way internal data cache in one processor design. But we're getting ahead of ourselves. Split instruction/data caches will be discussed in the next section.

A piece of code like the example in Figure 1.4 might do best in a four-Way design simply because it is using the same set address for the data table, the stack, the calling routine, and the subroutine. Feel free to draw yourself an imaginary trace of the program in Figure 1.4, then see how it would behave in direct-mapped two-Way and four-Way caches. I decided against illustrating it step by step, showing what would get written into cache when, since it would consume several times the space of the example shown in Figure 1.11.

2.2.3   Unified vs. Split Caches

One way to realize some of the benefits of a two-Way cache, without incurring the problems, is to split the cache into two parts, one for instructions, called the **instruction cache,** and one for data, called the **data cache.** This is called a **split** cache architecture, and the alternative is, not surprisingly, dubbed a **unified** or **unified instruction-data** cache. All discussions so far have assumed that the cache is a unified design. The advantage of the split cache is immediately obvious if you look at the piece of code given as an example in Figure 1.4. The code thrashes at times when data accesses conflict with code accesses and vice versa. If a split cache were used in the example of Figure 1.11, the stack push/pop in steps 5 and 7 would not conflict with any of the other steps shown, and the copy of the program counter would still reside within the cache at the Return instruction at the end of the subroutine. In a split cache, accesses to the data space, as well as to the stack, would occur through the data cache, and the instructions would be accessed through the instruction cache, reducing the thrashing about the same degree as it would be reduced by using a two-Way architecture. The disadvantage is that one of the caches might fill up faster than the other, and there is no way that the full cache could gain access to unused lines in the opposite cache. Worst case would be that the instruction cache would thrash significantly while the data cache would rarely be accessed, or the other way around. Either case is extremely software dependent.

Probably the nicest attribute of split caches is their inherent simplicity. Split caches are simpler to construct than two-Way caches for several reasons. First, each side can be designed as a simple direct-mapped cache, completely independently of any considerations of the other half of the cache. Second, most processors indicate whether the current read cycle is an instruction or a data fetch via a pin which becomes valid as soon as do the address outputs. This means that the outputs of the appropriate data RAM can be enabled as soon as the cycle begins, much the same as in a direct-mapped unified design, loosening the timing constraints not only on the cache-tag RAM, but also on the cache data RAM and the control logic. Some split-cache architectures simply treat the instruction/data output from the processor as the most significant set address bit. Third, in a split cache, there is no decision about which Way to replace a line in. Instructions are automatically put into the instruction cache, and data is automatically placed into the data cache. Fourth, the caches do not have to match each other in size. Instruction caches should be larger than data caches in most general computing applications, but when real number crunching happens in such applications as array processing, small instruction caches will be adequate, while large data caches are a requirement. Another unusual benefit is that altogether different policies can be used in the two caches. There is no reason why the data cache cannot be a highly associative design, while the instruction cache might be direct-mapped. Should you choose to implement a split-cache architecture, look through this book once to help decide on a set of policies for the instruction cache, then do it again for the data cache. Your design might look unorthodox, but will be more likely to outperform your competitors'.

You can look into different ways to split the cache. Most processors not only indicate whether the current access is for an instruction or data, but many will also disclose user/supervisor mode and whether or not the request is for a stack operation. You just might be able to realize a lot of the advantages of a multiway cache without incurring the speed headaches simply by using any or all of these status signals to enable different split caches.

2.2.4   Write-through vs. Copy-back

Way back in Section 2.1.3, I deferred explaining what action the cache took during a write cycle. This was because there are several means of handling write cycles in caches, or **write strategies,** and the decision impacts the cost as well as the complexity of the cache. Even in this section, I will be deferring until Chapter 4 the explanations of some of the more specific problems involving write cycles.

There are two fundamental strategies defining the behavior of the cache during a write cycle. One is called the **write-through,** or **store through (ST)** cache, and the other is a **copy-back, write back, deferred write, nonwrite-through,** or **store-in** cache **(SIC).** Given all these options, this book will exclusively use the terms write-through and copy-back, since they are both common and are not easily confused with one another. Naturally, once a write strategy is implemented in hardware, it becomes a **write policy.**

In a write-through cache design, either of two courses of action is taken. This is key in designs which can process some write cycles in no-wait states, some of which will be described in Section 2.2.6. In many designs, the cache is updated if a hit occurs, and the cache ignores the write cycle if a miss occurs. In others, the line is automatically invalidated (**write invalidate**). This approach is used to get over certain speed limitations of the hardware. With a third alternative, a line in the cache is written to whether the write cycle is a hit or a miss. This last course of action is called a **write update** and is usually taken to remove the need to check for a cache hit before writing to a line in a direct-mapped design. The cache controller can begin the write cycle just as soon as the processor indicates that a write cycle has begun. The cache example of Figure 1.15 uses a write update policy. Naturally, in a multiway cache, updating cache lines on miss cycles would not work, since the controller would not know which Way to update until a cache hit or miss had been detected. Imagine the problem of having an updated and an old copy of the same address in the same line of two different Ways of the cache!

The difference in throughput between updating the cache on a miss versus not updating on a miss appears to not yet have been deeply explored. Intuitively, it seems that most programs would read data before writing it, with the exception of data being pushed onto the stack, and with the initialization of memory-based pointers, where an immediate value would be written to a main memory location before being read, then rewritten a number of times. If the cache designer has the option of choosing either of these two approaches, it would be wise to discuss it with the programmers. No matter which approach is used, the write-through cache *always* updates main memory during all write cycles.

The copy-back cache does *not* always update main memory, but reduces main memory accesses by writing data to the cache alone at a much higher speed than that data could be written to main memory. This has three major advantages. First, write cycles become much faster than they would be if a main memory cycle were the penalty for every CPU write; second, some write cycles, like loop counters and stack entries, will only be written to the main memory a fraction of the number of times that the CPU tries to write them. Third, the processor is on the main memory bus a lower percentage of the time. This last factor is a concern in tightly coupled multiprocessing systems, where the speed of the entire system depends on the main memory bus traffic (we'll handle this in depth in Section 4.2).

These advantages come at a cost, however. Housekeeping in copy-back caches requires a lot of thought, especially in multiprocessing systems. The most basic concern is how to handle the data which has been written to the cache, but not to the main memory. At some point, the main memory will need to be updated with the fresher data which is in the cache. An opportunity for this usually occurs when the updated line is to be removed from the cache. Obviously, if this data were simply overwritten, as it would be in a write-through cache, new data would be destroyed, and the data integrity of the entire program would suffer. Therefore, a method must be implemented for the updated line to be transferred to main memory once it is to be re-

SET ADDR	VALID BIT	DIRTY BIT	CACHE-TAG RAM	CACHE DATA RAM
0	1	1	Address Tag 0	Dirty Data
1	0	?	N/A	Garbage
2	1	0	Address Tag 2	Valid Data
3	1	0	Address Tag 3	Valid Data
4	1	1	Address Tag 4	Dirty Data
5	0	?	N/A	Garbage
6	1	1	Address Tag 6	Dirty Data
7	1	0	Address Tag 7	Valid Data

Figure 2.14. The Dirty bit signifies whether a cache line contains data which is more up to date than the matching address in the main memory.

moved from the cache. The process of writing data back to main memory when it is being replaced in the cache is called **eviction** or **deallocation.** (The evicted line is called the **victim.**) Some less-often-used terms for eviction cycles are copy-back, write-back, **copy-out,** and **victim write.** I'll stick with the word "eviction" so that there will be no misunderstanding about whether I'm talking about the cache's write policy or the cycle being processed.

One very simple method of implementing a copy-back cache would be to write every Valid line which was being replaced back into main memory, whether or not it had actually been written to by the processor. This would make the cache waste a considerable amount of bus bandwidth with unnecessary main memory write cycles, due to all the evictions of lines which had not been written to by the CPU. Another problem with this method is that all line replacements would take twice as long as would line replacements in a write-through cache, since write-through line replacements require only a main memory read cycle. To avoid this burden, the cache is usually implemented with a means to signify whether a line in cache is more current than the main memory location it represents. The simplest method is to use another bit for each line in the cache, and this bit is called the **Dirty bit.** Data which has been written in the cache, but has not been updated in the main memory is tagged as **Dirty** by the cache controller's setting this bit. Like the Valid bit, there is usually a Dirty bit for every line in the cache (Figure 2.14). During a cache miss cycle, the line to be replaced is examined, and, if its Dirty bit is set, the current contents of that cache line are evicted back into main memory.

The Dirty bit is not the only means of signifying the Dirty status of a cache line. More complex methods are in wide use and will be examined in Chapter 4. In general, these other methods take advantage of the fact that more than three states can be encoded by the two bits normally used for the Valid and Dirty bits. The non-Valid state can exist with the Dirty bit either set or cleared, and only one of these states is really necessary to the protocol. The leftover state can be used to signify another cache line state.

Just as a point of interest, some split-cache designs use a copy-back data cache, but don't even have logic to accommodate write cycles in the instruction cache, since such cycles just don't happen.

2.2.5 Line Size

In Section 2.1.3, we deferred the true definition of a cache line to this section. A cache **line** is the smallest portion of the cache which has a unique address tag. Some researchers call this unit a **block,** others an **entry.** Those who use the term "block" use the words **"block fill"** to describe the line fill defined in Section 2.1.3.

In the caches in our illustrations so far, all lines have been one word long. Another way to describe them is to state that each word in the cache has its own address tag.

There are two reasons to use **line sizes** longer than a single word. First, if the line is two or four words in length, the cache-tag RAM need only be one-half or one-quarter of the depth of the cache data RAM. Although this is not a big money saver in discrete caches since static RAMs of different densities don't differ too widely in price, the reader can appreciate the savings in die size if a longer line is chosen for an integrated cache design where the die area consumed by a static RAM is directly proportional to the size of the RAM array, and where die cost is more than proportional to die size (see Figure 2.15).

The second reason to choose a longer line size is because multiword transfers from main memory (**burst** or **burst refill** transfers) can be designed to perform much faster than the number of individual transfers which would be required to fill the same number of cache words. If the whole cached system is designed around multiple-line transfers from main memory to the cache, the design can make superior use of available bus bandwidth. This is easy to see and is illustrated in Figure 2.16. With individual transfers, the processor/cache subsystem must output an address for every transaction at the beginning of that transaction. After a bus latency time, the data for that address is placed upon the bus, and the processor subsequently can change the address to request the next word. This is shown in Figure 2.16a. Figure 2.16b shows a burst transfer cycle. The address of the first word of the burst transfer is output, and the data for this word is transferred with the same latency as before, but the main memory realizes that a burst trans-

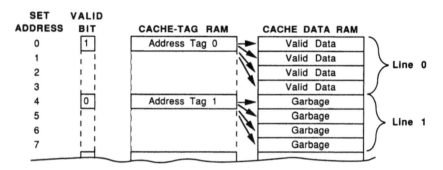

a) Single-word line.

SET ADDRESS	VALID BIT	CACHE-TAG RAM	CACHE DATA RAM	
0	1	Address Tag 0	Valid Data	Line 0
1	0	N/A	Garbage	Line 1
2	1	Address Tag 2	Valid Data	Line 2
3	1	Address Tag 3	Valid Data	Line 3
4	1	Address Tag 4	Valid Data	Line 4
5	0	N/A	Garbage	Line 5
6	1	Address Tag 6	Valid Data	Line 6
7	1	Address Tag 7	Valid Data	Line 7

b) Four-word line.

SET ADDRESS	VALID BIT	CACHE-TAG RAM	CACHE DATA RAM	
0	1	Address Tag 0	Valid Data	
1			Valid Data	Line 0
2			Valid Data	
3			Valid Data	
4	0	Address Tag 1	Garbage	
5			Garbage	Line 1
6			Garbage	
7			Garbage	

Figure 2.15. The difference between single-word and multiple-word lines. (a) In a cache with a single-word line, every word stored in cache has a corresponding cache-tag entry and Valid bit. (b) In a multiword line cache, there is only one Valid bit and only one tag entry for every *N* words stored in the cache.

fer is occurring and outputs the second, third, and fourth (or more) words a single CPU clock cycle apart from each other to allow that line to be refilled at the maximum possible rate. For a four-cycle refill, this is dubbed a 2:1:1:1 refill, since the first data is returned after the second cycle, and every following cycle presents data to the cache without wait states (if there were a wait state on each cycle, the refill would be dubbed 3:2:2:2).

This approach obviously takes advantage of the principle of locality, and it is easy to illustrate that there is a point after which it stops helping the system and becomes a burden. The subject of exactly where it becomes a burden is of quite some debate. I will argue my point from two extreme cases. First, look at the cache with single-word lines. As just mentioned, it takes an

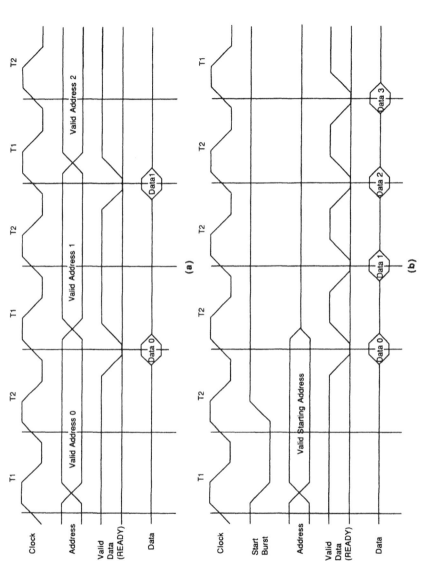

Figure 2.16. Individual word transfers versus burst transfers. In individual read cycles (a), each access consumes two cycles: one for address output, and the other for data input to the CPU. Burst transfers (b) output the address only once, expecting data from a number of adjacent addresses to be returned as a result.

address output and a data input to update any single word in the cache. After this, the CPU can start to run again, perhaps without incurring another cache miss. However, there is a latency cycle for each and every word updated within the cache. On the other extreme, let's look at an example where the entire cache is a single line, no matter if the cache is 512K bytes deep! A single address represents the entire cache, and either the entire cache is a hit, or the whole thing has to be replaced. A couple of mechanisms will make the system with this cache perform worse than any uncached system. During a read miss cycle, the CPU will be held up as the entire line is being replaced. For a four-word line, the 512K-byte cache example would require 131,072 (128K) bus cycles to complete, which is probably longer than most loops which the processor would execute. The other problem is easy to see if you look at a typical piece of code, like the one shown in Figure 1.4. Most programs execute simultaneously out of several spaces. This is what makes associativity work. If there is only one line in the entire cache, any stack access would require a line refill, then the code pointed to by the stack would require a refill, then the data space accessed by that code would require a line refill, and so forth *ad nauseum*. Although a certain degree of thrashing will occur in a one-word-per-line cache, it is pretty intuitive that anything we might do to reduce the number of distinct addresses contained in the tag RAM would produce more thrashing. It's as if the different spaces, which seemed to occasionally step upon each other, were given bigger shoes in order to step upon each other even more. Unfortunately, there is no globally optimum line size. According to some measurements, a line size of two words is optimum. Other researchers will swear by an eight-word line size. Some researchers point out that the miss rate can continue to decrease with increasing line length even though the performance of the system stops improving.

One very nice approach which some designers use to increase the speed of line replacement is to make the cache-to-main-memory interface use a wider word than the CPU-to-cache interface. As an example, assume that the processor uses a 32-bit word and that the cache's line size is four words. The cache can be designed to actually be 128 bits wide (4×32), but will only present 32 bits to the CPU through some sort of multiplexer (Figure 2.17). Every time there is a cache miss, the cache will conduct a 128-bit interaction with a 128-bit main memory in a single latency. This quickly solves the problem of the CPU's waiting for burst cycles to complete, but does not solve the problem of increased thrashing. Most designers assume that thrashing is the lesser of the two evils. Mitsubishi semiconductor has taken this same approach with a chip they call the "Cache DRAM." This IC is a 4-megabit DRAM with an additional $4K \times 4$ SRAM element. On a cache miss, a 64-bit cache line is moved from DRAM to SRAM and vice versa within a single clock cycle. Since the external data path is 4 bits, a system with a 32-bit bus would use eight devices, causing the line replacement to be a total of sixteen 32-bit words, all in a single clock cycle! This makes sense mostly because the array inside any SRAM or DRAM is often square and subsequently has a very wide internal word, which it internally narrows for the outside world (like the multiplexer shown in Figure 2.17), and also because within a single chip, the penalties of wide words are not nearly as severe as the board space and chip count penalties implemented using industry-standard discrete devices.

At the time of this writing, there are two different camps in microprocessor internal cache line burst refill sequences. The first is the one used by IBM and Motorola for the internal caches on the Power PC microprocessors, where the lower two word-address bits are used to specify which word is being replaced within a four-word line. The bits count upward, starting with the exact address of the cache miss. The other camp consists of the Intel PC processors. These caches will either count up or down, depending on whether the missed address is an odd or an even number. Both counters wrap around the two lower bits of the missed address and don't carry any increment into the higher order bits. At first flush, the Motorola algorithm might appear to be more practical, since code executes in a forward order.

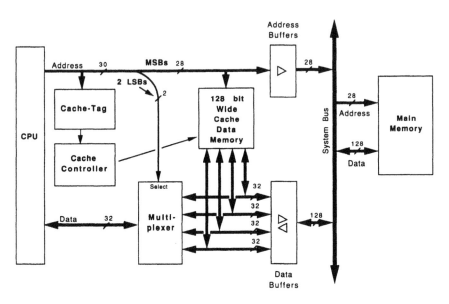

Figure 2.17.   Using a wide bus between main memory and cache to allow single-cycle, multiple-word line replacements.

This viewpoint neglects the fact that stacks, which are also stored in the cache, count backward when being read, as do certain other data structures. Another less obvious point is the fact that since the counter wraps around after overflowing, any cache miss will necessarily fill the cache line with the same four words, no matter which sequence is used. Although I am sure that someone will perform a study at some time in the future which will show a marginal difference between the two sequences, I honestly doubt that line re-fill sequences make much difference to the performance of the cache.

Long lines make a lot of sense in older systems designed using ECL CAMs. Recall that high-speed CAMs only come in a 4×4 density, forcing any 32-bit address system to use eight of these devices simply to decode four lines' worth of addresses. If such a system had 2K lines of cache, the cache directory would have to use over four thousand parts! There is an overwhelming incentive in such a system to use a smaller cache and to make the line size as long as possible. A cache with a 16-word line could automatically use one less CAM per four lines. A 256-word line would use two less CAMs, for a total of six CAMs per four lines. Actually, most processors use only the lower two address bits for byte addressing, so the latter case would even work with line sizes as short as 64 words.

Write policy is also a factor in line size decisions. If a write update rather than a write invalidate policy is chosen (in which a write miss overwrites an existing line in cache), and if the write is shorter than the line length, how does the cache signify that only a portion of the line is valid? There are several methods of handling this, and we'll explore two here.

The first method is **write allocation.** When a write miss occurs, the balance of the cache line being written is fetched from main memory, and the write data is merged into the line as that line is written into the cache. In more discrete steps, once a write miss has been detected, the cache controller starts a line replacement cycle, possibly evicting a Dirty line from the cache, performing a main memory read of the data which will be copied into the replaced line. Data from the address which is being written to is either not transferred from main memory or is immediately overwritten by the CPU's output data. At the end of the cycle, the cache line is filled with main memory data with the written word updated. Some designers also call this function a **merge.** Figure 2.18 shows write allocation graphically. In this example, the CPU encounters a write miss while attempting to write a byte to an address which is not represented in the cache. The line is updated from main memory, then the appropriate byte is overwritten in the cache. Whether or not the write data is sent to the main memory depends upon the write policy of the cache, but, in any case, the first write miss to any cache line will incur a significant penalty, since an entire line must be fetched before the processor can proceed. One way some designers have gotten

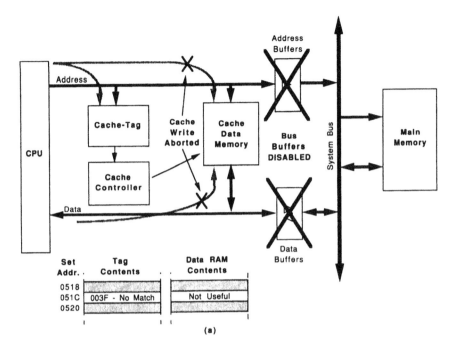

Figure 2.18. Write allocation in a write-through cache. When a cache write miss is detected, the write cycle is aborted (a), and the processor is put into a wait state. A line is then read from main memory into the cache data RAM (b), and the corresponding tag is updated. The processor is then allowed to proceed with the write cycle, writing simultaneously to the updated cache line and to main memory (c).

around this problem is to post writes to the cache, but this can cause the cache hardware to become inordinately complex.

The second method involves **sectoring.** Those who call lines blocks call sectors **sub-blocks.** In the preceding example we assumed that all cache to main memory transactions involved entire lines. When the CPU encountered a miss while trying to write to a portion of a line, the line was replaced by a matching line via write allocation. That line used a single Valid bit to indicate its authenticity. A sectored cache design allows the smallest writeable data unit (usually a word) to have its own Valid bit, so that each cache line contains several Valid bits, one representing each sector or sub-block. This is illustrated in Figure 2.19. Readers will note a strong similarity between this diagram and Figure 2.5, where the line is a single word long. The cache data and the Valid bits for every word have been kept, but the cache-tag RAM has been economized to have only one-fourth as many entries. This approach is often used to save silicon on integrated cache controllers.

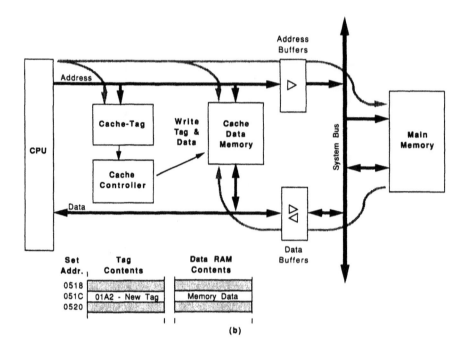

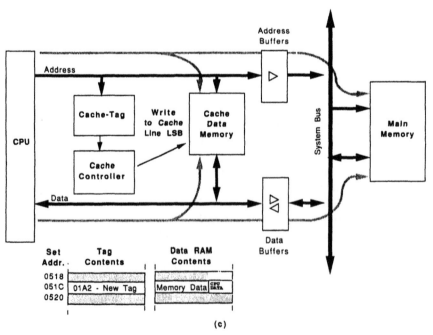

Figure 2.18. (*continued*)

When a cache read miss occurs, the target line is invalidated, and the re-quested word is brought in and added to the cache. Only the Valid bit for that word is set. By spatial locality, we would be drawn to conclude that some nearby word would be requested by the CPU soon. When this word was in-deed requested, if it fit within the same line, the cache controller would up-date the cache and set the Valid bit for that word within the line, so that now two Valid bits would be set. Only those words that the CPU actually re-quested would be brought in from main memory; however, each word would require an entire bus cycle, rather than the abbreviated cycle af-forded by burst refills. In our example of a write miss, all Valid bits for the line being replaced would be cleared, and the Valid bit would be set only for the word being written into the cache (Figure 2.20). This allows cache write miss updates to occur at the same speed as the write cycle would if the cache were not updated. This beats having to wait for the multiword read cycle re-quired in a wire allocated system. If a write buffer is used, or if this method is used with a copy-back policy, the write cycle can happen as fast as the CPU can operate. An added benefit in systems using sectoring is that the main-memory-to-cache interface can now be handled on a word-by-word basis, which is important if the cache is added to an older bus architecture which cannot support burst read cycles.

Looking back on the last few paragraphs, we see that a lot of trouble arises from trying to cache write miss cycles. Of course, the simplest way to handle the entire problem is to disallow line replacements on write misses in the first place. Write-through caches are unlikely to realize much benefit from cacheing write misses, since data is usually read first, then written to the same location unless it is the first stack push to a given address. Although a policy of disallowing line replacements on write misses could cause an in-

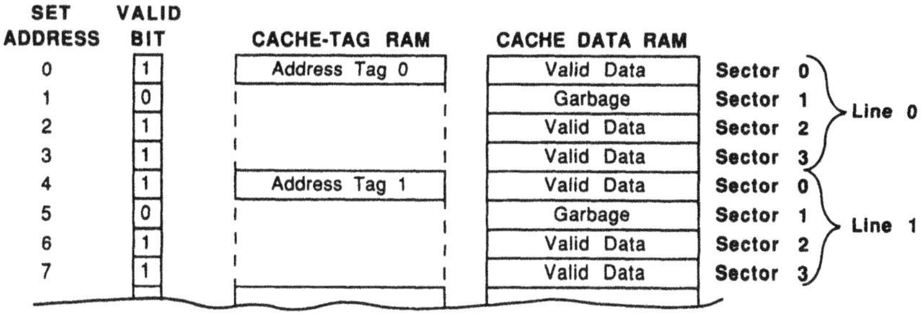

Figure 2.19.   The organization of the cache-tag RAM, Valid bit RAM, and the corresponding cache data RAM in a sectored cache design. Each line has a cache-tag entry, and each sector has a Valid bit. This is similar to the long line cache in Figure 2.15b but adds a Valid bit for each sector.

(a) Before Miss cycle

SET ADDRESS	VALID BIT	CACHE-TAG RAM	CACHE DATA RAM
0	1	Non-Matching Tag 0	Valid Data
1	0		Garbage
2	1		Valid Data
3	1		Valid Data
4	1	Address Tag 1	Valid Data
5	1		Valid Data
6	0		Garbage
7	1		Valid Data

(b) End of Miss cycle. New Line in cache. Only one sector valid.

SET ADDRESS	VALID BIT	CACHE-TAG RAM	CACHE DATA RAM
0	0	New Tag 0	Garbage
1	1		Missed Sector
2	0		Garbage
3	0		Garbage
4	1	Address Tag 1	Valid Data
5	1		Valid Data
6	0		Garbage
7	1		Valid Data

(c) Second sector read from same address added to new cache line.

SET ADDRESS	VALID BIT	CACHE-TAG RAM	CACHE DATA RAM
0	0	Address Tag 0	Garbage
1	1		Valid Data
2	1		New Sector
3	0		Garbage
4	1	Address Tag 1	Valid Data
5	1		Valid Data
6	0		Garbage
7	1		Valid Data

Figure 2.20. Line replacement in a sectored cache. Before the miss (a), the tag bits for set addresses 0–3 do not match those output by the CPU. The CPU's output address should be mapped into the cache's set address 0, causing the replacement of the tag and data for that address and the invalidation of all the other sectors in that line. When a second sector (c) is read into the same cache line, the data and Valid bits are updated, but the matching tag is left alone.

crease in bus traffic in copy-back caches, even here the penalty would be slight.

2.2.6 Write Buffers and Line Buffers

A simple write-through cache design works with a microprocessor to reduce the effective main memory read cycle time; however, it has no effect upon main memory write cycle time. Effective main memory write cycle time can be improved through the addition of a **posted write buffer** or, more simply, a **write buffer,** to perform (quite naturally) a **buffered write.**

In a write-through cache designed without a posted write buffer, the microprocessor must complete a main memory bus transaction every time it performs a write cycle. This will cause it to suffer the associated system bus delays. However, in a system using a write buffer, the microprocessor writes the data to the cache and writes the data, address, and pertinent status signals to the write buffer (but not to the system bus) during a write cycle. The microprocessor then continues to access the cache, while the cache controller simultaneously downloads the contents of the write buffer to main memory. This reduces the effective write memory cycle time from the time required for a main memory cycle to the cycle time of the high-speed cache.

The use of write buffers can nearly remove the performance differences between write-through and copy-back caches. Just as studies have been performed to determine the most cost-effective cache size and associativity, similar studies have focused upon the appropriate depth of write buffers. For economy's sake, many designs use a single level of depth. Some semiconductor companies have produced four-level write buffers and claim that this configuration will allow zero-wait write cycles 99.5% of the time, but it is patently obvious that the appropriate depth of write buffers, like most other cache design trade-offs, depends greatly upon such phenomena as main memory access time and the write cycle activity of the program being run.

Write buffers cause their own set of problems. Let's examine the case of a stack push followed shortly by a pop, where the push was a write miss which was not written into the cache. Naturally, the pop will also suffer a read miss cycle. Even if the write buffer is only a single level deep, there is the possibility that the data from the push will not have made it into main memory before the pop is executed. Unless care is taken, the pop will read main memory before main memory is updated with the pushed data. A simple way around this is to disallow the cache from performing a line update until the write buffer's contents have been loaded into main memory. A forced write from the write buffer to main memory is called a **drain** of the write buffer. Another answer is to always update the missed line on a write miss.

The problem gets far trickier when a multilevel write buffer is used. Either the write buffer must be entirely depleted before the cache can continue with the line update, or the write buffer must satisfy the request for data. Certain commercially available write buffers allow this last approach and behave as if they were fully associative caches for any data they contain which has not been written to main memory. This is sometimes referred to as a **victim cache** and is touted as a one- or two-line fully associative cache used to reduce thrashing one or two lines at a time. No matter where the data is in the queue, if a read cycle requests that data, the write buffer will supply the data back to the CPU rather than the cache or main memory. A version of this approach is also known as a **pollution control cache.**

Byte gathering is a nice feature which is offered on certain multilevel write buffers. In programs which perform text manipulation, and in some older revisions of programs which might have been written for an architecture which previously supported only narrow data, the processor might find itself writing twice or four times to the same word address in order to update individual bytes or pairs of bytes within that address. As an example (Figure 2.21), let's say that a four-letter word was being written, one byte at a time, to address 09AF 45ED. In this example, the processor outputs the same address four times and outputs a separate byte write command each time. If our write buffer had four levels, all four would quickly become filled during this operation. A byte-gathering write buffer notices the similarities between the addresses and keeps updating bytes within the word, which has yet to be written to main memory. The hardware for doing this is the same as is used by the write buffer to satisfy read requests with pending write buffer data, since either one is enabled by address matches. In a more severe case, a string might be written to two locations, with the same data being written alternatively to two addresses. Byte 0 goes to 0000 0000, then to FFFF FFFF; then byte 1 is written to 0000 0000, then FFFF FFFF, and so forth. In a byte-gathering write buffer, two buffer locations would collect the data to these two locations, no matter what the order in which the data were presented. In caches which use multiword cache lines a similar mechanism called **write combining** combines separate word writes into a single cache line write.

One outcome of all of this is that the traffic on the main memory bus doesn't look a thing like the traffic on the CPU's pins. A cache miss which is unfulfilled by the write buffer data can place a read request on the main memory bus before the preceding write cycles have been downloaded from the write buffer. A succession of alternating byte writes like those just illustrated would slim down to two simple four-byte word writes. To put it another way, a string of eight single-byte writes, followed by a read cycle, might appear on the main memory bus as a read cycle followed by two four-byte word writes. This greatly disturbs the order in which events occur on the sys-

CYCLE 1
Write least significant byte
to address 09AF 45ED.

Level	Address	Data			
3	N/A	N/A			
2	N/A	N/A			
1	N/A	N/A			
0	09AF 45ED	N/A	N/A	N/A	Valid

CYCLE 2
Write word to address
0000 0000

Level	Address	Data			
3	N/A	N/A			
2	N/A	N/A			
1	0000 0000	Valid Word			
0	09AF 45ED	N/A	N/A	N/A	Valid

CYCLE 3
Write second least significant byte
to address 09AF 45ED.

Level	Address	Data			
3	N/A	N/A			
2	N/A	N/A			
1	0000 0000	Valid Word			
0	09AF 45ED	N/A	N/A	Valid	Valid

CYCLE 4
Gain control of the bus.
Write buffer location 0
to main memory.

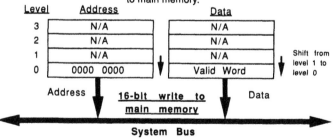

Figure 2.21. Operation of a byte-gathering write buffer during interspersed multiple-byte writes to the same address.

tem bus (as if the randomness of the main memory read cycles was not bad enough due to the cache's absorbing most of the program's locality). The degree to which the write and read cycles are out of order is referred to as **write ordering, read ordering, sequential consistency,** or just **consistency.** Write ordering is called **strong** when write cycles and read cycles occur on the system bus in a sequence close to that followed by the CPU. The strongest ordering is called **processor ordering,** indicating that cycles appear in exactly the same order on the bus, as on the processor. If the sequence is completely jumbled, the write ordering is referred to as **weak.** Without covering this in too much depth, let's simply observe that write ordering can become important in I/O or multiple-processor transactions where a location is read, and, according to its value, a correction factor is written to a different address. A subsequent read, to determine the effect of the preceding write, could conceivably be placed upon the system bus before the preceding write had made it through the write buffer. Naturally, there are few systems where this will actually occur, but in real-time systems, this could cause some hard-to-find instabilities.

Write buffers are not used only at the CPU-to-main-memory interface. Certain processors have such unforgiving write cycle timing that their caches cannot possibly accept write cycles at zero wait states. Some designers solve this problem by putting a single-level write buffer between the CPU and the cache. In other designs, the apparent speed of main memory can be accelerated through the addition of a write buffer to the main memory itself. Although write cycles are still delayed by the system bus latency, the main memory write cycle time is hidden from the processor.

Write buffers can also be used profitably in a copy-back architecture in what is known as **concurrent line write-back, fly-by write-back,** or **background write-back.** Concurrent line write-back is a method of hiding eviction cycles from the processor. They are hard enough to explain that the diagram in Figure 2.22 will be used to help. In a typical read miss eviction cycle, the evicted line is copied back to main memory before the read cycle for the replacement line is allowed to begin. This amounts to a doubling in the effective main memory access time, which is a pretty bad deal. In a concurrent line write-back, the read cycle is the first to occur. This can be accomplished in either of two ways. In the first, which is called **buffered line fill,** the replacement line is read into a **line buffer** (something like an incoming write buffer, writing main memory data into the cache) and is used to satisfy the CPU's immediate needs. Later on, when the CPU is off doing something else, the evicted line is written into main memory, and the line buffer is written into the cache. This can involve some pretty tricky timing, especially since the cache is nearly never left alone by the CPU.

The second approach to performing a concurrent line write-back is simpler, but can slow down line replacements if the main memory is signifi-

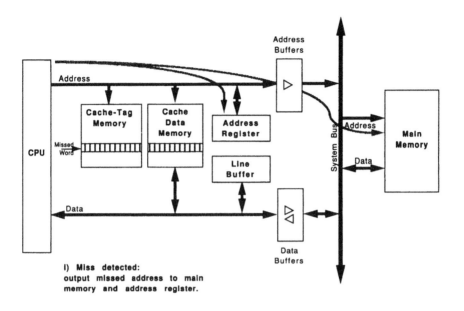

i) **Miss detected:**
output missed address to main
memory and address register.

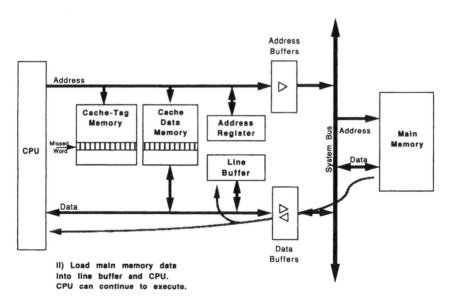

II) **Load main memory data
into line buffer and CPU.
CPU can continue to execute.**

Figure 2.22. Concurrent line write-back implementations using line buffer for read data
(a), and write buffer for evicted line (b).

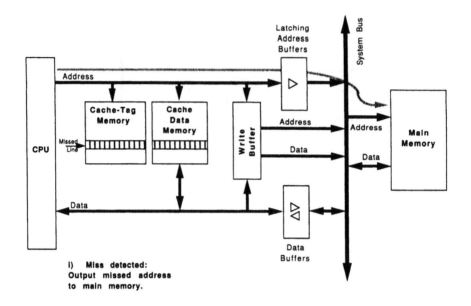

I) **Miss detected:**
Output missed address
to main memory.

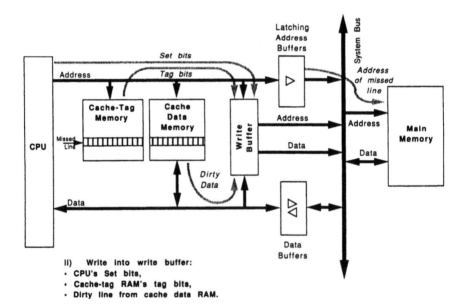

II) **Write into write buffer:**
- CPU's Set bits,
- Cache-tag RAM's tag bits,
- Dirty line from cache data RAM.

Figure 2.22. (*continued*)

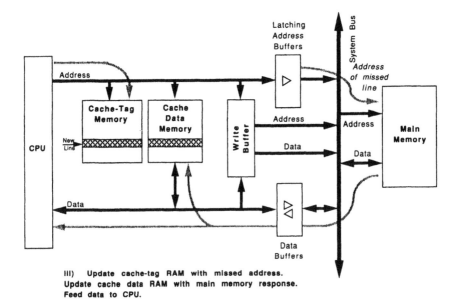

iii) Update cache-tag RAM with missed address.
Update cache data RAM with main memory response.
Feed data to CPU.

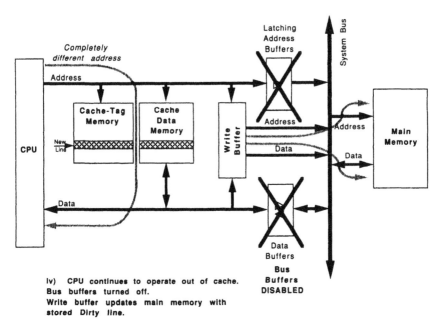

iv) CPU continues to operate out of cache.
Bus buffers turned off.
Write buffer updates main memory with
stored Dirty line.

Figure 2.22. (*continued*)

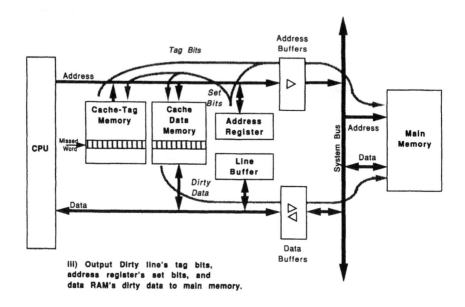

iii) Output Dirty line's tag bits,
address register's set bits, and
data RAM's dirty data to main memory.

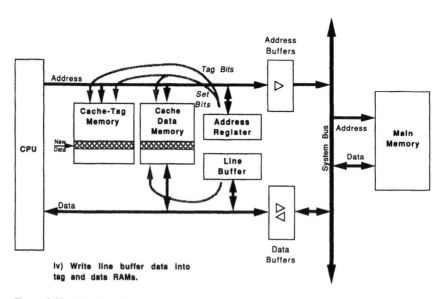

iv) Write line buffer data into
tag and data RAMs.

Figure 2.22. (*continued*)

cantly fast and the cache line is long enough. With this method, once the read miss is detected, the main memory read cycle is initiated. At the same time that the cache controller is waiting for a response from the main memory, the evicted line is being loaded into an outgoing write buffer. Hopefully, the write buffer takes less time to fill than the main memory's access time, so that the main memory data is not languishing, waiting for the cache controller to finish moving the evicted line into the write buffer. As soon as both the main memory data is available and the evicted line is completely copied into the write buffer, the main memory data is presented to the CPU and copied into the cache as a line update. Once the line update is completed, the CPU can continue to operate out of the cache, while the write buffer copies its contents into main memory as a background task.

While either of these methods is pretty complex, the advantage of halving the effective main memory access time is well worth the effort. For this reason, the approach of allowing two things to happen at once is called **concurrency** or **bus concurrency** and is a sought-after feature in cache designs. Just like write ordering, concurrency is called strong if a high number of events can overlap and weak if few events overlap. If you think about concurrency a little, it will become clear that one means of increasing concurrency, namely, write buffers, serves to mess up the write ordering, or consistency, of the cache. In other words, systems with weak concurrency will exhibit strong consistency, while systems with strong concurrency will exhibit weak consistency. Good grief!

Line buffers are not only helpful in mastering concurrency, they tend to speed up line replacements in any sort of cache which supports multiword lines. The designer has two options when deciding on a line refill strategy. An option which does not require a line buffer is to hold the processor in a wait state until the entire line has been refilled. After the complete refill, the processor is allowed to continue. This stands to reason, since the data path into the processor's internal cache is tied up with the cache line refill and cannot be easily made to service the needs of the CPU as the data is being fed in from outside. It is not uncommon for such systems to use a **line fill order** or sequence of lines burst into the cache of **data requested last** (also called **desired word last** and **critical word last**). The line fill starts with a different address than that required by the cache miss, and ends with the missed word.

Line refill strategies based upon line buffers can be called **streaming** caches. The missed word is fed to both the line buffer and the CPU simultaneously, then the CPU is allowed to continue, perhaps to request the next word in the line, which might be the next word being updated in the line buffer at that exact moment, or even to read from a completely different cache line as the rest of the missed line is being read into the line buffer.

Other streaming cache designs which are based on sectored caches without line buffers allow simultaneous execution and cache line update at the expense of the line update possibly being interrupted by CPU-to-cache interaction at a location away from the address of the line update, resulting in the cache only updating a portion of its line. This is dubbed an **aborting** line fill, since the CPU has the capability of discontinuing the line fill in order to service a miss at a different address. Of course, this can also be done in a non-sectored cache design if the designer doesn't mind invalidating the entire line on the miss which aborts the line fill. On the other hand, if the line fill is allowed to continue, and the CPU is caused to wait for the second miss to be serviced, the line fill is called **nonblocking** (the CPU cannot block an ongoing line fill). Most caches with line buffers use a nonblocking strategy. It's anything but intuitive why one strategy would be any better than the other. Streaming caches go by a variety of names (like everything else in this book) such as **bypass, load forwarding, early continuation,** or **early restart** designs. Examples of streaming caches are found in most modern processors.

In general, if a line buffer is used to accelerate a cache line replacement, a **wrapping fetch** is used (the miss may happen at the middle of the line, in which case the burst wraps around until the entire line is fetched). The line fill order of wrapping fetches is called **desired word first, data requested first,** or **critical word first.**

Certain caches perform **prefetches** in anticipation of the next line to be missed by the cache. In general, the line following the last line fetched is prefetched and stored in the line buffer, with the assumption made that all misses are compulsory; that is, the fetched line has not previously resided in the cache. Caches which prefetch in anticipation of the next miss are called **fetch always** or **Class 2** caches. Conversely, caches which only fetch missed lines are called **Class 1, fetch on demand,** or **fetch on fault** caches.

After you've read through this section, look it over and count all of the new buzzwords shown in bold print. And then decide whether you would rather be a cache designer or a Tibetan monk!

2.2.7   Noncacheable Spaces

Certain spaces in main memory should not be cached. The most obvious example is portions of the main memory address range which are used as device inputs. This is especially important in processors which don't differentiate between memory and I/O addresses, like Motorola's 680x0 series. Should the processor be looping while awaiting a change in the status of a switch panel, for example, no change will be noticed if the first reading from the switch panel was cached. Some processors also use a portion of the main memory address range for communication with coprocessors. Once again, the data cannot be assumed to be static, so a cached copy might become out of date. Lastly, multiprocessor systems often communicate via flags which are set and cleared in dedicated main memory locations. No communication can occur if the main memory flag that one processor sets cannot be read by another since the other is reading a cached copy.

All of these examples are reasons for accommodating **uncached addresses** or **noncacheable addresses (NCAs)** within the cache. The method of implementing this is very simple. An address decoder signals to the cache that the current memory request is within a noncacheable space. The cache controller, in turn, disallows the selected line from being updated within the cache. In a way, the cache controller treats the cycle as neither a hit nor a miss, but causes the cache to behave as if it did not exist during this particular cycle.

The exact implementation depends on the freedom of the system designer to change the system architecture. In some systems, all of either high or low memory can be declared noncacheable, and the cache will ignore addresses with the top bit either set or cleared. In other systems, each add-in I/O board will signal which portion of its own address space is noncacheable through a dedicated signal on the backplane. The most difficult case is the addition of a cache to an architecture which previously existed without caches. In such systems, the usual approach is to implement an address decoder as a part of the cache, right next to the CPU, and to feed all possible noncacheable addresses to the cache controller, even for devices which might not be installed in the system. Naturally, this will impact cache performance if the decoder disallows the cacheing of several spaces where the I/O device in question does not exist.

2.2.8 Read-only Spaces

Along the same lines as the noncacheable space is the **read-only** space. This is a cacheable address where the cached line is updated during cache miss reads only, and not on write hits. Read that last sentence again because it doesn't seem to make sense. Why would a cache want to contain the last data read from a main memory address and not to update that data when the same main memory address was written?

This peculiar concept owes its existence to the fact that certain I/O board designers overlay the main memory write addresses of their I/O devices' output registers with a PROM containing the I/O device's driver. There are actually two memory spaces residing at the same address: a read-only space and a write-only space. The write-only space is the output registers of the

I/O device. The read-only space is the I/O driver PROM. Naturally, the PROM would do well to be cached, but since the PROM's contents don't get revised as the CPU writes to the I/O device's registers, the cached version of the PROM's contents cannot be changed when this write cycle occurs. This problem, sometimes called **write side effects,** tends to occur largely in PCs, whose main memory space is limited, so designers use the PROM-I/O overlap to save room.

The simplest method of handling this problem is to mark all addresses within a certain range with a read-only or **write protect** bit as they are cached. Once again, an address decoder is used, but this time the decoder's output is sent directly into a separate bit, similar to another Valid bit, as the cache line is being updated. This bit automatically disallows any change to the contents of the cache data RAM during any write hit cycle at the read-only address.

This approach is used in certain secondary cache controllers. The write protect bit is used to allow an address to be cached, but not overwritten, in the secondary cache. The secondary cache controllers further use this bit to disallow the processor's internal primary cache from even containing a copy of the location. This prevents the inevitable updating of the primary cache's copy during a CPU write cycle, since the CPU's internal primary cache usually does not have a read-only bit (see Section 2.2.10).

2.2.9   Other Status Bits

All of the housekeeping bits described in the preceding sections can be called **status bits.** This category includes Valid bits, Dirty bits, read-only bits, LRU bits, and anything else which is stored along with every other cache line, but is not data or an address tag.

If you do a little math, you will find that you can reduce your cache's overall bit count through judicious use of status bits. A good example is the use of sectored lines, or longer lines, to get rid of tag entries. While these approaches might not help out much with discrete cache designs, on-chip caches can really take advantage of any opportunity to reduce transistor count. This makes it even more important to measure the actual performance of all of your design options before committing to a specific cache design. Another way to save memory bits is to disregard more significant tag bits if these represent address bits which are not used by the system.

There are other reasons to add status bits to a design. **Control domain identifier** bits can be used to identify the user level of a cache entry. Sometimes these are used to determine which cache entries should be invalidated during a task switch in a multitasking operating system. In some cache designs, task numbers are stored to counter aliasing problems which might otherwise crop up in a logical cache design. The logical cache in Figure 1.15 uses this approach with the processor's function code bits FC0–FC2.

Lock bits are used to force an entry not to be removed from the cache. This can help speed up interrupt response in time-critical software applications, such as real-time operating systems. Lock bits make most sense in a multiway cache, but can also find their way into direct-mapped designs. A **reader's/writer's lock** is a bit which can keep unauthorized processors or processes from overwriting the contents of a cache line.

No doubt you will run into other caches which use status bits in some unique manner. They are easiest to understand if you just think of them as markers for the individual lines of the cache. We'll see designs in Chapter 4 where cache line states are encoded to reduce the number of status bits used to store a line's state.

Now let's move on to some approaches which do not interplay with the number of status bits in each cache line.

2.2.10   Primary, Secondary, and Tertiary Caches

You can't have gotten this far in the book without having determined that caches do a good job during their hit cycles, but don't really speed up miss cycles at all. The question then becomes one of a cost/performance trade-off, pitting the optimum cache size and speed against the practicalities of building such a system. Microprocessor designers are confronted with the trade-off of die size versus cache size for a processor with an on-chip cache, since an on-chip cache can naturally be made to run significantly faster than anything that involves signals being routed off of and onto the processor chip itself.

Let's work with a hypothetical case where the processor has been designed with a small, but very good cache, and slow DRAM is used to implement main memory in order to keep the memory array's cost down. How can such a system be made to operate faster? The designer is going to try to minimize the access time of the main memory during on-chip cache miss cycles, and although tricks like interleaving main memory help, they are effective only to a certain point. A very valid approach to this problem is to build a larger but slower cache outside of the chip and to use this cache to accelerate the apparent access time of main memory during an on-chip cache miss cycle. In a system where two caches are cascaded in this way (see Figure 2.23), the cache more intimately tied to the processor is called the **first-level** or **primary** cache, and the cache which is placed between the CPU/primary cache subsystem and the main memory is called the **sec-**

ondary or **second-level** cache. More levels may be added, of course, and these would be called **third-level** or **tertiary** for the cache between the secondary cache and main memory, and so on. Some architects use the terms **Level 1** or **L1** for the primary cache, **Level 2** or **L2** for the secondary cache, **Level 3** or **L3** for the tertiary cache, etc. Whichever terminology is used, the cache which is closer to the processor than the one being discussed is called the **upstream** or **predecessor** cache, and the cache closer to the main memory is called the **downstream** or **successor** cache.

Rest assured that the world has not become all that complex yet. Although the author has seen a number of systems with secondary caches, systems which use more than two cache levels are extremely rare at the time of this writing, although some multiprocessor systems use a shared tertiary cache for processors which each have their own primary and secondary caches.

There are other reasons to use a multilevel cacheing scheme than the one just mentioned, such as saving die size on the CPU chip. Certain processor architectures have designed-in cache controllers which automatically limit the size and policies of the primary cache. Another reason is that the size or type of cache which is desired to fit between the CPU and the main memory might not be implementable with state-of-the-art static RAMs. Large RAMs tend to be slower than small ones, so a designer might be caught compromising between a small, fast cache and a large, slow one. The problem can be broken down so that both a small, fast cache and a large, slow one are used together as the upstream and downstream caches in the system, thereby reducing the level of compromise which must be made. This same approach has been discussed as an approach to be used within a single chip, where the processor chip contains the CPU plus a small primary and a large secondary cache. Wait a minute, you say. Won't both on-chip caches operate at the same speed? Not really. The larger a RAM grows, the more levels of logic required to implement its address decoder. Followers of the RISC argument, where the cycle time of a CPU is reduced by minimization of the critical path logic delay elements (Section 3.1), will observe that by reducing the cache size the critical path can be made that much faster. In this sort of chip, the cache and CPU are designed closely together, with all efforts going to the reduction of cycle time. We'll show some examples in Section 5.2.

One last reason, and probably the most common one used to rationalize the use of a secondary cache, is that the system designer is chartered to use an industry-standard CPU which has an internal cache which was not designed with the current system in mind. A good example is that of a multiple-processor system designed around any of the many currently available processors featuring write-through caches. Caches in multiple-processor systems are usually designed to minimize system bus traffic far more than is

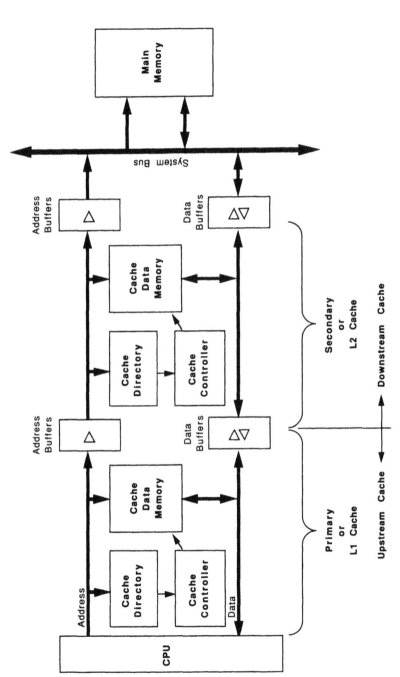

Figure 2.23. Primary and secondary caches. Note how little difference there is between any two levels of cache from the perspective of so simple a block diagram. Any number of levels of caches can be implemented.

possible using a write-through cache, so designers of such systems often choose to supplement the on-chip write-through cache with a secondary copy-back cache.

Naturally, the design of the secondary cache depends greatly upon the kind of traffic expected out of the primary cache. It is safe to say that the activity demanded of the second cache will look nothing at all like that required of a primary cache. A secondary cache is generally idle, while a primary cache is almost never idle. The balance of read to write cycles can be completely reversed between a primary and a secondary cache, the hit rate will probably be significantly lower, and the sequence of requests will probably exhibit a much more random behavior, with both temporal and spatial locality playing a smaller role. How can it all be so different? We'll examine this one piece at a time.

First, let's assume that the processor normally would perform one write cycle for every ten read cycles (this once again is a function of the code being run on the machine) and that the primary cache is a write-through design which satisfies a flat 90% of all read cycles. This is a pretty typical scenario. Since the design is write-through, the primary cache will not intercept any of the write cycles, so that 10% of the processor's cycles automatically get passed through to the secondary cache as writes. How many read cycles does the secondary cache see? Well, if the other 90% of the processor's cycles are reads, and 90% of these are satisfied by the primary cache, then 10% of them make it to the secondary cache, or $10\% \cdot 90\% = 9\%$ of the overall CPU cycles. This means that the secondary cache will see more writes than reads, and, if the primary cache has a higher hit rate than 90%, the balance will be even more skewed toward write cycles. This flipflop would not occur in a system using a copy-back primary cache; however, the writes from the primary to the secondary cache would only occur upon cache evictions, so there would be no bearing for temporal locality as far as write cycles were concerned. The eviction might occur either a very short or a very long period after the write cycle actually had occurred.

Downstream caches never exhibit anywhere near the hit rates of the primary cache, and with good reason. As we saw in Figure 2.9, the cache's hit rate tapers off with increasing cache size. The improvement in hit rate can be viewed as a differential, $\Delta H / \Delta S$, where H is the hit rate and S is the size of the cache. If the primary cache offers a hit rate of 90%, and the secondary cache brings the hit rate up to 95% (Figure 2.24), then the secondary cache is only cutting the miss rate in half, thus exhibiting a hit rate of 50%. This brings up questions about the value of secondary caches. Why pay for so little an improvement? If we look at the problem from the bottom up, we see that the miss rate of the single-level cache system is 10%, and the miss rate of the two-level cache system is 5%, meaning that the bus traffic in the two-

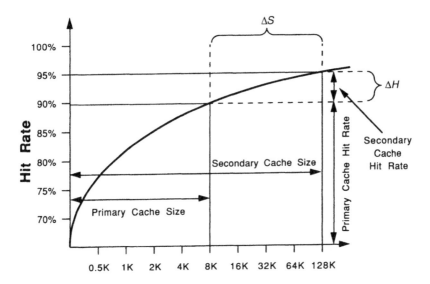

Figure 2.24.   Incremental hit rate of a secondary cache. A very large secondary cache can exhibit a really small hit rate in comparison to the hit rate of the smaller primary cache. Most designers focus on miss rate improvements in order to rationalize using multiple levels of caches.

level system is half that of the traffic in the single-level system. This is a key improvement in multiprocessing systems, as was discussed in Section 1.8, and is also very important in systems which have long main memory latencies. (By the way, Figure 2.24 is fictitious data, so don't try to use it to prove any points or to design your own cache.)

If the downstream cache has the same line size as the upstream cache, then it stands to reason that the only hits the downstream cache will have are from the upstream cache misses which are caused by conflicts. This is simple to see. The secondary cache will only be filled with the same data as is requested by the primary cache at the same time that it is being loaded into the primary cache. The only way that this data will stay in the secondary cache but will be removed from the primary cache is if the primary cache has a conflict which causes its copy of that line to be overwritten, yet the same conflict does not occur in the secondary cache, due to either a larger line size or a larger address space. For this reason, the downstream cache should either be considerably larger than the upstream cache or should use a line size much larger than its upstream neighbor.

Some designers choose to assure that the contents of a primary cache are excluded from being contained in the secondary cache. Why hold redundant data in both of these places? This is a more efficient use of the two caches, but sometimes this added efficiency gets in the way of the implementation of other good cache policies. We'll examine one called "inclusion" in Section 4.1.1. Sometimes, too, the exclusion of primary cache data from the secondary cache becomes extremely difficult, and the alternative not only shortens the design cycle, but also might reduce the complexity and chip count of the cache control logic.

Secondary caches can also be used to implement good screening mechanisms in multiple-processor systems, a topic which will be described in depth in Section 4.1.3. In a nutshell, the less often a system intrudes on the CPU/primary cache subsystem, the faster that subsystem will operate. A secondary cache can filter system intrusions from the primary cache and only allow interaction by potentially meaningful transactions.

2.3   STATISTICAL PREMISES

Figure 2.9 was used to illustrate both the diminishing returns of increasing cache size and the hit rate improvements offered by increasing the associativity of a cache of a given size. Although the figure gives a good impression of the potential of cached systems, it is not at all accurate. True cache statistics are highly dependent upon the exact target system, both hardware and software, and there is no substitution for determining the exact characteristics of your own system. Unfortunately, most designers don't have the resources available to test the various combinations of caches which they might implement, so a graph like this one might be the fallback for certain design decisions.

In general, the curves are a reasonable estimate of the performance to be expected of a cached system. Several papers have been written in which actual measurements are provided, and they usually don't follow curves as smooth as those in the graph. Many exhibit lumps which may be attributable to the maximum size loop which a programmer is comfortable writing, or limits to the size data set being used, and some performance curves actually cross each other, showing a cache using certain policies performing better than another for small cache sizes, but worse for larger caches!

2.3.1   The Value of Choosing Policies Empirically

If we are to be purists, the cache must be designed only after significant statistics have been collected to indicate the performance trade-offs of certain policies and cache sizes against all others. More probably, the designer will go on from this text to read a few of the available papers, then make decisions based on statistics which were measured upon an altogether different system running software completely unlike the programs the target system is to use.

This can lead to bad decisions, since the statistics in these papers have been collected on systems which are so completely different than the current design that some of the more subtle trade-offs which were determined to make the paper's system perform better might actually impede the operation of the newer cache. Real-time multiprogrammed systems tend to do better with higher associativity levels than are required in simple single-tasking operating systems like MS-DOS. The main memory bus protocol can have a significant impact on the choice of replacement algorithms.

The following section should be discussed with the system programmers in the hopes that they can help you out by providing tools to help measure the cache's true performance.

2.3.1.1 Simple Methods of Measuring Performance Software modeling is an inexpensive way to test possible cache strategies against each other. Usually, the target processor is used in an uncached system, with a simulator actually intercepting all memory accesses. The simulator is made to emulate different sorts of caches, and the model is made to run programs which will be run on the target system. A great disadvantage to software modeling is that it runs more than an order of magnitude (and quite possibly two orders of magnitude) more slowly than the same program would run on the uncached system without using the model. This is pretty easy to understand, since each instruction of the target code must be hand-fed via the model software to the processor, and statistics must then be stored for each reference made. The large addition to the execution time means that the exercise of trying several different cacheing strategies on a large software base can consume quite a bit of time. Nonetheless, the low cost and ease of implementation of this method make it a popular alternative.

A less popular and considerably more expensive alternative is hardware modeling. A typical hardware cache simulator consists of the most full-blown cache the designer could hope to use, with the addition of switches to change or remove one variable or another (examples might be cache size, write policy, or associativity). The target programs are then run with the various features enabled or disabled, and the resulting execution times are used to decide upon a system's implementation. Naturally, such a system can take a considerable effort to debug. To simplify the designer's life, such systems are sometimes run at a scaled speed, like half or one-quarter of the final system clock speed. As long as all parameters are scaled equally (CPU clock, main memory latency, bus clock, etc.), valid measurements can be obtained, and good decisions can be made regarding the optimum cache strategy.

Two other simple methods involve the use of traces of example executions. There are two sorts of traces: hardware and software. Hardware traces usually are performed by placing an apparatus upon the bus which will measure real-life address activity in such a way that statistics can be compiled to reveal an optimum cache strategy. One method is to make a hardware model of the example cache-tag RAM for a possible alternative and to measure the miss rate it would have. The cache-tag RAM only has to run as fast as main memory, so making one which allows the simulation of several different cache architectures is a simple task. Although it would be reasonably easy to design another sort of trace machine which counted simple statistics on the number of main memory accesses within certain address ranges (possibly by using nothing more than a logic analyzer), these statistics reveal nothing about the locality of the program being run, and end up not being very useful.

Software traces, often called code profiles, are even simpler to implement: however, they lack somewhat in resolution. Those used in most cache research are implemented in microcode, but can only be run in systems which allow the microcode to be modified. The simplest sort of software trace is driven by the nonmaskable interrupt in a real-time system. If the system being used for traces doesn't have an interrupt of this sort, it is often not too difficult to set one up. At the beginning of the interrupt routine the program counter is pushed onto the stack. The trace routine is layered into the normal interrupt service routine, and looks at the stack to keep statistics on the location of the program counter. The program counter is not the only address generator which can be traced by software tracing. All other pointers can be examined as well, once again at the expense of latency in the interrupt service routine.

As with the simpler hardware method just mentioned, care will have to be taken to assure that the interrupts are not so widely spaced that issues of locality are lost. On the other hand, causing too many interrupts might slow the system down to the point where it would operate as slowly as a software model.

One good reason to use traces is if the scenario in which the target system is to run cannot be simulated adequately at a much lower speed and if the cost of a hardware model cannot be justified. Examples include a single node in a network of other computers or a widely used multiuser system, either of which depend greatly upon timely interaction, with uncontrollable outside sources to be measured realistically.

Certain compilers support profiling by inserting extra instructions into the compiled code when a profiling option is invoked. This is a great way to gather information about the program counter and what the code is doing, but does not often do a lot to help you see what's happening in the data space. If your main thrust is to optimize code accesses, this is a workable solution. At least one programmer I know of profiles his code by measuring the length of loops using a ruler on an assembler listing (generated either by a compiler's output, or from disassembled object code) and figuring the average number of times each loop is executed. He can use this to determine the percent of time the program counter resides within any single location.

2.3.2   Using Hunches to Determine Policies

Of course, now that you have an understanding about how you can measure your own cache statistics, that doesn't mean that you are going to do it. Maybe you don't have the time, or, quite possibly, your marketing department has told you the only features which a customer will buy (sadly enough, hardware specifications are usually more deeply scrutinized by potential customers than are benchmarks). This is where you must depend upon your (or somebody else's) intuition.

For those who haven't the time, I hope that the intuitive approach taken in this book is found to help. As an example, it should be pretty clear from what has already been discussed that a design which falls downstream of a write-through cache should focus more attention on write cycle performance than on read cycles, or that an increase in the associativity or even size of a write-through cache often pales in comparison to the benefits (or complexity) of converting the design to a copy-back cache, or that wait states are so bad that there is no cache strategy which is worth incurring one. I should also hope that the reader has the time to read some of the more academic studies on cache performance. Although this book does not try to categorize which papers are of value, there are plenty of them out there, and it is a simple task to find one paper you feel good about and to get copies of every paper in its bibliography. Still, remember that the papers were written about a different system than yours, running different software on a different CPU across a different bus structure. In cache design, the only absolute truths are the ones describing how your cache works with your software on your system. Nothing else really matters. One step to be sure of is that you argue every decision with your peers. Nothing helps work out the bugs in advance more than having to defend your assumptions.

For those of you who have to design a cache to some arbitrary specification because somebody told you to, don't despair. Look a little deeper. Maybe there is something you learned in this book which can be coupled with the restrictions you have been placed under which can turn a less optimal strategy into a near-stellar one. You are probably learning that there are so many variables in cache design that there must be one or two options you have so far neglected to take advantage of. One of the nicer points is that many of these options require little or no additional hardware and can be had for the simple price of a little more effort in the design/debug cycle.

2.4   SOFTWARE PROBLEMS AND SOLUTIONS

So far, we have assumed that the cache designer is burdened with solving the cache design problem without any help from the software side of the house. This usually happens to be the case, but in those instances where the programmers and designers are able to work together to solve the problem, there are certain simple rules which can be used to drastically simplify the design of the cache.

Most often, the real challenges encountered are due to the fact that the cache is being designed to accelerate the performance of a system which has been around for several years. The software is already written in a certain way, and the cache might need to maintain compatibility with existing hardware which has anomalies which must be accommodated. In altogether new designs, however, the cache designer has the luxury of working with the design team to help define the overall system specification.

2.4.1   Trade-offs in Software and Hardware Interaction

It is easier to understand hardware/software cache design trade-offs with some examples. One good example is the problem of cache validity, as described in Section 2.1.3. The software solution is to disallow the cache from satisfying any CPU bus cycles until a bootstrap routine has made certain that all cache lines have been overwritten with valid data, after which the same program sets a flag which enables the cache to respond. The hardware solution is to maintain a Valid bit for every line and to reset all Valid bits through a hardware reset mechanism before allowing the cache to respond. Obviously, the hardware method will be more costly to reproduce.

This sort of valid/invalid criterion is not only a problem at startup, but also occurs during direct memory access (DMA) activity, where an outside device modifies the contents of main memory, but not necessarily the corresponding contents of the cache memory. The brute-force hardware method of handling this problem is to invalidate the entire cache whenever the bus signals supporting DMA write cycles occur (several more elegant methods will be detailed in Chapter 4). The software method of handling the problem is to have the operating system invalidate either the entire cache or the appropriate section of the cache whenever a context switch is invoked.

Another example is a bit tougher to explain here, mostly because it involves multiprocessors, the subject of Chapter 4. In a multiprocessing environment, processors often communicate via locked read/modify/write instructions. One processor writes to a main memory mailbox location to tell another processor what it is doing. This problem is similar to the problem of I/O addresses mentioned in Section 2.1.3. If the processor which is to read the mailbox location refers to a copy of the location in its cache instead of reading the actual main memory, the main memory will be updated by the writing processor without the reading processor ever noticing. The software solution to this problem is always to map the mailbox locations to the same physical memory address. It will then be simple for the cache designer to disallow that address range from being cacheable. In multiprocessing systems which are not in control of the mailbox locations, some extremely sophisticated intercache communications protocols must be worked out. These are sufficiently complex that I won't go into them here, but will wait until we arrive at Chapter 4.

2.4.2 Maintaining Compatibility with Existing Software

If you review several cache designs, you will start to notice the bizarre twists which sometimes must be added to account for ways in which existing software has been written.

Probably the biggest headache for many cache designers is the software timing loop. The timing loop runs at exactly the right speed as long as the processor is clocked at exactly such and such a frequency, and might even depend on a certain main memory latency. This type of programming pretty well does away with the possibility that the hardware can undergo improvements. The only really clean way to deal with such a problem is to nail down the location of the timing loops for the program(s) under question, and to disallow these from being cached, meanwhile assuring that the processor clock is never improved. A simpler alternative is to allow the user two operating modes. It has become the terminology in the IBM PC world to dub the two operating modes in systems so equipped as normal mode and turbo mode.

In certain real-time systems, interrupt latency must be exactly the same, no matter when the interrupt occurred. This is not easily accomplished in cached systems. Say the interrupt service routine were written to count the number of interrupts and to respond to the interrupt with a high or low output, depending on the previous interrupt activity. Naturally, the interrupt routine and the record of previous interrupt activity will be stored in main memory. The routine runs the possibility of thrashing on certain interrupt cycles and not thrashing on others, meaning that the interrupt latency will be variable. Add to this the chance that the program being run between the interrupts will at some times overwrite some of the interrupt routine and at other times will leave it alone. Two simple approaches to this problem are to disallow the cache from working during the entire interrupt response or to disallow the cacheing of those locations involved in the interrupt service routine. The latter solution might be a little too drastic, since the interrupt service routine, at a minimum, involves not only the service routine's code space and an associated data space, but also the stack. Disallowing the cacheing of the stack will have a negative impact on the performance of the entire program!

For those who have chosen to use a logical cache implementation, care must be taken to understand any tricks which programmers may have played with the logical to physical address mapping. Address aliases can be used very artfully to improve the communication between routines, but they are really tough to account for in a logical cache design. Once again, a heavy-handed, but useful, approach is to simply disallow the cacheing of any page which might be used in this manner at some time.

2.5 REAL-WORLD PROBLEMS

Compared to the rest of the book, this is a really mundane section. Here, we will not cover the tricks and techniques of artful cache design, but will tackle the tougher problem of getting the hardware to run, and to run reliably in such a way that it can be mass produced.

It's pretty reasonable to assume that the cache designer is going to use the fastest processor available. After all, caches are a way to make up for the disparity between true main memory access time and the access time required by the CPU to run at maximum throughput. This disparity does not become a problem until the designer uses the fastest CPU speeds. Also, the cache is usually a more expensive means of increasing throughput than is the use of a faster CPU (although this might not be the case, as was shown in Figure 1.1).

At the fastest CPU bus speeds available, the CPU/cache subsystem cannot be examined only as a digital system with the problem of logic bugs, but the timing must be scrutinized and derated, circuit boards must be designed to accommodate high frequencies, and the designer must be resigned to a lot of sleepless nights.

Most high-speed system designers allow themselves time to get the system working thoroughly at a scaled-down speed, like 10% of the maximum CPU speed, then to gradually increase the clock frequency to full operation until all timing bugs have been found and removed. Although this sounds slow, less methodical methods seldom can be used more profitably.

2.5.1 Parasitic Capacitance and Bus Loading

Designers who are working for the first time with cycle times of under 50ns are often surprised at the care and attention required by high-speed systems' bus signals. At lower speeds, the few nanoseconds consumed by capacitive loading might have been mentioned in a thorough timing analysis (if one were performed), but could easily be accommodated by using a slightly faster, slightly more expensive part. At 20ns cycle times, once the processor's output delay and set-up times are accounted for, the designer finds that the cache will require the use of leading-edge component speeds even before derating calculations are made. Inaccurate derating can hurt in two ways. Overoptimistic derating can cause the cache simply not to function, whereas overconservative derating might keep the cache from ever being designed, possibly allowing a competitor to beat you to the punch.

High-speed processors tend to be specified into small (50pF) loads for three reasons. First, processor manufacturers don't want to lose yield simply because they tested their parts under overly stringent loading, possibly on a pin which nobody uses anyway. This is a way for them to cut themselves some slack. Second, to drive large output loads at high speeds, high-current output drivers must be used. The consequences of designing these high-current drivers into a processor chip are many. All ICs are designed within strict power budgets. Fast circuits require more current, so the more of the budget's current which is diverted to the output drivers, the less there is available for the faster parts of the processor; hence, the processor must be made to run more slowly. That's not a good deal for a processor which is being pushed to the highest speeds. High-current output drivers also generate a lot of noise on the processor's internal ground, which can confuse some of the internal thresholds, leading to slower performance or even bit errors and lockups. The last reason for the CPU manufacturer to specify outputs into a light load is that the test equipment tends to come from the tester manufacturer looking like a light load, and the addition of heavier loading is somewhat of a burden and a puzzle to the CPU manufacturer. If additional loading is to be put onto the tester, what exactly should it look like? It seems that no two system designers can agree on what the "typical" output load looks like to a CPU chip.

A generally accepted method of derating is to add 1ns of propagation delay to a signal for every 20pF of loading above the specified output loading of the processor or other driving device. This works for light drivers like CPUs and memories, but some logic outputs can drive either more or less, and the device's data sheets should be consulted if that data is given. Although I've never heard a consistent number to use for the capacitive effects for printed circuit card traces, one number is 1pF per inch. This adds up really fast, so careful layout is a must.

As an example, let's derate a CPU output which is driving the address inputs of four 128K × 8 cache data RAMs and three 128K × 8 cache-tag RAMs, plus an address buffer along a 30-inch trace (this sounds huge, but is about

Table 2.1.   Capacitive derating on the address bus of a typical cached system.

Load	Capacitance (pF)	Notes
Tag RAMs	21	Three 7pF inputs
Data RAMs	28	Four 7pF inputs
Address buffer	7	
PC board traces	+30	30 in. · 1ns/in.
Total capacitance	86	
Less: CPU rated output drive	–50	
Derating capacitance	36	
Times: Derating factor	*0.05ns/pF	1ns for every 20pF.
Derating	1.8ns	All tags, etc., must be 1.8ns faster than figured in timing calculations without derating.

as short as you can run such a trace on a two-sided PC board). The address buffer and all the RAMs will be given 7pF input capacitances, and the processor is specified into 50pF. Table 2.1 shows how the typical derating equation would look for the lower address bits in this system.

Why does this only apply for the *lower* address bits? Remember that these are the set bits, so each set address bit must be routed to the address inputs of all the tag RAMs plus all the data RAMs. The tag bits only must go to one tag RAM and the address buffer (unless a discrete comparator is being used, which will add a load). Remember that no tag bits are used in accessing the cache data RAM. Also, the loading will be different for the address bits which are lower than the set bits in a system using multiword lines or sectoring. Further, bidirectional buses must have these equations performed for each driver on the bus. This may sound as if it only pertains to the data bits, until you realize that the addresses in a copy-back cache are obtained from the tag RAMs during line evictions. We will see in Chapter 4 that there can also be episodes in which the CPU/cache subsystem's address inputs will be driven by the address buffer. There will be an awful lot of these little calculations in a high-speed system!

One method to get around some of these derating issues is to use **multichip modules (MCMs)**. Multichip modules are a hot topic of conversation at the writing of this book, but have not been put into widespread use. The Intel Pentium Pro is one of few widely available MCMs. In an MCM, the CPU, the cache, and all buffers to the outside world are mounted onto a substrate, preferably without previously having been packaged. The advantages to this technique are that the input capacitance is lower for devices which are not packaged, and the module substrate is capable of carrying signals using shorter connections at a lower capacitance per inch. Further, if all of the signals which are not required to be placed on a module output pin are allowed to use smaller I/O swings, the charge/discharge cycle of the node capacitance becomes smaller, allowing the module's chips to be run at a higher speed. The downside to MCMs is that the manufacture of modules is costly and tends to require the use of sole-sourced RAMs and logic. Add to this the cost of rework should a single chip upon the module fail, and the costs go through the roof! Testability is also a big problem. In the near term, it appears that MCMs will remain the domain of vertically integrated firms' highest performance and highest cost systems. A reasonable compromise is to use a carefully designed module made of packaged parts on a standard circuit card, as is being done by Intel with their standard processors.

Another nagging real-world concern is clock skew. Clock skew can result from mechanisms as obvious as the use of different buffer outputs to drive two different devices' clock inputs, usually motivated by heavy loading on the clock lines. The worst case of this is if two different buffers in two different packages are used to drive two versions of the same clock signal. One device may be particularly fast and be mounted in a cooler part of the board, while the other device is allowed to get warm and, even at cooler temperatures, runs at the slow end of the devices shipped by the component manufacturer. Heat slows silicon down. Less obvious are the times that clock skew comes from mismatched loading on two identically buffered but separate clock lines, or from deviations in trace length between two clock paths. Sometimes, the skew which causes the problem comes from two different taps on the same signal line, where these taps are simply too distant from one another. The methods often used to prevent clock skew from becoming a problem are to drive carefully placed underloaded clock lines with hefty signals all coming out of the same package. Some designers simply use the same octal buffer for all clock outputs (pin-to-pin skew is not tested or guaranteed on these devices), but there are devices available which are designed and tested specifically for this function, which have much stronger current drive than the octal buffer, and are tested and guaranteed to maximum pin-to-pin skew. Certain clock driver circuits go so far as to use a phase-locked loop to synchronize one of the clock driver's output pins with the reference input.

Resistive loads can also help systems avoid pitfalls due to delay-line effects. Any conductor, unless properly terminated, will reflect power back in the direction from which it came. This is fundamental transmission line theory. If both ends of a PC board trace are improperly terminated, the waveform can adopt a severe ringing which may even pass back and forth across an input threshold, causing false triggers of registers, erroneous write cycles into RAMs, or even a reading as the opposite logic state of the value represented on a data line. Once again, there are many schools of thought on this subject, all of which will be left to better qualified sources to explain. PC board layout techniques are neither the forte of the author nor the subject of this book. Still, don't overlook this important issue.

Designers whose products are aimed at the U.S. market must worry about complying with Federal Communications Commission (FCC) radiofrequency emissions regulations. This ties in with the clock skew and termination issues just discussed and is a challenge which will be noted but not discussed here. Let's just say that it is one more in the list of concerns facing the high-speed cache designer.

2.5.2   Critical Timing Paths

Figure 2.10 shows the critical timing path of the cache-tag RAM in a direct-mapped cache. For most systems, this is the real hot spot and will be the most difficult timing problem to solve. The use of integrated cache-tag RAMs and cache controllers is often determined by the speed required of the cache-tag RAM. In some architectures, the cache controller is a single chip which accepts address inputs, and outputs a Ready signal back to the CPU. Although this is a fast approach, it is usually implemented using ASICs, so the cache-tag RAM is never as large or as fast as the state of the art in static RAM design. Other implementations involve putting all of the cache control logic except the cache-tag RAM within the CPU chip itself to reduce chip transitions, or to include the tag comparator into either the cache controller chip or the cache-tag RAM chip. Only the slowest designs have the luxury of allowing the use of a discrete cache-tag RAM, followed by a discrete comparator, followed by the cache control logic.

One observation which pops out when considering the problem of designing a cache-tag RAM and downstream logic with sufficient response time is that the problem might be difficult for direct-mapped caches, but with multiway caches it becomes really nasty.

Back in Section 2.2.2, we saw that the tag on a multiway cache is used to gate the output of the data RAM, whereas the data RAM in a direct-mapped system starts the cycle in an enabled state. An approach used by at least one cache controller is to implement the two-Way architecture using a **most recently used (MRU)** bit to signify the Way most recently accessed for the line being read. The MRU bit is just an inverted version of the LRU bit discussed in Section 2.2.2. Using this approach, the cache data RAM starts the cycle with the most recently used Way's outputs enabled, just as a direct-mapped cache starts a cycle. This allows the cache-tag RAMs to be as slow in this sort of two-Way design as they would be in a direct-mapped architecture. Time is only lost on a Way miss where the Way which was initially enabled is the wrong one, and the CPU is delayed until the proper Way can be selected. It is easy to conclude that the highest miss rate which would be likely to occur in such a cache would be about 50%, and, with the operation of this particular design, that Way miss only costs a single cycle. Intel's designers seem to believe that the Way miss rate is actually significantly lower than 50%. The actual performance benefit of a two-Way architecture over a direct-mapped version would need to overwhelm the detriment to overall cache bandwidth of these added wait states in order for this concept to improve system performance. It is not intuitively obvious that the MRU-based, two-Way cache would outperform an equivalent-size direct-mapped cache. Only measured statistics could prove or disprove this argument.

Other vexing timing difficulties can occur in the data loop. Figure 2.10 shows the path of the addresses out of the CPU, through the cache data RAM, and into the processor's data input pins. If the processor has no internal cache, it will tend to consume a few CPU clock cycles every time it requests memory data, and the cache data RAM's timing might be tight, but not impossible. Processors which have internal caches tend to use multiword lines and fetch the entire line at one time, using the burst cycle described in Section 2.2.5. Naturally, there is a speed benefit of allowing the burst refill to run just as quickly as possible, so the designer will attempt to implement a zero-wait data RAM in the design. The first cycle is easy to match. The address is output over a full CPU cycle time before the data is required. However, the address stays valid until after the first word is fetched, skewing the timing on the other cycles to the point that the access time of the remaining cycles is the CPU clock cycle time less the CPU address output propagation delay and the CPU data input set-up time.

Some designers use interleaving to solve this timing problem, where the cache or main memory is four times as wide as the CPU's data bus, and multiplexing is used to perform the burst sequence automatically, based on the CPU clock rather than on the CPU address outputs. (A DRAM which is interleaved this way will usually have a couple of wait states only at the beginning of the cycle and will thus be called 4:1:1:1.) Other designers place outboard burst counters between the CPU and the RAM, so that they can reduce the clock to burst count propagation delay. Today's most popular cache data RAMs have included the counter on-chip.

Back in Section 2.2.6, we spent a lot of time and buzzwords on describing the use of line buffers and early continuation (where the CPU is allowed to continue to operate as a multiword line is being updated in the cache). It might save you some time and effort to find out whether or not the internal cache of the processor you're designing with uses early continuation. As a case in point, one acquaintance of the author went to lengths to design a secondary cache around the Motorola 68030, which supported the 68030's burst cache line refill mechanism. Oddly enough, the burst design *under-*

performed a similar design without burst support. Why? Because the 68030's internal cache does not support early continuation. To better understand the problem, look at Figure 2.25. If all instructions execute in the minimum amount of time, and if the instructions all execute in line without intervening accesses to other addresses, as is shown in the figure, the burst will work no faster than the discrete cycles. In a lot of instances (probably 75%, since the line is four words long), however, only a portion of the line will be used before the processor needs to access a completely different address. With the 68030's nonblocking design, the burst must be completed before the CPU's need to look elsewhere can be accommodated, thus stopping the CPU from performing any work during this contention.

Another point of difficulty in the design of high-speed caches is the production of well-timed write pulses, especially for cache write cycles which are allowed to occur at zero wait-states, either because the cache adopts a copyback policy or because a write-through design employs a write buffer. There are two sources of problems with high-speed write cycles: skew and noise. Write pulse skew is caused by the use of separate silicon to time the write pulse and the data and address inputs to a RAM. If the write pulse is generated by the same clock on the same piece of silicon as the data and address, all of these signals move together over temperature, voltage variations, and IC manufacturing process variations. No matter what the environment, the timing is accurate to a fare-thee-well. In systems which buffer the address inputs or the data I/O to the cache, or systems which use different silicon to generate the cache data RAM's write pulse than that used to generate the RAM's address and data inputs, the designer must assume the possibility that these different ICs will come from different manufacturers and will exhibit different propagation delays, different temperature tracking (not to mention that each chip will probably be at a different temperature at all times), and all other worst case possibilities which will cause the data, address, and write pulse inputs to arrive at wildly fluctuating intervals with respect to each other. A common way to get around this problem is to use synchronous static RAMs in the cache design, since the synchronous SRAM uses no write pulse, but instead uses a separate clock input to sample address, data, and write enable inputs all at once. We won't go into synchronous SRAMs in depth here, but the timing waveform of a write cycle of a synchronous SRAM is shown in Figure 2.26, and it is easy to see that the write cycle can have a lot of margin and still be performed at very high speeds.

Synchronous SRAMs also neatly solve the noise aspect of high-speed write pulses. Assume that you have succeeded in collecting the appropriate logic to precisely time the write pulse to the address and data inputs to the cache data RAM. At 50 MHz clock frequencies, the transmission line effects of a printed circuit card become significant, and fastidious board layouts be-

a) Individual accesses

	Cycle 0	Cycle 1	Cycle 2	Cycle 3	Cycle 4	Cycle 5	Cycle 6	Cycle 7	Cycle 8	Cycle 9
First Instruction	O/P Address	Input Data	Decode	Execute						
Second Instruction			O/P Address	Input Data	Decode	Execute				
Third Instruction					O/P Address	Input Data	Decode	Execute		
Fourth Instruction							O/P Address	Input Data	Decode	Execute

b) Four-word burst

	Cycle 0	Cycle 1	Cycle 2	Cycle 3	Cycle 4	Cycle 5	Cycle 6	Cycle 7	Cycle 8	Cycle 9
First Instruction	O/P Address	Input Data				Decode	Execute			
Second Instruction			Input Data				Decode	Execute		
Third Instruction				Input Data				Decode	Execute	
Fourth Instruction					Input Data				Decode	Execute

Figure 2.25. Why bursting in nonblocking caches is no faster than individual zero-wait accesses. Note that the first instruction in the burst sequence in (b) is not even decoded until cycle 5, resulting in the timing of the fourth instruction to be the same for burst (b) and nonburst (a) approaches. If the processor doesn't need all four burst addresses, then the instructions which were requested will not be decoded in such a cache until all of the unnecessary addresses have been fetched.

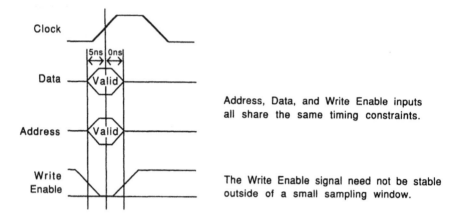

Figure 2.26. A synchronous write cycle. The write enable input is not sensitive to random edges or ringing which occur outside of the sample window. Also, write cycles can be decided upon much later in the memory cycle with synchronous parts.

come a must, as well as proper termination with impedance-matched loads at both ends of the write pulse line. Still, reflections will occur at every change in the trace due to a solder joint, a device pin, or even a corner of the trace, and when these reflections are added to the original signal, they might cause the write pulse to appear to ring, not being stable as a high or low level at the onset of the write cycle, and hanging around or recurring after the cycle is over. This causes headaches because the write enable must be a precisely timed pulse, rather than a voltage level. Synchronous SRAMs look at the write enable input as a level, which can go through countless transitions before the sampling window and which can bounce up and down without consequence after the window has passed.

2.5.3   Bus Turnaround

There are three main reasons that a cache design would have a potential for bus contention. The first is if the cache design satisfies a burst cycle using interleaved RAMs. The second is the case where a multiway architecture is used, and the cache controller must decide, in the minimum amount of time, which of two RAM banks is to be used to satisfy a data request. The third is in caches which interleave data and instruction caches to simulate a Harvard architecture. In all of these examples, the problem is to turn one RAM off and the other on in the minimum amount of time. Overlap of the outputs of two or more RAM banks is to be avoided at all costs, since the resulting contention causes high power dissipation, ground noise, radiofrequency interference (RFI), stress on the RAMs' output pins, and other concerns.

One problem with attempting to interleave RAMs this way is that the specifications for static RAMs are not adequately tight to ensure that bus contention will not occur. Some manufacturers are addressing this issue by guaranteeing minimum and maximum turn-on and turn-off times, but this is the exception, rather than the norm. Because of this, designers are often forced to assume that the turn-on and turn-off times will lie anywhere between zero and the maximum specified for the part. More venturesome designers assume that the parts cannot respond in 0ns, and will find some number which makes them comfortable, but the margin in the maximum and minimum numbers still slows down the interleaved system unless the designer chooses to ignore the effects of bus contention (at least until the system needs to be debugged).

Certain CPUs use separate data input and output pins, at quite a cost in package pin count, just to get around the problems of contention caused by bus turnaround, when the CPU stops inputting data and starts to write. This approach helps to solve the problems of synchronizing the outputs of the CPU to the outputs of the cache data RAM.

CHAPTER 3

CACHE MEMORIES AND RISC PROCESSORS

3.1 THE RISC CONCEPT

Management consultants and business authors today admonish American businesses to throw away old adages and the tried and true methods of the past and to try different modes of thinking. This is exactly what happened at IBM's T.J. Watson Research Center during the late 1970s.

Until that time, the increasing integration afforded by advances in semiconductor processing were welcomed as a means of increasing the complexity of the CPU. Old architectures offered simple constructs like load, store, and add using simple addressing modes. With higher levels of integration, programmers could be offered single instructions which would multiply and divide or perform subsets of simple series approximation functions on multiple memory-based operators using highly sophisticated addressing techniques. This approach does a lot to increase code density.

The research at IBM showed that the majority of the CPU's effort was spent performing simple load and store functions and not using sophisticated addressing. This should come as no surprise. What *is* surprising, though, is that the ratio of loads and stores to any other sort of operation is so high that the advantages of streamlining any other instructions or adding more complex instructions were found to be insignificant in comparison with the effects of increasing the speed of load/store instructions. Further research at various universities showed that compilers turned out faster code if they were restricted to using only a subset of a rich instruction set, focusing on those instructions which executed most quickly, no matter how simple their operations were. This is even the case for Intel's CISC processors, starting with the Pentium. Intel has taken pains to deliver optimizing compilers to software houses to assure that new software takes best advantage of the processor's throughput. Throw away sophisticated address modes! Get rid of any high-level instructions! Just speed up the loads and stores!

Let's look at a numerical example. Say a compiler turns out a piece of code which executes (based upon traces) in the following ratio:

Loads from simple addresses	40%
Stores to simple addresses	40%
Branch/jump/push/pop	5%
Register-to-register operations	3%

This should all appear to be perfectly reasonable and believable, especially to those who, back in the era of the 386, were sorely disappointed at the lack of a sizable performance increase in their PCs after the addition of a costly math coprocessor. In this example, if the loads and stores using simple addresses can be made to operate faster by 2.5% $(1 - 39/40)$ then the references to more complex addresses can run twice as slowly and the program will still run equally fast.

3.1.1   The CISC Bottleneck

So who cares? Designers of CPUs do! The maximum clock speed of a CPU is set by two simple factors: gate propagation delay and the number of gates in the critical path. All processor designs are somewhat circular. The data or instruction must travel around a circular path in time to be clocked into a register during the next clock cycle. Pipelined systems expedite this process (except in certain cases) by adding registers to intermediate points within the circle and clocking at a faster rate (see Figure 3.1). The minimum clock cycle time of any CPU is set by the maximum delay length path between register clocks. In CISC processors, the added complexity of a richer instruction set adds gates, one at a time, to this critical path.

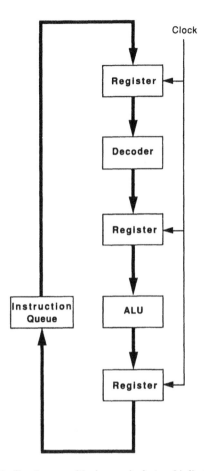

Figure 3.1. A typical pipelined system. Maximum clock speed is limited by the length of the longest delay between pipeline registers.

Those who know about Turing machines are aware that a surprisingly diverse range of problems can be solved through the use of an incredibly simple machine. If the speed of a CPU is set by a delay path which involves ten gates, and if we can remove a single gate by stripping out half of the instruction set, it might be worthwhile to remove this gate and all of the instructions it supports in light of the fact that the CPU has just gotten 10% faster. Using the compiler statistics just shown, a 10% improvement in all of those instructions which did not involve the complex references would allow the complex references to take as much as six times as long to calculate without impacting system performance! At this point, it becomes pretty obvious that software alternatives for more sophisticated instructions at a higher speed might actually be a very good trade-off in comparison with hardware implementations which might pose a burden upon all other instructions.

The reduced instruction-set computer (RISC) approach is to find the optimally small instruction set, based upon concurrently reducing both the instruction set's size and the cycle time of the CPU. As is the case with so many studies, the exercise ends up being anything but objective, and several RISC architectures have thus been spawned. Still, instruction sets for RISC processors are so similar that one acquaintance of the author claims that it would be impossible to tell which processor's instruction manual was being read if the reader started at the middle. All RISC CPUs focus heavily on simple loads and stores, with the arithmetic and logical operations only occurring between registers. CISC CPUs, on the other hand, often allow memory to be used as both source and destinations for arithmetic and logical operations, and are more likely than not to support some rather exotic address modes.

3.1.2   The RISC Architect's Goal

The objective in the design of a RISC CPU is that the most frequently needed instructions are optimized to run as quickly as possible, at the loss of complexity in the instruction set. CISC CPUs will often boast of instructions which perform the task of an entire subroutine of lower level instructions but might take as many as 30 cycles to execute. The utility of the reduction in executed code, and the consummate increase in code density, must be traded off against the speed at which more frequently encountered instructions are executed, just as was illustrated in the statistics of the example given in Section 3.1.

The big goal in RISC architectures is to be able to execute as many instructions as possible every cycle. To accomplish this, designers tend to make extensive use of pipelines, even to the point that branch prediction is used as a method of attempting to fetch the appropriate instruction before it is actually requested by the processor. In one very simple form of branch prediction, as an instruction is being fetched, the address of the next memory location, which is very probably the next instruction which will be used, is already being output to the memory system. Of course, more complex algorithms are also used, but this one will suit our purposes.

As long as the code runs in a linear fashion, and as long as no main memory data accesses are made, the processor can indeed execute an instruction on every clock cycle. When a data access is made to main memory, an extra cycle is consumed, increasing the cycles per instruction number by some fraction (although this can sometimes be hidden from the CPU by allowing it to process other instructions which do not require the data being loaded by the main memory access). Also, when a branch is taken, since it would not have been predicted by the simple prediction unit chosen here, at least one cycle is wasted while the output address changes from the reasonable estimate to the actual address required by the CPU. This is sometimes countered by architectures which allow the execution of the instruction following the branch instruction, whether or not the branch is taken.

RISC CPUs tend not to support instructions as complex as a jump to subroutine, since several cycles can get gobbled up both as the program counter is loaded with the destination address and as the prior contents of the program counter are pushed onto the stack (which usually resides within main memory). This would have the effect of increasing the number of clock cycles per instruction required to process code, a cardinal sin in the world of RISC CPUs. Instead, subroutines tend to put the program counter into a register and to let the compiler worry about the ins and outs of context switching.

3.1.3 Interaction of Software and Hardware

A large portion of the overall RISC equation is supported by superior software. Some RISC sales-support programs go so far as to provide models of systems with different cache configurations, so that a designer can test a variety of cache policies with a particular piece of code before determining how a system is to be constructed. Of course, none of this will pull together if the complex references we might have abandoned in the earlier example are replaced by a piece of poorly configured code. To get all the speed possible from a piece of fast hardware, the software needs to make the best possible use of the specific processor being supported.

The whole RISC solution then depends not simply upon optimization of the hardware (based once again upon the measurement of statistics), but also upon the use of optimizing compilers which will skew the compiled code's statistics further in the direction of accelerating the processor's throughput.

3.1.4 Optimizing Compilers

How do compilers optimize code, and what impact can this have on cache performance? After having read this much of this book, you should realize that I'm trying to raise your awareness of the importance of understanding the interaction between the software run upon a system and the hardware's overall performance. By understanding how your particular optimizing compiler works, you will be better able to optimize your cache's strategy.

In Section 3.1.2, branches were briefly discussed. A processor often consumes an extra cycle every time a branch is taken in order to give the program counter time to reload itself. This means that any loop will run more slowly than would a linear piece of code where the same few instructions were run one after another in repetition. The percent speed improvement is inversely proportional to the length of the loop. Optimizing compilers will look at loops which use a fixed number of repetitions, determine if the number of repetitions is not so great that the code would get too large if the loop were straightened, examine the speed trade-offs of leaving the loop intact versus straightening it out (sometimes called unwinding), based upon loop length, and will then decide whether to use the loop or a linear piece of highly repetitive code (see Table 3.1).

In a similar manner, an optimizing compiler will decide whether to leave a subroutine as a subroutine or bury multiple copies of the subroutine within the few code locations where it is called. Subroutine calls not only have latency due to the reloading of the program counter, but they can also require massive amounts of stack support to save and restore contexts, causing high latencies which can be completely removed through this optimization procedure.

RISC architectures focus more attention on registers and have register-rich CPUs. This means that the compilers to support these CPUs will focus a lot of attention on means of turning frequent memory accesses into register accesses instead, with the result that external data transfers are disproportionately small in comparison with the number of instruction calls.

Other than making disassembled code difficult to follow, what does all this mean to the cache designer? First, the use of straight-line code instead of small loops tends to make longer line lengths a more reasonable alternative, since a higher number of sequential accesses is likely to be made within this sort of optimized code. Second, in both Chapters 1 and 2, we explored the importance of more highly associative caches in systems which would suffer from thrashing due to conflicts stemming from subroutine calls and their ensuing stack operations. If several of the subroutines are pulled into the calling routines, there will be fewer address conflicts and stack accesses, thus slightly reducing improvements afforded by using higher cache associativities. Again, the code will be more in-line, rather than broken into subroutines, so longer lines will be more feasible than they would be if a nonoptimizing compiler were used. Third, if data is being shuffled around between registers the majority of the time, and if data loads and stores are dramatically reduced by the use of optimized code in a register-rich machine, the designer should focus a bigger effort on getting the most out of the instruction cache rather than the data cache. This last point is amplified by the fact that optimized code for a small instruction set will be significantly larger than will its nonoptimized CISC equivalent.

Table 3.1. Compiler support for optimized RISC code.

Level	Optimization Name	Explanation
High-level		At or near the source level: Machine-independent
	Procedure integration	Replace procedure call with procedure body
Local		Within straightline code
	Common subexpression elimination	Replace two instances of the same computation with a single copy
	Constant propagation	Replace all instances of a variable that is assigned a constant value with that constant
	Stack height reduction	Rearrange expression tree to minimize resources needed for expression evaluation
Global		Across a branch
	Global subexpression elimination	Same as common subexpression elimination, but this version crosses branches
	Copy propagation	Replace all instances of A which have been assigned the value X ($A = X$) with X
	Code motion	Remove from a loop any code which generates the same value during each iteration of that loop
	Induction variable elimination	Simplify/eliminate array-addressing calculations within loops
Machine-dependent		Depends on machine knowledge
	Strength reduction	Many possible examples, such as replacing multiply by constant with faster shift/add sequences
	Pipeline scheduling	Reorder instructions to improve pipeline performance
	Branch offset optimization	Choose the shortest branch displacement which reaches the target

Reprinted with the permission of Electronic Design Magazine.

3.1.5 Architectural Trade-offs

Processor architects have to trade off the speed of their design versus a lot of the features it may offer. If the number of instructions per clock cycle is to be maximized, the instruction, operands, and destination must all be accessible to the CPU at the same time, rather than being accessed sequentially. Furthermore, one site at which some large delays can arise is within the memory management unit. The approaches to these trade-offs determine two important aspects of cache design, both of which have been used to reduce gate delay paths in certain RISC processor designs.

3.1.5.1 Harvard vs. Von Neumann   Von Neumann architectures are so prevalently used nowadays that the terms Harvard architecture and Von Neumann machine are hardly heard. As a refresher, we'll just say that, while a Von Neumann machine has a single address space, any portion of which can be accessed as either instructions or as data, a Harvard architecture uses two separate fixed size spaces: one for instructions and one for data. This automatically implies that a Harvard machine can load or operate upon data in a single cycle, with the instruction coming from the instruction space via the instruction bus, and the data either being loaded or stored via a data bus into the data memory (Figure 3.2a). It is also implied that a Von Neumann machine (Figure 3.2b) must fetch an instruction, then load or store an operand in two separate cycles on a single data bus within a single memory space.

Naturally, any machine hell-bent on performance will try to reduce the number of instructions which require two accesses to main memory. One way to gain incredible speed advantages in any sort of CPU is to allow both instructions and data to be accessed simultaneously. There are two basic ways to do this. The first is to design a register-rich Von Neumann architecture, in which most of the instructions operate upon the data contained within two registers rather than on data held within memory. In a register-rich RISC machine, an instruction is accessed, performing some function on

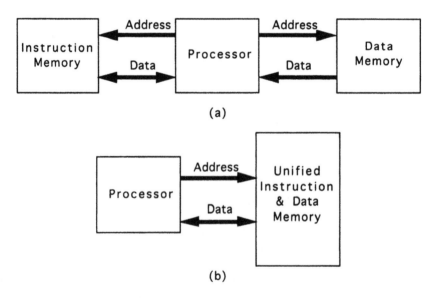

(a)

(b)

Figure 3.2.   Harvard architecture versus Von Neumann machines. The Harvard architecture (a) uses two memory spaces to allow the simultaneous access of data and instructions. A Von Neumann machine (b) gives up half the bandwidth of the Harvard architecture to gain the flexibility of allowing data and instructions to take variable amounts of the same memory.

the data between two on-chip registers, and the data is written back into one of those registers, all within a single cycle. (Actually, the processor's internal pipelining spreads any one instruction across several cycles, but because several instructions are being operated upon at any one time, the effective instruction execution time is under one clock cycle.) An optimizing compiler for a register-rich architecture tries to assure that the operands which will be used most frequently will be mapped into registers (which are in short supply), and that the less-often-used operands are never mapped into registers, but reside within main memory. With this approach, a great portion of the data accesses will be hidden from the bus, and the bulk of the bus activity will revolve around instruction fetches, forcing accesses to be more sequential than they would be in a machine which interspersed instruction and data operands more randomly. This intuitively implies that long lines might be a very good cache strategy for such a machine, and that an instruction cache alone might improve throughput as much as would a combined cache.

Other RISC processors use a Von Neumann-style unified memory space for the main memory, but to split the caches into instruction and data spaces, causing the CPU–cache subsystem to appear to be a Harvard architecture (see Figure 3.3). Data and instructions come simultaneously from

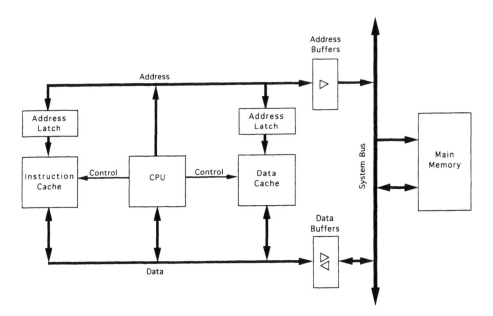

Figure 3.3. Certain RISC processors use a Harvard cache and a Von Neumann main memory to try to get the best of both worlds.

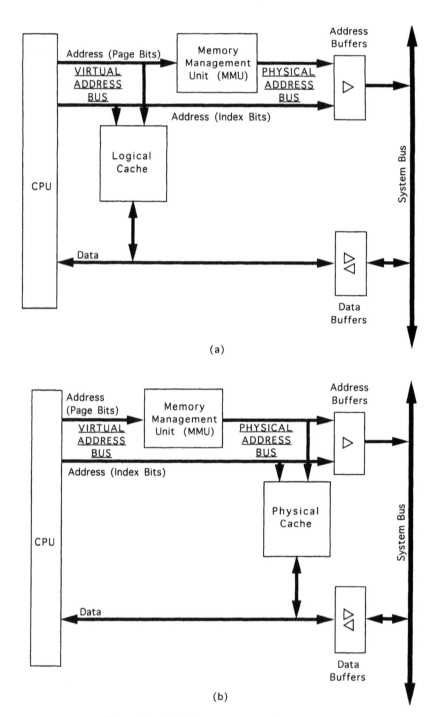

Figure 3.4. Logical (a) and physical (b) caches.

two different memories on two different buses. A single internal accumulator provides one operand and stores the results. Now an instruction fetch and a data load/store can occur within the same cycle, yet the overall system still has the main memory flexibility of a Von Neumann machine. This approach makes the processor's performance less dependent on the size of the CPU's register set.

The Harvard approach has two advantages. First, less care needs to be taken by the compiler in managing the contents of the registers to assure that data contained is likely to be needed both soon and often. Second, in register-rich machines with high orders of pipelining, there is the possibility that a later instruction will need data produced by an earlier instruction before that data has actually emerged from the pipeline. Such problems are handled via scoreboarding, a process in which certain flag bits are used to signify whether the data in a register is the most current available. This process is messy to implement and causes delays when an instruction must be stalled to wait for one of its operands to become available.

3.1.5.2 Physical vs. Logical Caches Back in Section 2.2.1, we discussed the attributes of logical versus physical caches. It would appear in keeping with the RISC philosophy of reducing gate delays to simply use logical caches in a RISC design. You probably recall that the logical cache is on the processor side of the memory management unit and its delay, while the physical cache is downstream of the MMU's delay (Figure 3.4).

Some RISC processors get around the MMU delay problem by increasing the depth of the pipelining in the processor, thereby hiding the delays from the cache. This may have challenged the designers, but simplifies a problem which we will encounter in Chapter 4, that of maintaining coherency in a logical cache.

3.2 FEEDING INSTRUCTIONS TO A RISC CPU

It would be careless to design a fast CPU and then force it to wait on a slow memory interface. Thus we come up with a race between the RISC processor and the cache. One processor architect even recommends designing the cache for optimum speed and hit rate before designing the processor. This seems a tad extreme, since it would be difficult to optimize the cache hit rate if you did not know what kind of code the compiler was going to spit out, and the compiler will optimize based upon the processor's architecture. The bottom line is that the entire system must be designed as a whole, with each part influencing the design of all others. Even a wonderful cache, coupled with a bad main memory, can underperform a system with an inadequate cache but a very well-designed main memory.

As with any CPU, RISC processors perform the majority of their main memory accesses to fetch instructions. Just as with CISC CPUs, then, the designer who focuses most attention upon optimizing instruction accesses is the designer who produces the best cache. The cache designer can borrow a page from the RISC processor architect's notebook, to wit: Reduce gate delays by simplifying the design. Most designers of RISC CPUs advocate placing both a tiny primary plus a larger secondary cache, rather than a single larger cache, right on the chip, so that the primary cache can be built with the absolute minimum number of gate delays. The smaller an SRAM, the fewer gate delays there will be in the address decoder.

3.3   PROBLEMS UNIQUE TO RISC CACHES

The whole RISC philosophy falls apart if the cache cannot support the processor's voracious appetite for data. Remember that the RISC assumption is that the processor's clock rate is accelerated through the reduction of delay paths in the critical timing loop. The cache is an integral part of this loop. What good is it to design a bodaciously fast CPU only to tie it up upon every single instruction cycle with a cache access delay?

Supporting zero-wait hits can be quite a problem at high clock rates. Simply getting onto and off of a piece of silicon can typically cost around 3ns (assuming TTL I/O levels are used). Since the cache RAM and the CPU are often two different pieces of silicon, 6ns can disappear in the interchip communications. Even if the balance of the delays amounted to 0ns, the maximum clock frequency of such a system would be 166 MHz, already below the clock speed of most current processors!

To overcome this problem, processor designers always place at least one cache on the CPU chip itself. There is a pretty good argument in favor of doing this, since even small caches tend to exhibit relatively high hit rates. This does not absolve the cache designer from speed problems however. Problems of RISC secondary cache design are still vexing, and at the time of this writing generally require the use of extremely high-speed synchronous SRAMs.

Of course, the same pin loading problems mentioned in Section 2.5.1 get you in spades in a RISC cache, especially at the high clock rates at which RISC CPUs are now offered. Derating, which was negligible at lower clock rates, becomes a determining factor at higher speeds. The approach taken with most architectures is to implement the cache data RAM using the widest possible devices at state-of-the-art densities. By reducing the number of devices being driven by the CPU's address bus, the deleterious effects of capacitive loading can be kept at bay.

CHAPTER 4

MAINTAINING COHERENCY
IN CACHED SYSTEMS

A statistic that is often quoted decrees that the most common cause of quarrels between married people is money. Why would such a statistic creep into a book about cache memory design? Because the parallels between some kinds of money arguments and the issue of cache coherency are both profound and down-to-earth.

Let's assume that the majority of the money arguments start with something like one of these examples:

"Why don't you enter it on the check register when you withdraw money from the automatic teller machine? Now you made us bounce three checks!"

"You charged $900.00 onto the Visa account and *forgot* to tell me? No wonder my credit was declined at the restaurant in front of my boss!"

"That was the money we were saving to go to Hawaii!"

"So what *did* happen to that $100 cash in your wallet, anyway?"

In all of these cases, there is money (or credit) which is community property to both members of the marriage, which one party spends without telling the other. If we move from married couples over to computers, and we change the community property over to the memory space, we can see that there are potential catastrophes if the same data is being manipulated by two different devices without either somehow informing the other of its actions. Each member of the couple thinks she or he has a mental picture of what is in the bank or what has been charged on the credit card, just like a cache memory is supposed to contain an accurate copy of the appropriate contents of main memory. When one or another of the couple alters what is in the main memory, then the other must be informed. Likewise, whenever any device on the system bus updates either main memory or a cache location which is to be copied to main memory at a later time, it must assure that no other device can harbor a misunderstanding about the freshness of the data in the main memory.

Such problems have been solved in a number of software databases. Imagine the problem of booking airline seats. United Airlines has a data base which can be accessed simultaneously by about 2,100 telephone ticket agents at each of three offices in the United States alone. Likewise, hundreds of travel agents in the United States are on-line and also have the power to book a seat on a flight. In a worst-case scenario, there could be a single seat remaining on a flight from New York to Chicago, and, at the exact same time, everybody who was on the system tried to sell that seat to a customer. If the problem were not solved, about 3,000 people might be assigned the same seat on the same airplane!

Cache coherency is the term given to the problem of assuring that the contents of the cache memory and those of main memory for *all* caches in a multiple cache system are either identical or under tight enough control that stale and current data are not confused with each other. Like any other cache buzzword, there are less-often-used alternatives to the word coherency, namely, **consistency** and **currency.** The term **stale data** is used to describe data locations which no longer reflect the current value of the memory location they once represented. As I type this book, the new version of this chapter is stored in the computer's main memory, while a stale version resides on the computer's hard disk. The next time I save the file, the disk and the main memory will contain the same data at the same locations and will be coherent with each other until I again start to type.

4.1 SINGLE-PROCESSOR SYSTEMS

At first flush, most designers assume that coherency is only a problem in multiprocessor systems, or possibly in systems with copy-back caches. It seems as if a write-through cache in a single-CPU system would never have coherency problems. This is untrue due to any activities which are not under control of the processor, in other words, input and output activities.

The simplest example is that of a memory-mapped polled I/O device, which the processor is continually reading to determine the status of a single bit. We used the same example to illustrate the use of noncacheable areas in Section 2.2.7. If the cache contains a copy of the memory-mapped I/O location, and the CPU refers to the cached copy rather than to the I/O device, the processor will never see any change in the I/O bit's status, since it will be reading the stale or incoherent value in the cache rather than the real value being input from the memory-mapped I/O location.

This situation is easy enough to correct by mapping the I/O location into a noncacheable address. The problem gets tricky when an alternate bus master can write into the main memory without CPU intervention. A master is any device which can command the main memory to perform read and write cycles, rather than requiring the CPU to perform these cycles for that device. The most typical examples in single-processor systems are DMA devices like disk controllers or video interfaces.

Taking the disk controller example, visualize, if you will, the CPU initiating a DMA transfer of a portion of a program from a hard disk to main memory at a time after the entire cache has been filled with copies of main memory addresses. Some of these cache locations will doubtlessly be copies of main memory locations which will be overwritten by the incoming DMA data. If these cache locations stay out of sync with the contents of main memory, the newly fetched code will execute in all the uncached addresses, interspersed with cached copies of the old program. As if this were not bad enough, in copy-back caches, outputs from main memory to DMA devices also can cause problems since the data which the CPU thinks it is sending to the DMA output device is the most current, but if a portion of this block is still residing Dirty within the cache, then some stale piece of data will end up going to permanent storage instead. These two problems will be addressed in the following portions of this section.

Perhaps this would be a good place to differentiate between cache policies and cache and/or bus protocols. **Protocol** is the word used by cache architects to express the means by which caches, processors, main memory, and alternate bus masters communicate with each other. The cache policies determine the interaction of the cache with the CPU and the software and set the hit rate of the cache. The protocol is the vehicle by which all the subsystems within the system assure that coherency is maintained and that bus collisions do not occur. In this chapter, either all the coherency mechanisms must be designed around both the cache policies and the bus protocol, or the bus protocol must be designed around the cache policies and the coherency mechanism.

4.1.1   DMA Activity and Stale Cache Data

During a DMA transfer, the current bus master (the DMA device) can write into main memory locations which may also be replicated within the cache. The cache controller must be able to assure that the contents of the cache memory continue to faithfully resemble the replicated main memory locations, rather than to contain copies of how the main memory used to look.

The simplest method is called a cache **flush,** and involves invalidating the entire directory every time there is a DMA write cycle. Three of the most common methods of doing this are as follows: 1) to use special invalidate hardware to write an Invalid state to the Valid bit in every cache line, 2) to use a special cache-tag RAM which has hardware reset capability to do the same, and 3) to reset the main Valid flag which gates the tag's comparator output to the CPU (assuming Valid bits are not used in the design). The best that can be said about this method is that it works and is trivial to implement, as long as the cache is a simple write-through implementation. The worst thing about it is that it forces the cache to refill itself after every DMA write cycle. In certain cases this is not so bad. In a PC running DOS, the CPU is always stalled for the duration of the DMA block move, so the added penalty of several subsequent cache line refill cycles is not so noticeable. On the other end of the spectrum, a flush can be devastating in a system using a multitasking operating system like UNIX which attempts to dispatch another task once it requires DMA activity for the first one. The alternate task would ideally be performed out of the cache, so that the DMA activity and the processor activity would not interfere with each other.

Another more efficient way to assure coherency on DMA transfers is to provide hardware that watches all system bus cycles and checks their addresses to alert the cache if one of its locations is being affected.

A **bus watch** or **snoop** mechanism is a simple means of assuring that any pertinent system bus cycle to main memory updates or clears the appropriate cache location. On main memory write cycles, if the addressed location is replicated in the cache, or, in some designs, if that location merely has a high likelihood of being contained within the cache, it will be overwritten or invalidated, depending on the design. A term occasionally used for the process of invalidating a line on a snoop write hit is **back invalidation,** which implies that the invalidation is happening in a direction other than the normal direction in which cache updates occur. Most designers refer to the process as if the cache is watching the system bus and usually use the term snooping, while others look at it as if the system bus is looking into the cache and call the process **interrogation** or say that the system bus **inquires** the cache about its contents. Another, less widely used, term is **cross-interrogate,** which sounds like a lawyer's way of describing the process of the current bus master looking for potential coherency issues within other caches. The problem with the terms *interrogate* and *inquire* is that they imply that the requesting device requests the data first from any existing cache before looking in main memory. In true-to-life designs, caches generally watch the bus and take action when a coherency problem is likely to arise. It's like somebody inside looking out as compared with another person outside looking in.

In a copy-back cache, the snoop logic must also watch out for main memory reads which should be satisfied from a Dirty word in cache, rather than by a stale word in main memory. The DMA device, often a disk, will need to be sent the most up-to-date copy of a memory address, rather than the data which is actually contained within the main memory.

In a snooping cache design, a cache-tag RAM continually monitors main memory bus activity. This can be performed by a separate cache-tag RAM which holds an identical copy or a superset of the cache's actual directory (more on this later) or by the cache's actual directory.

Those designs which use the cache's actual directory fall into two classes. The most common class is one in which the cache is multiplexed between the main memory bus and the processor. This is often called a **dual-ported directory** or a **dual-ported tag.** In some designs, a snoop cycle starts by stopping the CPU, thereby disabling its access to the cache. The DMA address is then routed to the cache-tag RAM, and, in the case of a DMA write to main memory, the location can be either compared and written Invalid (if there is a DMA hit), compared and left Valid, with new data written to the cache data RAM (once again if there is a hit), or simply invalidated (whether or not there is a hit). The choice of these alternatives is another one of the myriad of system-dependent trade-offs, since the first two require read/write cycles, which cause the CPU to be disabled for more precious time, yet the last and fastest alternative will assuredly step on a number of innocent, nonmatching cache locations, which will then need to be updated upon a subsequent access cycle, once again costing CPU speed. Just like every other cache decision, there are no easy answers as to which of these three is the best for your system. It all depends on the size and associativity of the cache and, probably to the largest extent, upon the structure of the software being run upon the machine.

Other approaches involve multiplexing the tag RAM in such a way that snoop cycles are invisible to the CPU, or handing the CPU the snoop address and requesting the CPU itself to perform the housekeeping via dedicated hardware, as is done in most processors. The multiplex approach doesn't slow the CPU down, but can only be used if the processor gives the bus up for a significant percentage of the overall operating time. The CPU-based invalidation mechanism can cause significant delays in processing time, as each invalidation usually consumes several CPU cycles.

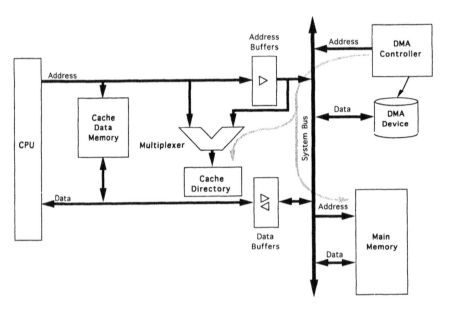

Figure 4.1. Snoop line invalidation using a multiplexed cache-tag RAM. The multiplexer must be inserted into the cache's critical tag address input timing path.

A multiplexed cache-tag RAM in a discrete cache implementation saves little expense and does not reduce chip count because it requires a multiplexer on the address inputs of the cache-tag RAM between the system and local buses (Figure 4.1). The delay caused by this additional logic can prevent a design from keeping up with a fast CPU. This approach does make sense in an integrated cache implementation, like those on most processor chips, since the multiplexer might already be in the critical path and simply need to be widened, and, even if it is not, it could probably be implemented at less than a 1ns speed penalty to the cache-tag RAM's access time.

Another twist to this is referred to as **DMA through cache,** where a DMA device is essentially tied to the CPU/cache bus rather than to the main memory bus (Figure 4.2). During the DMA, the processor is isolated from the CPU/cache bus, and the DMA device reads and writes to and from both the cache and the main memory in exactly the same method as that used by the CPU. Even the cache controller doesn't know that a DMA is taking place. Although this shuts the CPU down for the duration of the DMA, when the DMA is over, the cache is coherent and is likely to contain at least several useful locations, depending on the write miss policy chosen. Probably the best write policy which could be used in a write-through cache of this sort would be to not replace a line on a write miss, since 1) there may have been useful code or data in that line, which the processor would need after a DMA, and 2) during a DMA transfer, there is often a lot of data transferred which is not used for quite a while. It would be too bad if the DMA overwrote an often-used cache copy of an address with something which would not be likely to be used, but happened to be in the same sector as some useful information. It's easy to see why some designers call this approach a **read-through** cache, although this term really only tells half of the story.

One interesting side benefit of the use of a DMA through cache approach is that Valid bits can be completely avoided. If the DMA data is the only data which is cached (i.e., ROM, EPROM, I/O locations, and so forth are mapped into the noncacheable space), then the cache only contains random data at those addresses which have not received DMA data since power-up. Which is worse: to execute random bits from DRAM or from cache? It really makes no difference. As long as the code is debugged to the point that legitimate data alone is accessed (data which comes from the hard disk, rather than random power-up bits), then that data can be supplied by either cache or main memory, with the only difference being the speed at which it executes.

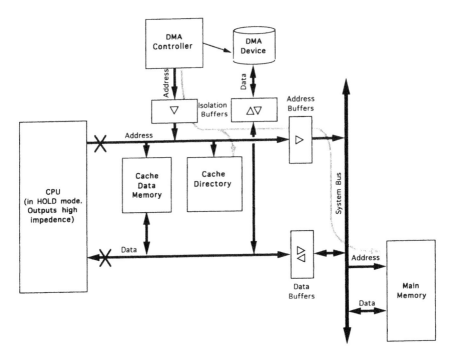

Figure 4.2. The DMA through cache approach ties the DMA device onto the cache/CPU bus and communicates with main memory as would the CPU. The CPU cannot operate during these DMA cycles.

A second class of snoop mechanism uses a duplicate tag to snoop the main memory bus. Depending on the cache design, these can be either very simple, very costly, or completely free but very difficult to understand. Let's move from the simplest to the most complex.

Dual cache-tag or **dual directory** systems offer a higher operating speed, asynchronous operation, and a greater degree of system design flexibility than multiplexed cache systems at a similar chip count, but require slightly more expensive components.

In a dual cache-tag RAM system, there are two identical directories: one which monitors the CPU's address bus and one which monitors the system address bus. A copy of the contents of the local cache-tag RAM is replicated in the system cache-tag RAM. At first guess, it would appear that a special effort needs to be made to assure that the snoop-tag RAM contains the same information as the cache-tag RAM. This is actually a trivial problem. During any cache line update (Figure 4.3), the cache address bus is connected to the main memory bus, so both the snoop-tag RAM and the cache-tag RAM will be seeing the same address at the time that the cache-tag RAM is updated with the tag of the new line. It then becomes simply a matter of using the same write pulse to update the snoop-tag RAM as is used to update the cache-tag RAM.

When the CPU is operating out of the cache and another master write occurs, the system bus address is compared against the address in the system bus cache-tag RAM. If there is a DMA write hit (implying that the main memory address being accessed is copied in the cache), the snoop-tag RAM will notice a match, causing the cache controller to stop the CPU and invalidate or update the matching location. Both the snoop-tag RAM and the cache-tag RAM entries should be invalidated at this time to assure that subsequent snoop hits to a previously invalidated location will not occur. There are even systems which use the same parts, a snoop-tag RAM in addition to a full cache, but upon a snoop hit, flush both the snoop-tag RAM and the directory's cache-tag RAM via their reset input pins. While this is a drastic approach, this system would experience fewer cache flushes than would a system which flushes the directory upon each and every DMA write cycle. It's a little surprising that the flush-on-snoop-hits approach is used at all, given that the complexity of the cache controller is nearly the same for both of these types of coherency mechanisms.

Before we progress to more sophisticated coherency mechanisms, this might be another good place to harp on one of my favorite subjects in this book: the need to consider the software being run on a system when choosing cache strategies. The complexity of the coherency approach really shouldn't be greater than what is required by the operating system being used. Once again, let's use Intel-based, single-processor PCs as an example,

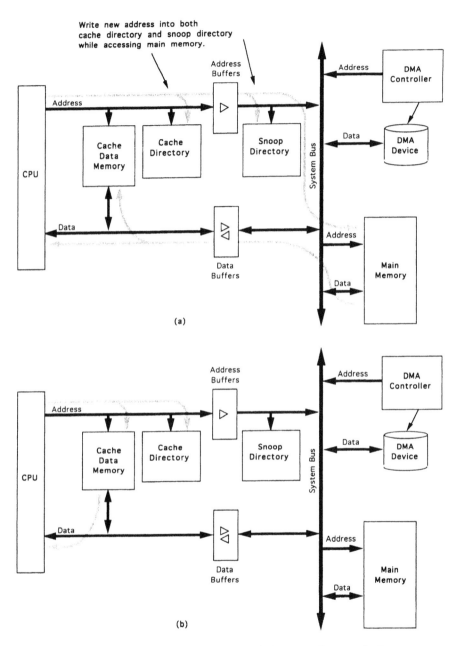

Figure 4.3. Using an additional directory to snoop the bus. (a) When a cache line is updated, the same tag and set bits appear on both sides of the data bus buffers, so the snoop and cache directories can be simultaneously updated. (b) When the CPU is not using the bus, simultaneous DMA/snooping and CPU/cache operations can occur.

and let's only consider those which use DMA for disk I/O and nothing else. Should the design be targeted solely at MS-DOS or Windows 3.1 applications, snooping might not be an important feature in a cache design. In simpler operating systems, the CPU is not allowed to operate during DMA accesses, so system performance is not improved by reducing the number of invalidate cycles to the cache during this CPU idle time. On the other hand, in systems using UNIX or other more sophisticated operating systems and in multiple-processor systems, a significant performance improvement can be realized by reducing needless invalidation cycles, since in these cases the processor operates simultaneously with other bus master devices.

The next coherency mechanism in the scheme of ascending complexity involves the principle of **inclusion.** This sort of design is used where the snooping tag is bigger and not necessarily of the same associativity as the cache directory. First, let's see why anyone in their right mind would attempt to do this, then let's explore why it works.

Say you were trying to build an external snooping mechanism for the internal cache of a processor with an 8K-byte, four-Way, set-associative unified internal physical cache, with a line size of four words (16 bytes). It appears that the easiest thing to do would be to replicate the internal cache's directory. How many chips would this take? Putting on our math hats, we see that four separate cache-tag RAMs would be needed, one for each of the four Ways, and that each cache-tag RAM would need to have a depth of [8K bytes/(4 Ways · 16 bytes per line)] = 128 locations. Assuming that there are 30 address bits, 28 of which are used to address cache lines, and since 7 bits would be used as set bits to get into the 128 tag locations ($128 = 2^7$), the other 21 bits would be the tag bits. Add one Valid bit and the overall cache-tag RAM requirement would be four 128×22-bit snoop-tag RAMs. If we were to use the industry's currently most widely available integrated cache-tag RAM, which comes in an $8K \times 8$-bit organization, a total of 12 devices would be needed to implement the tag alone (22 bits/$8 = 3$, times four Ways)! By using inclusion, this can be whittled down to two $8K \times 8$ integrated cache-tag RAMs hooked up in a simple direct-mapped configuration. Let's see how.

If the snoop-tag RAM can always be caused to contain a superset of the cache's directory, then the snoop-tag RAM can be used to verify all invalidation cycles before these cycles are passed on to the actual cache. This way, a lot of fruitless invalidation attempts to the cache (and subsequently a proportional number of unnecessary CPU wait states) can be screened out and discarded by the snoop-tag RAM. The name "inclusion" indicates that the contents of the entire cache directory are included within the contents of the snoop-tag RAM.

Forcing the snoop-tag RAM to be a consistent superset of a more complex cache's directory may appear difficult at first for a couple of very good reasons. First, a cache with a higher associativity than the snoop-tag RAM will be able to put a copy of a main memory location into any of a number of cache locations, while a less associative snoop-tag RAM will be limited and in certain cases will not be able to concurrently contain a set of addresses which would easily fit within a more highly associative cache directory. Second, the cache may not disclose enough to the outside world to allow the snoop-tag RAM to determine which line is being updated. Most processors do not tell the outside world which internal cache lines are being replaced. If the cache's directory and snoop-tag RAM have such a hard time understanding each other, how can their status as subset and superset be maintained?

The answer is surprisingly simple: inclusion. There are two basic precepts to inclusion:

1. Any tag entry written into the cache directory is also simultaneously written into the snoop-tag RAM.
2. Any tag entry that is removed from the snoop-tag RAM (whether by a bus snoop or by replacement) is simultaneously forced out of the cache.

Astute readers will instantly note that with some processor designs data can be dropped from the cache without the snoop-tag RAM being updated. The snoop-tag RAM will subsequently be prone to experiencing snoop hits on addresses which no longer exist within the cache. This is the reason why the snoop-tag RAM becomes a superset of the cache directory.

Another item which the two rules above don't mention concerns address tags which are put into the snoop-tag RAM, but not into the cache. This might occur if the snoop-tag RAM sported a larger line size than the primary cache. Once again, the snoop-tag RAM in this case simply becomes a superset of the cache directory.

Even if the cache is a four-Way design and the snoop-tag RAM is direct mapped, the four-Way cache can't contain anything with an address not copied in the snoop-tag RAM, since, at the same time that the location was being added to the cache, its address was put into the snoop-tag RAM. And if every address which is invalidated in the snoop-tag RAM is also invalidated in the cache itself (whether or not it still exists within the cache), then there can be nothing remaining in the cache which is suddenly missing in the snoop-tag RAM.

Now that we have assured ourselves that inclusion can indeed guarantee that the contents of the cache directory are a subset of the snoop-tag RAM, we should examine the drawbacks.

Probably the most important drawback is that the cache in a system using inclusion can never stay full. It is inevitable that lines which could have continued to reside within the cache will be forced out because of problems fitting them within the less-associative snoop-tag RAM. This causes the cache to exhibit a slightly lower hit rate, and will cause a time loss to refetch the invalidated line from main memory if that line is needed again. This is a good reason to assure that the snoop-tag RAM is appreciably larger than the cache directory, so that it reduces the number of lines forced out of itself and subsequently forced out of the cache. On the other hand, if too large a snoop-tag RAM is chosen, more false invalidation cycles will be passed on to the cache, thus slowing the system down. There is no free lunch! (As an aside, we have not considered how small the snoop-tag RAM can get. Believe it or not, the snoop-tag RAM could be *smaller* than the cache-tag RAM and inclusion would still work. If the only items which are allowed to reside in the cache have addresses which are copied within the snoop-tag RAM, then only a fraction of the cache-tag RAM *smaller* than the snoop-tag RAM will end up being used in such a system. This would work, but would be a shameful waste of the unused portion of the cache.)

A second apparent drawback is that inclusion may dramatically increase the number of invalidation cycles presented to the cache. Each and every time an address is removed from the snoop-tag RAM, a cache invalidation cycle occurs. This will be the case whether or not the address being removed from the snoop-tag RAM actually still exists within the cache, and whether the snoop-tag RAM entry was invalidated due to a bus snoop cycle, or because of a cache line update which caused a snoop line to be overwritten. Although this looks bad, it is really a strong advantage of inclusion.

Most cache invalidation cycles will be triggered by the replacement of a valid entry in the snoop-tag RAM. This only occurs during a cache miss, and, during cache miss cycles, the CPU is stopped and cannot proceed until it receives the new data. Since an entry is being replaced in the snoop-tag RAM, several cycles will pass before the new data is available to the CPU, and this wasted time can be used productively to invalidate a line within the cache itself! In this way, most of the cache invalidation cycles are forced to coincide with a time when the CPU would ordinarily be stopped. Only those bus snoop cycles which pass through the snoop-tag RAM screen are permitted to stop the CPU in order to cause a performance-threatening invalidation cycle.

If a secondary cache is used in a system, inclusion can be used to allow the secondary cache to prescreen bus traffic and limit the number of false invalidation cycles which are passed on to the primary cache. The secondary cache's tag can get a second use as a snooping tag at a very small cost. A negligible quantity of additional logic is usually required to support inclusion using an existing secondary cache. The set bits output from the primary cache/CPU subsystem will contain the same value which is to be driven into the primary cache to invalidate the primary cache line, so a set address latch is needed. This latch can be absorbed into the lower bits of an existing address buffer, so the cost in additional chip count is usually zero. The tag bits required by inclusion are supplied from the secondary cache's directory. Very few additional terms usually need to be added to the cache controller state machine, so the cache controller's complexity is not dramatically increased.

Dirty inclusion is similar to inclusion for cache hierarchies in which the upstream and downstream caches both use copy-back write strategies. With Dirty inclusion, a secondary copy-back cache would contain a line marked Dirty for every line marked Dirty in the primary cache; however, some Dirty secondary lines would not necessarily be marked as Dirty in the primary cache. This allows a line to be evicted from the primary cache without causing any write traffic to occur on the interface between the secondary cache and the main memory. The secondary line does not get evicted until the secondary cache needs the line to accept new data, and secondary line updates are less frequent than primary line updates, so the traffic stays down. Another advantage of using Dirty inclusion is that snoop read hits to a Dirty line in a copy-back cache must be supported from the cache rather than from main memory. If the secondary cache is to prescreen bus write cycles before allowing invalidate cycles to pass through to the primary cache, then it also makes sense to allow the secondary cache to prescreen read cycles. This can happen if the status of every secondary line is the same as the status of the primary line. This is not to be construed to mean that the Dirty line in the secondary cache would always contain the same data as the Dirty line in the primary cache. For this to happen, the primary cache would have to be write-through and would have to update the secondary cache every time the CPU updated the Dirty line. Instead, the status of the secondary line is updated to Dirty when the primary line is first taken Dirty, and maintains the status for snoop cycles, even though the data from the secondary cache cannot be guaranteed to be coherent in the event of a snoop read hit. Therefore, all snoop read hits to Dirty secondary cache lines must be sent to the primary cache. Still, this beats sending all bus read cycles to the primary cache.

4.1.2 Problems Unique to Logical Caches

Probably the biggest difficulty encountered in logical caches is the problem of address aliases, first described in Section 2.2.1. The difficulty stems from the fact that two separate virtual addresses may be mapped into the same physical address. Another way to say this is that two virtual addresses which share the same offset addresses but have different page addresses might be mapped by the operating system into the same physical page and would therefore share the same offset within the same physical page (in other words, the same physical address). This is one way that tasks in a multitasking system communicate with each other (for example, system calls from an application program).

During any DMA write into main memory, cached copies of the address written into by the DMA device must also be either updated or invalidated. If two virtual addresses are mapped to the same physical address, there is the possibility that there will be two copies of the same main memory location in the cache. Both will become stale when another bus master writes to the main memory.

Of course, there are lots of ways to solve this problem, the least sophisticated of which is to flush the cache upon every DMA write cycle. More elegant solutions involve disallowing the cache from using as set address bits any CPU output addresses which lie within the page number bits of the MMU. Although this puts a severe limitation on the size of the cache in many cases, it completely does away with the possibility that within a single Way or cache (in a nonunified cache design) there will be two concurrently cached copies of the same physical address which represent two different logical addresses. Think about it. The only way that two separate logical addresses could be mapped to the same physical address is if the two logical addresses had the same offset bits but different virtual page numbers. A large cache, which used some page number bits as set bits, might be able to maintain two different copies, at two different set addresses, of the same physical address, but a cache which had its set bits limited to be a subset of the offset addresses could never have two copies of the same physical address since they would both end up being mapped to the same set address.

The other rule in applying this approach is that only a unified, direct-mapped cache should be used in a snooping logical cache design. During a DMA, the set bits of the DMA address can then be fed into the cache-tag RAM's snoop mechanism, and the tag outputs that set address's virtual page number (see Figure 4.4). This can only work if the set bits are the same on both sides of the MMU, agreeing with the restriction requiring the set bits to be a subset of the page offset address bits. The MMU is then called upon to translate the tag's virtual page number output into a physical page number which can then be compared with the DMA's tag address bits. If a hit is discovered, that cache line is invalidated. If this sounds like a slow process, that's because it is, but think of how much slower it would be if two snooped tags had to process their tag bits one Way at a time through the MMU in a nonunified cache or a multiway design! One alternative is to invalidate all entries with matching set address bits, but this might be difficult to implement and would needlessly invalidate a disproportionate number of innocent bystanders. It is nearly impossible to perform a clean snoop invalidate process in any way which does not require the CPU to stall during the entire snoop cycle, so logical snooping cache designs are usually kept simple just to avoid large speed penalties during snoop cycles.

Although I have never seen such a machine, I would not doubt that some

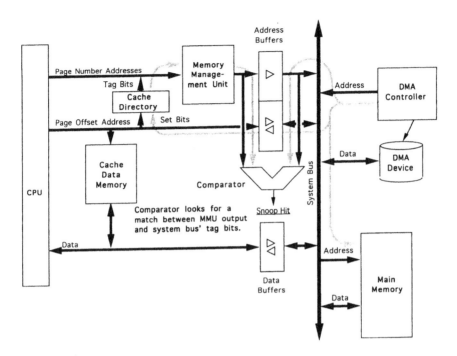

Figure 4.4.   Snooping addresses in a logical cache. The set bits of the DMA address are put onto the CPU bus, and the cache-tag RAM outputs that set's logical tag bits. This logical tag is then translated into a physical page number by the MMU, and the page number is compared with the corresponding bits of the DMA access (a snoop hit).

are implemented with reverse translation schemes to map physical addresses back into all the relevant virtual addresses, then to allow several Ways of a highly associative cache to snoop the newly created virtual address. This would allow the logical cache to be nonunified or more associative and would also remove the cache size restriction caused by requiring the set bits to be a subset of the page offset bits. I just hope nobody I know is saddled with the job of designing such a monster.

Discussion of the aliasing problem often centers around context switches, which are more of a software way of describing those times during which DMA activity is likely to occur. Most concern about aliases in general is centered around context switches in both cached and uncached systems, since the MMU mapping of main memory and disk is very similar to the mapping used between the cache and the main memory. If you have the opportunity to discuss your cache design with the software designers who conceived your operating system, go ahead! You'll both be surprised at how many problems you have in common, and you'll probably help broaden each other's perspective.

4.2 MULTIPLE-PROCESSOR SYSTEMS

In tightly coupled multiple-processor systems, especially those in which any processor can perform any task in any part of memory, the problems of cache coherency are pretty big. Just as a refresher, we'll go over the nomenclature *tightly coupled* and *loosely coupled* again, since they were first defined in Chapter 1. A tightly coupled multiprocessing system is designed to allow main memory to be equally accessible from each processor. Loosely coupled systems, on the other hand, are made of two or more processors, each of which has a private memory space. Examples of both sorts of system are shown in Figure 4.5. The connection between the processors in a loosely coupled system can be a shared portion of main memory, FIFOs, dual-ported memory, or even a serial link like a local area network, or a dedicated interprocessor communication channel, as is used on the Inmos Transputer. Hypercubes use loosely coupled architectures. Since the processors in a loosely coupled system each have their own main memories, there is absolutely no reason why any memory locations in the two individual main

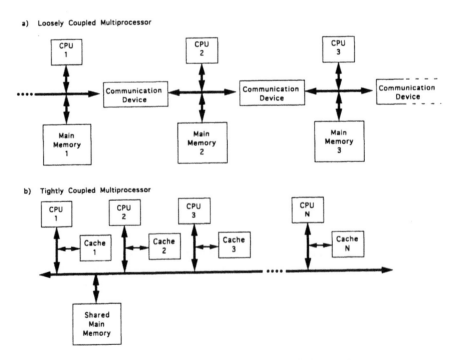

Figure 4.5. Examples of loosely coupled (a) and tightly coupled (b) multiprocessing systems. Main memory is shared in tightly coupled systems.

memories should need to match each other, so no steps need to be maintained to assure cache coherency beyond those which would be required in a single-processor system to avoid incoherent cache copies of the input/output activity of the processor.

One very simple means of assuring that caches in a tightly coupled system stay coherent is to set up a noncacheable space in memory called the **coherency domain.** Since the data in the coherency domain is not cached, that data is always the most current. This is a communication space, which is arbitrated between processors. The coherency domain approach was used by systems like the Honeywell Series 66, early versions of the Intel i860, and the Elxsi 6400. This approach is also available via a status bit in the MMU's page descriptors in certain microprocessors. The major drawback of using such a scheme is that it becomes restrictive to the programmer, since all programs must waltz around the coherency domain with any piece of data or code which is not intended to be shared. Invariably, the portion of memory set aside for the coherency domain will always be found to be too small for certain applications and will consume too large a portion of the memory space for others. Naturally, coherency domain approaches can only be used in systems where the software is defined at the same time as the cache architecture, rather than the cache being designed to accelerate the performance of an existing CPU/software combination. This occurs all too rarely.

There are other, more flexible approaches available if the hardware and software are being defined at the same time. One of these is the use of a **sophisticated** protocol, in which a customized compiler generates and stores bits corresponding to different main memory addresses to tell the cache which main memory spaces are cacheable and which are shared. The use of the special compiler disallows these caches from being software transparent, so they are not selected for use in systems where source for the code to be used is unavailable. Those protocols which do not depend on compiler support are called **naive** protocols and will make up all of the examples given at the end of this chapter. Naive protocols are the more useful of the two in the widest variety of applications, but they are also harder to understand than sophisticated protocols.

4.2.1 Two Caches with Different Data

It's pretty obvious that a tightly coupled system with two or more cached CPUs can run into situations where the two CPUs' caches each have a copy of the same main memory location. One of the main reasons to use a tightly coupled architecture rather than a loosely coupled architecture is to allow arbitrary memory locations to be shared between the different processors, and these shared locations will perform more slowly if they are not allowed to be cached.

In Section 4.1.1, we looked at the problem of assuring that DMA write cycles update their appropriate cache locations and explored several of the means used to implement coherency. In tightly coupled multiprocessor systems, similar means must be taken to assure that any main memory write cycle from one processor updates the other processors' caches where appropriate.

One method which has somewhat fallen from grace is the use of a single cache to support multiple CPUs, as is shown in Figure 4.6. The Univac 1100/82 used such an approach to support two processors, and Futurebus+ allows for such a configuration. This can be made to work if the CPUs can be interleaved with each other; however, today's and tomorrow's CPUs often run at such high speeds that no discrete primary cache could be designed to be fast enough to service the bandwidth needs of the interleaved CPUs. Another problem is that a dual processor using the same cache is about twice as likely to thrash as a single processor operating out of the same cache. Last, in systems using on-chip primary caches, a shared secondary cache is sometimes used to reduce bus traffic. If all of the CPUs in the system are tied to the same cache, the bandwidth limitation simply gets moved from the CPU–main memory interface to the cache–CPU interface, rather than being reduced.

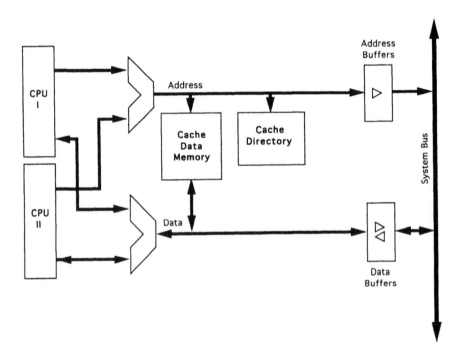

Figure 4.6.   One cache serving two CPUs. This tends to cause thrashing since the two CPUs are in contention over the allocation of the cache.

4.2.2 Maintaining Coherency in Multiple Logical Caches

Coherent logical caches in single-processor systems have a lot of restrictions, which were outlined in Section 4.1.2. The same restrictions apply to logical caches in multiple-processor systems. The most important is that the cache set address bits must consist of a subset of the MMU's page offset bits of the memory-mapping scheme, unless the designer wants to go to some pretty extreme measures to maintain coherency.

Let's look back at the mips R4000 as an example of how extreme those measures can become. Read this closely, because the scheme used in the R4000 is very involved. The R4000 was designed for multiprocessor systems and used a logical primary cache and a physical secondary cache. The secondary cache screened primary snoop invalidates through inclusion. The primary cache was eight times larger than the size of a page of main memory, so three of the page numbers in the MMU were mapped into the set bits. This implies that there can be aliases within the primary cache for which the secondary cache must snoop.

A drastic way of solving this problem would have been to invalidate all primary cache locations which had any likelihood of matching an updated main memory location. On a secondary snoop hit, all right of the primary cache locations with matching page offset address bits would be invalidated. This would have worked, but would reduce the performance of the cache by causing unnecessary invalidations.

The way mips solved the problem was to make a physical secondary cache a necessary part of the system and to use inclusion, assuring that every primary cache location was replicated within the secondary cache. Each of these secondary cache locations contains three **color** bits, directing the secondary cache to the corresponding primary cache location. These three bits are stored at the secondary cache line's set address, just like the tag bits and the line status bits.

When there is a secondary snoop hit, the secondary cache merges its three color bits with the page offset bits to create a logical set address of the matching primary cache address. The primary cache location at this logical set address is then invalidated. Multiple cached copies of the same main memory locations cannot exist in a system using this sort of inclusion, since both logical copies would map to the same physical secondary cache address, and there is a one-to-one mapping of primary cache locations to their secondary counterparts. If there were not this one-to-one mapping, each secondary line would have to store multiple coexistent sets of color bits to account for every possible alias.

Let's see what would happen if the CPU attempted to put aliases of a location into its primary cache. Say there exist primary and secondary cache copies of a main memory location, and the processor wants to read (and cache) a different logical address which will map into the same physical address. This will be treated by the primary cache as a miss/refill cycle, and by the secondary cache as a hit. The color bits are checked against the three lower logical page bits and will be found not to match, so the secondary cache would treat the cycle somewhat like a miss cycle, performing its inclusion housekeeping by invalidating the primary cache location which has matching offset and color bits, yet the secondary cache's copy would not be invalidated or evicted. A new copy of the secondary cache data is then copied into the new primary cache address, and the only part of the secondary cache line which would be modified are the color bits, to reflect the new logical address which that cache line represents. No main memory accesses take place, even if the secondary cache's line contains modified data. As I said before, this is complex and might not be deemed worth the effort.

4.2.3   Write-through Caches as a Solution

The problem of assuring that two or more caches in a system stay coherent with each other really boils down to the issue of how to handle write cycles. DMA writes into main memory must be accommodated by the individual caches, and writes performed by another processor must not disagree with the data subsequently held in another cache for the same memory location.

A very direct means of assuring that this happens is to cause all write cycles, whether from a DMA device or a cached processor, to be placed on the main memory bus. Write-through caches send all of their write cycles to main memory, either directly or through write buffers, so they are an obvious choice for this sort of system. This approach is the one used in IBM's 3033 processors, as well as Sequent's Balance 8000 system. All write cycles on the bus are snooped by all caches, and write snoop hits will cause any cache with a matching address to invalidate or replace its copy of the data being updated. As previously mentioned, some systems flush the entire cache on a write snoop hit.

This last option is even less desirable in a multiprocessor than in a DMA system, since write cycles from other processors will be small, frequent, and random in nature, rather than the occasional large block data transfer which is typical of DMAs. If each bus write caused all caches in the system to flush, the number of cycles which would be satisfied by any processor's cache would be almost zero.

One problem revolves around the use of write buffers. Assume that a processor writes data for a certain address into a write buffer, and another processor is simultaneously reading from the same address in main memory. Should the second processor first receive the now-stale data from main memory, with the data being invalidated or updated immediately after its use, when the write buffer is finally granted access to the bus? In most designs, this is not really a problem, since the processors are not synchronized to begin with. Other designs, however, shorten the response from one processor's write to another's read by configuring write buffers to snoop the bus, just as a cache would, and to either abort the other processor's read cycle until the write buffer is emptied into main memory or to supply the data directly from the write buffer to the requesting processor. A third option is to grant write buffers higher priority during bus arbitration than is granted to any reading device. This will always allow the write buffers to empty before any possible read conflict arises.

4.2.4 Bus Traffic Problems

Now that we've seen the advantages afforded by write-through caches from the perspective of multiprocessor coherency problems, let's look at the same caches from the perspective of bus traffic. Bus traffic is a real concern and is often a reason to add a cache to any system, especially multiprocessor systems. Naturally, the less bus traffic, the better, but by no means does the designer want the system's bus to come anywhere near saturation.

First, let's work under the assumption that all bus cycles occur with no wait states. This is just a temporary assumption to clarify. We'll return to reality a little later. As we have done before, let's assume that 10T of all CPU cycles are write cycles, and since the caches used are write-through, all of these writes are propagated to the main memory bus, both to be written to the main memory and to be snooped by all of the other caches in the system. Let's also assume a 5% read miss rate on the cache, and since the read cycles make up 90% of the CPU's I/O cycles, read misses will account for 4.5% of all CPU cycles.

Write cycles and read misses will occur pretty randomly. If they were completely predictable, the system would quickly synchronize itself, and up to six processors (100%/[10% + 4.5%]) would run as fast as they could on such a bus before there were any signs of a problem. This does not happen in the real world, though, and every added processor will cause arbitration and associated overhead, so the bus will cause added processors to show diminishing returns long before six processors are installed. (Still, remember that we are basing this analysis on some assumed numbers. These numbers are extremely dependent upon the cache design, as well as on the software being executed. Sequent's Balance 8000 was said to be able to sustain up to 12 CPUs before saturation, and it used write-through caches.)

Now, let's see what happens when a wait state is added. Assuming this means that every bus cycle is twice as long as it was in the previous case, the bus would quite simply become saturated with half as many processors. Diminishing returns would most probably become glaring even when the second processor was added.

Just to add insult to injury, let's now consider the fact that all of these main memory bus cycles will be in contention with each other for bus usage, further piling up the wait states. Most multiprocessor bus arbitration algorithms cost at least one extra wait state, even if the bus doesn't happen to be in use at the time.

I'm sure that you are looking at the example and saying "There's a lot to be gained by increasing the read hit rate and by making sure that the main memory system is as fast as possible," and you're right, but high-speed systems are nearly impossible to design with zero-wait buses, and read hit rates can only be pushed so far. What's the next option? Well, since the write cycles are the most frequent users of the bus (10% vs. 4.5% in this example), doesn't it make most sense to go after them?

Say your write-through cache, with its 5% miss rate, can be converted to a copy-back cache with a similar write miss rate. Suddenly, the bus is needed not for all writes plus 5% of the reads for 14.5% of all CPU I/O cycles, but for only 5% of all CPU I/O cycles. This looks well worth the effort, but in a multiple-processor design it can cause a lot of difficult problems. The next section will address these.

4.2.5   Copy-back Caches and Problems Unique to Copy-back Caches

We have now decided that bus traffic would have a far lower impact in a system if it could be reduced by using a copy-back cache, so we want to know if there are any special considerations which would cause difficulties in a copy-back multiprocessor cache design. There sure are!

By their very nature, copy-back caches maintain data which is allowed to be incoherent with the associated main memory location. How in the world can a cache location be coherent from cache to cache, yet be incoherent with main memory? Well, maybe it doesn't always have to be! There is every possibility that a written location belongs solely to a single processor, for example, a loop counter or a private pointer. The locations which are shared between processors, however, must always match from cache to cache. Although this seems like a place where the code would need to be written to support the protocol, this is not the case, and we will soon see that the method of assuring that the shared write cycles are appropriately communicated, while private writes are not, is not as difficult as it may seem.

Just to take a quick break from all of this complex talk about multiple processors, let's look at a simple software-controlled mechanism for assuring that DMA read cycles use the most up-to-date copy of a piece of data in a uniprocessor system with a copy-back cache. This problem is trivial in comparison with the problems encountered in a multiple-processor system, since the CPU initiates all DMA activity, and the process of assuring coherency can be tacked onto the routine which allows the DMA activity to start. In multiple-processor systems, the communication between processors is less tightly controlled and can happen more or less randomly in bits and pieces.

To support DMA coherency in uniprocessor systems, some processor instruction sets provide the user with an instruction which initiates a copy-back cycle on all Dirty cache locations. This is typically called a cache **purge** cycle, since the process purges all of the Dirty locations out of the cache. If the program controlling the start of a DMA from memory (possibly a write to disk) commences by performing a purge instruction, there will be no Dirty locations when the next instruction is allowed to execute. Intel's IntelArchitecture, with its internal write-through cache, provides a write-back invalidate data cache (WBINVD) instruction to support external copy-back caches, but all the instruction does is to raise a flag and expect the external cache controller to stop the processor from executing any further I/O activity until all Dirty external copy-back cache lines have been updated in main memory. Cache designers are sometimes frustrated at the duration of an instruction which must inspect the status of every cache line and might even need to perform four or eight times as many write cycles as there are lines in the external cache! Worst yet, some processors support an **export** instruction, which is aimed at turning the purge process into a software loop, rather than a hardware purging mechanism. The export instruction, when used in a purge loop, will send a copy of a single Dirty line within the cache back to main memory, so that that individual main memory location is made coherent in main memory. Naturally, purging the cache under software control does nothing to solve the random snoop read hits by alternate processors in a multiple-processor system, so let's move onward to the more challenging task of assuring coherency via hardware for arbitrary coherency conflicts.

In the write-through design suggested in Section 4.2.3, main memory was viewed as the holder of "the truth." Any cache looking for data could always go to the main memory to get the most current copy of the data. In a single-processor copy-back cache design, the most current copy of a main memory address might be held in either the main memory or in the cache, and the location of the most current version is indicated by the cache line's Dirty bit. Obviously, the location of the most current version becomes more obscure in a multiple-processor system.

Something which might instantly spring into your mind is that, if replicas of all the tags and Dirty bits for all caches were available in a centralized location, then each cache which was performing a read cycle would be able to direct its read cycle either to the main memory or to the cache which held the most current copy of the data. CDC computers and Chips and Technologies' M/PAX multiprocessing chip set operate this way, in what is referred to by the following variety of names: **directory-based, memory-based, global directory,** or **memory tagging.** In a directory-based system (Figure 4.7), every memory location or group of memory locations which has the same length as a cache line (sometimes called a block, and sometimes not) will also contain one or two extra bits per processor. These bits indicate the status of that memory block as a cache line in one or more caches. The status might indicate that processors A, B, and F contain a copy of the data and that it has not been modified. In another block, the status bits might indicate that only processor D has a cached copy, and this copy is the only valid one in the system. In some more elaborate systems, the status bits might indicate that D, E, and F contain valid copies, but the copy in main memory is not coherent with these. All of these status bits must be reset upon system initialization.

In any case, the main memory acts as a referee and must be constantly aware of the status of the caches of each processor. This simplifies the design somewhat, since all monitoring functions are assumed by a single unit. On the other hand, the number of processors used is not arbitrary, but is limited by the number of main memory bits allotted to keeping the status. It might be tempting to put these bits onto the processor board, so that processors could be added indefinitely at will, but then expansions and reductions in main memory size would require simultaneous modification of all processor boards.

This approach is not quite as simple as the preceding text might suggest, because some means must be chosen to disallow the concurrent existence of two or more copies of the same main memory location during a time when one processor wants to write into its cached copy of that location. If

A		B		C		D		E		F		Data Bits
Valid	Dirty	Valid	Dirty	Valid	Dirty	Valid	Dirty	Valid	Dirty	Valid	Dirty	Each main memory location is equivalent in size to a cache line.
1	0	1	0	0	0	0	0	0	0	1	0	Line 0 — Valid copies in A, B, and F.
0	0	0	0	0	0	1	1	0	0	0	0	Line 1 — D has only valid copy, and has written to it.
0	0	0	0	0	0	1	1	1	0	1	0	Line 2 — D, E, and F have copies, and D has written to all.
0	0	0	0	0	0	0	0	0	0	0	0	Line 3 — No cached copies exist.
0	0	1	0	0	0	0	0	0	0	0	0	Line 4 — Cache B has only copy.
1	0	0	0	0	0	0	0	0	0	1	0	Line 5 — Valid copies in A and F only.
0	0	1	0	1	0	1	0	1	0	1	0	Line 6 — All except A have valid copies.
1	0	1	1	1	0	1	0	1	0	1	0	Line 7 — All have copies, and B has written to all.

Figure 4.7. Organization of main memory in a memory-based coherency architecture. Bits within main memory keep track of the location and coherency of cached copies of each line-sized main memory location.

all cache writes first had to check for copies of the same line in other caches, the main memory bus would be saturated with cycles interrogating the status of various lines of main memory. For this reason, many protocols disallow the existence of multiple cached copies of a Dirty line.

A much more popular method of assuring coherency in multiple copy-back caches is to use the inherent snooping mechanisms built into each cache. These systems are called **cache-based.** Several recipes can be used to assure that data will remain accounted for and that there can never be more than one copy which the entire system agrees is the most current at any particular instant. Any cache line's state can be changed by either a CPU cycle or by a snoop cycle.

The most widely used multiprocessor copy-back cache coherency protocols are those dubbed **write-once.** Some call these protocols **write-first.** In write-once protocols, the first write cycle to a location held in cache is also written onto the main memory bus. In other words, a cache line is treated as it would be in a write-through cache for the first write cycle. Why is this done? Well, it allows the other processors to snoop the write cycle and invalidate their own copies of the same line. It is key to this scheme that they invalidate their copies rather than update them, since this will be the only bus write the writing processor allows to go onto the bus. A processor's bus traffic will be a little higher for a write-once cache than it would be in a standard copy-back cache, but this is one of the penalties of maintaining coherency.

A processor must perform two kinds of writes. The first is the write to a private location, which, as we saw, would be something other processors would not want to see, like a loop counter. The second kind of a write would be for public data or data other processors would want to see. In a processor using a write-once protocol, the private data write follows a sequence where the processor writes to the bus the first time, invalidating any other cached copies of the same memory location, then, during all subsequent write cycles, writes only to the cache, at the cache speed rather than the main memory speed. Bus traffic would also be eliminated for all of these subsequent write cycles. The Dirty line is copied back into main memory only if it gets evicted during a line refill. Another way to look at this is that the cache controller assumes that the data is public on the first write cycle, but if it is able to write to the same location twice without intervening requests for the same information from other devices, then the controller determines that the location is private.

A write cycle to a public data location would unknowingly proceed in the same manner until another processor requested the data. If only the first write cycle had taken place, the other processor would update itself from main memory, and the processor which had performed the first write would be told that the first write was no longer the first write. Another write-once cycle would need to be performed to invalidate the second cache's new copy of the matching main memory location's data. If more than one write cycle had taken place before another processor requested a copy, then main memory would not be current, and the requesting cache would need to procure a copy of the contents of the cache line into which the first processor had been writing. The means by which this happens is called **intervention,** since the cache with the most current data must intervene, forcing the reading device not to see the current contents of main memory, but to see the updated data. Means of intervention will be investigated shortly.

It would appear that yet another status bit would be required on each cache line to tell the cache controller whether the write cycle was the first or some subsequent write cycle to this cache line. This is not the case, since a typical copy-back cache has all of the mechanisms to support an unused state. Recall from Section 2.2.4 that a typical copy-back cache uses two status bits: Valid and Dirty, yet there are typically only three states indicated by these bits: Invalid (clean or dirty), Valid Clean, and Valid Dirty (Figure 4.8). What if we had a more elaborate interpretation of the two bits which allowed us to use the spare Invalid state to keep better track of the cache line's status? This would allow us to store four states: Invalid, Valid-and-never-written-to-by-any-CPU, Valid-and-written-to-once-by-this-CPU, and Valid-and-written-to-more-than-once-by-this-CPU. (Cache designers don't use this terminology, but have far more brief nomenclature which we will examine shortly, in Section 4.3.) By doing this, we can no longer refer to the bits as Valid and Dirty, since their meanings are now encoded, but we still have the same number of bits, and the changes to the cache controller to support this new protocol are simple. The only state which requires the cache controller to intervene is the state in which the cache's copy of a piece of data is more current than that held in main memory. This is the Written-to-more-than-once state, which is sometimes referred to as the **Private** state, since it is the only state in which the data in the cache is not shared or coherent with the data in either main memory or another cache.

A protocol which offers a slight twist on the write-once algorithm is called **broadcasting** or **write broadcasting.** As opposed to the invalidation which is caused to happen by the first write in a write-once scheme, broadcasting cache protocols allow the recipients of the newly written data to keep copies in their caches of the data which was written to the bus by other CPU/cache combinations. Because of this, broadcasting caches must be supported with system bus cycles which differentiate between a broadcast write and a write which is intended to invalidate other cache's copies of the same line. Furthermore, a whole new set of states is required to account for the new approach. Some broadcasting protocols will be examined in later sections.

There are two kinds of intervention: **indirect data intervention** and **direct data intervention.** Both deserve thorough explanations. We'll start with indirect data intervention, which is by far the simpler of the two.

Valid Bit	Dirty Bit	Status
0	X	Invalid Line
1	0	Valid Clean Line. Matches main memory.
1	1	Valid Dirty Line. More current than main memory.

Figure 4.8. The three states in a typical copy-back cache design.

As previously stated, the problem to be solved exists when a cache detects a read snoop hit to a location which is marked Dirty. Indirect intervention caches will abort the snooping read cycle, gain control of the main memory, write from the snooped address to the appropriate main memory location (without CPU involvement), updating the line's status from a Dirty state to a clean Valid state, then relinquish the bus so that the other CPU can again attempt, and succeed, to read the data it needs. (The process of updating main memory during a snoop cycle is sometimes called **XI castout** for "cross-interrogate castout." Cross-interrogation, as we have already seen, is another term for snooping, and castout is actually eviction, but the creators of the term XI castout probably don't really mean eviction; they probably perform main memory updates and modification of the line's status to a Valid-and-never-written-to-by-any-CPU state, just like you and me.)

The reason this intervention is indirect is that the request for data in the snooped processor's cache is answered not by the snooped cache handing the data directly to the requesting device, but by the process of handing the data through main memory, a more indirect path. This is reminiscent of conversations in some old movies, where three people are in a room, and one tells another to tell the third something because the two of them are not on speaking terms. Some indirect data intervention protocols allow a device which has had its request aborted to watch the bus traffic and, if a write cycle to a matching address occurs, to grab a copy and continue with its read cycle, saving time and reducing bus traffic over protocols which require the read cycle to be retried.

Indirect data intervention does require special bus support. Either of two methods are used to abort bus cycles, depending upon whether the bus protocol does or does not support split transactions, and a mechanism must be provided to allow main memory updates from snooped locations to take priority over any other cycle from another processor, even if the other processor would normally be granted a higher priority in bus privileges.

In split-transaction systems (first defined in Section 2.1.2), a bus master issues a request and removes itself from the bus, awaiting a response from the executor of the task. The snooped cache in split-transaction systems sends an abort/retry message to the requesting device, then gains control of the bus before another request can be issued.

In systems without split transactions (where a bus master issues a request and stays on the bus until a response is recognized), either a higher priority request forces the requesting processor off the bus and puts it into a Hold state until the main memory update is complete, or an abort/retry signal causes the cycle to be restarted, but in the intervening time, a higher priority master, the snooped processor, gains control of the bus to update the main memory. It's pretty obvious that if the read cycle comes from a processor with a higher priority in attaining the bus than the snooped cache, and if the response to the snoop cycle is not allowed to temporarily take a higher priority, then the system will lock up while the higher priority processor waits for the data which the lower priority processor is not allowed to place into main memory.

Direct data intervention systems allow any responding cache to disable system memory on a bus read snoop cycle, and allow the data from the snooped location to be placed on the bus supporting instant communication between the snooped cache and the requesting processor. This is also called a **cache-to-cache transfer,** since main memory is not involved in the transaction. In these systems, either of two methods can be chosen for the problem of multiple cache copies of data for which there is no valid copy in the main memory. The simplest to understand is the use of **reflection,** a process by which the main memory has a snoop mechanism similar to the snoop mechanism on the caches of the other CPUs on the system. The snoop mechanisms on the other processors would typically use cache-tag RAMs to monitor the bus for matching address cycles. The main memory, on the other hand, consists of a single large, contiguous block of addresses, so all that it requires is an address decoder, in fact the same address decoder which is used to assign the memory space that the main memory would ordinarily be mapped to if not superceded by an intervening cache. If a processor starts a read cycle to an address which is stored as Written-more-than-once in another processor's cache, the snooped processor disables a response from main memory and places its own data on the bus, downgrading its status to Valid-and-not-written. The memory's snoop mechanism sees a read cycle which it was not allowed to support, so it grabs a copy of the data as it appears on the bus and temporarily places it into a write buffer in the main memory system itself. As memory latency allows, the new data is written into main memory. In the end, the caches and main memory all have copies of the same data, so the appropriate state for all cached copies of this line is Valid-and-not-written.

Direct data intervention systems which do not use reflection use a different set of cache states which are designed to allow multiple cache copies to exist of data which has not been updated within main memory. These are known as **ownership** protocols. Assume, once again, that one processor's cache contains a Dirty copy of a main memory location which another processor is requesting. When the cache containing the updated copy snoops this read cycle, it will supply the data to the requesting processor, as in the preceding example, but the main memory will not be equipped with means of updating itself when this transaction occurs. The main memory, in fact, is a traditional design which will only modify itself on system bus write cycles. The only time that main memory is updated in such caches is when the Dirty line is evicted from the cache. This requires a different set of states, since there can now be two Dirty copies of the same location in two different caches. This is where the concept of ownership comes into play.

In ownership protocols, the cache whose CPU modified the Dirty cache location is deemed to be the owner of that location. The owner, and no other cache, is responsible for the eventual update of main memory. Thus, when a Dirty line is replaced in the cache which owns that line, the Dirty line will be evicted from the cache and updated in main memory, whereas the replacement of the same Dirty line in a cache which does not own that line will not cause a main memory update.

So what do we call the case in which no cache owns a copy of a main memory location? This is not widely discussed, but about half of the papers written about ownership give main memory the ownership of any potential cache line which has not been claimed by any cache, while the others say that the line is **unowned.** Main memory ownership of a line balances things out and seems to make it easier to describe the actions taken in an ownership cache coherency protocol, so we will use that nomenclature for the rest of the book. When a cache with this sort of protocol needs to update a line, it will request the line from the owner, whether or not the owner happens to be, in fact, main memory.

One problem addressed by caches using ownership protocols is the difficulty of **pingponging,** which is something like thrashing, in that the state of a line changes frequently at the expense of both the timing on that line and increased bus traffic. Pingponging, besides being a hard word both to spell and to say, is the phenomenon of a line's being taken into and out of a Private state as its value is being interrogated by a cache which does not own it. In an indirect data intervention system, the bus would often be tied up as the reading cache performed abortive reads of the Private location, which the responding cache would answer via memory write cycles, subsequently allowing the reading device back onto the bus. Afterward, the copy which was being modified would again be taken Private, at the expense of a broadcast write, only to be further interrogated by the requesting cache. It wouldn't take too much of this to dramatically tie up a main memory bus.

As an example of how an ownership protocol might work, we'll describe a typical direct data intervention copy-back cache using four states somewhat similar to those previously used in the indirect data intervention example: Invalid, Valid, Valid-and-written-to-once-by-this-CPU, and Valid-and-written-to-more-than-once-by-this-CPU. "Hey!" you say, "This is almost the same as the last protocol we went through." Well, it is, and it isn't. Bear with us, and you will see the difference that direct data intervention brings to the party.

The last two states are the states which declare that this cache is the owner of the true copy. If we watch a given line through its various state changes, we will see a progression similar to the previous example until a snoop read hit is encountered. Say processors A and B both start out with Invalid lines and get read misses for the same main memory location. The lines will be updated, and their states will be changed from Invalid to Valid. Processor A might then write to this line, and its cache controller, upon seeing a transition in state from Valid to Valid-and-written-to-once-by-this-CPU, will broadcast the write to invalidate other copies on the bus. Let's let processor A write to the line again, raising the status of the line from Valid-and-written-to-once-by-this-CPU to Valid-and-written-to-more-than-once-by-this-CPU.

The copy in processor B's cache was invalidated by the first write, which was broadcast by processor A's cache to the bus, so on the next read miss to this address, the processor will again attempt to update the line. This attempt is now satisfied by the intervening cache from processor A, and the line's state is stored in processor B's cache as Valid, just as if the line had come from main memory. If processor B then replaces this line, no main memory write cycles occur, even though the copy in processor B's cache was more current than the copy contained within main memory. If processor A evicts the line, its cache will update main memory, and processor B's cache will snoop this update, but will not need to change the line's status. Ownership of the line has been relinquished from processor A's cache back to main memory.

Upon careful inspection, the reader will note that the owning processor (processor A) in this example has no idea about whether or not there exist copies of its Valid-and-written-to-more-than-once-by-this-CPU cache line in other processors' caches. To maintain coherency with these copies, the owning processor would have to place every write cycle onto the bus, removing any advantage to using a copy-back protocol. Something needs to be done to allow the cache to know whether write cycles must be broadcast or can remain Private. This requires that the state Valid-and-written-to-by-this-CPU be further divided into two categories: snooped and unsnooped. Unsnooped copies would perform immediate cache write cycles without performing any bus interaction. Snooped copies, knowing that another processor might have a copy of the Dirty location, would need to perform a bus write cycle to invalidate other copies; then the owning cache can take the line's status back to unsnooped. This is where a fifth state of an ownership will come in. We'll rename Valid-and-written-to-by-this-CPU to Valid-and-written-to-by-this-CPU-but-unsnooped, and make the fifth state be Valid-and-written-to-by-this-CPU-and-snooped.

Caches like this one tend to work only with certain bus protocols. The most common at this time (and probably the slowest version we'll discuss) are buses with daisy-chained hierarchies, wherein main memory only responds after all other devices have been given the opportunity to supercede it. If there are several caches tied to the bus, each has its opportunity to respond before main memory is allowed to finally satisfy a read cycle. Split-transaction buses are the next on the list, and, like their use in indirect data intervention systems, they allow the responding cache to give itself a time slot to respond before main memory's access latency, signaling to main memory that the cycle has been satisfied by another respondent. A third method involves the use of an auxiliary bus, which supplies the snooped data while the main memory bus is used exclusively for main memory transfers. The decision of which bus to read then is made on the processor board of the requesting CPU/cache, rather than as a system function. A different set of line states is required to support a two-bus protocol to reroute read cycles, depending upon where the reading processor expects to find the line it needs. Another method, which is used with the $N+1$ protocol discussed in Section 4.3.4 is the use of a **smart** main memory. A smart main memory keeps a bit for every potential cache line to indicate whether the line is or is not owned by main memory. You will not be surprised when I tell you that designers of such systems call the more common type of design, where the main memory keeps no such status, **dumb** main memories. Smart protocols are a hybrid between cache-based and memory-based protocols, with a leaning more toward the cache-based side.

Both write-once and ownership protocols sometimes take advantage of write allocation as a method of signaling the need for other caches to invalidate any existing copy of a cache line. This means that the only write cycles to the main memory will either be to noncacheable addresses (if they exist) or copy-back cycles, neither of which will cause invalidation, since no other caches contain copies of these lines. Buses used to support such protocols require a mechanism to allow line invalidations during snoop read hits rather than snoop write hits. It will become more clear as we examine such protocols in detail that the bus will be required to support two completely different read cycles, one allowing other caches to maintain existing copies of the requested line, and the other requiring matching lines to be invalidated. Some examples are **Read-for-Ownership** or **Private Read, Read Shared** or **Public Read, Write-for-Invalidate,** and **Write-without-Invalidation,** and they are described in Section 4.3. Although such states are closely tied to the maintenance of cache coherency, we will treat them as a bus protocol issue and will only describe them in enough depth to allow a thorough understanding of the cache's rather than the bus' operation. As a general rule, though, Read-for-Ownership cycles are used exclusively for write allocation cycles and not for satisfying read misses.

In sophisticated ownership protocols, however, the compiler instructs the CPU to indicate that a read miss will later result in a write cycle, so the CPU initiates a Read-for-Ownership on read misses to locations which the compiler has decided would best be immediately invalidated in all other caches, locations to which a write is imminent, even though they are brought into the cache via a read miss cycle. Most designs don't have the luxury of being able to have all programs compiled to suit the architecture of the cache, so they count on write misses of naive ownership protocols to generate their Read-for-Ownership cycles.

A really unusual benefit of an ownership coherency protocol is that the cache which owns a copy of a requested piece of data may respond more quickly than main memory, causing there to be certain combinations of hardware and software which will exhibit performance gains which are more than proportional to the number of processors contained within the system (Figure 4.9). Another way to put this is that two processors might perform at 210% of the throughput of a single-processor system, three processors at 325%, and so on. How can this be? Well, as more processors are added, there exist more fast cache locations which can supply data to other processors faster than can main memory, to the point that a large enough system, with just the right programs, would only use main memory as a place to put evicted lines or possibly as a staging area for DMAs. Of course, the benefit of

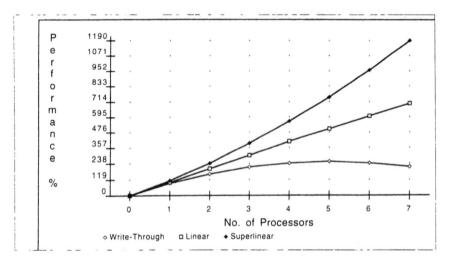

Figure 4.9. Throughput versus number of processors for three kinds of multiprocessing systems. The lower curve shows the effects of main memory bandwidth limitations, the middle line is an idealized linear ratio of performance to number of CPUs, and the top line shows superlinear performance, which can occur in systems using direct data intervention.

this phenomenon is highly dependent on the amount of interprocessor communication which is supported by the software comprising the benchmark.

Some multiprocessor systems use this concept to the hilt, and are sometimes said to cache their own portion of main memory. This is a point at which the delineation between cache and main memory becomes less clear, and what some designers would call cache, others would say is anything but a cache. Kendall Square Research Corporation was one such company with an approach they named Allcache, meaning that the entire main memory was implemented within the caches of several (from 16 to over 1,000) CPUs. One term for systems which have various portions of main memory physically split between all of the different processor boards within a system is **nonuniform memory architectures (NUMA).** In a nonuniform memory machine, the portion of main memory which is local to the CPU card responds to the local CPU far faster than the other processors, not just because of proximity, but because the local processor need not arbitrate for the system bus and is always given top priority for access to the local memory. From any processor's viewpoint, main memory will have a small fast address range, but all the rest of the address range will be slow. The way to get the best performance out of NUMA machines is to compile code which makes as many references as possible to the local, fast portion of main memory. This implies that the code must be designed to fit the hardware, which is often not an option available to the system design team. Naturally, the converse of a NUMA machine is a **UMA** or **uniform memory architecture** machine, where main memory is equally accessible to all processors, and any one address will respond to all processors with the same latency.

One last piece of bus support for multiple copy-back caches should be mentioned in this section, and that is the **backoff** command. In certain cache designs, backoff is simply a bus command which requires the cache immediately to stop interacting with the system bus. In copy-back cache coherency protocols, the meaning is different, and two types of backoff exist. A **full backoff** is what happens when a snoop hit is not serviced until the snooped cache is able to service the snoop cycle at its own convenience, possibly when the cache is not being used by the CPU. The alternative, a **restricted backoff** is where the snoop hit causes all CPU/cache interaction to come to an immediate halt so that the snoop hit can be instantly serviced. To my knowledge, there is not a large base of thought or research into the merits of one over the other; they are simply viewed as alternative snooping techniques.

4.3   EXISTING COPY-BACK COHERENCY PROTOCOLS

This section will show some real examples of existing multiple copy-back coherency protocols. You probably feel by now that this all gets very involved, so to help you out, we will go through illustrations in the form of tables for each of the protocols. These tables can be very helpful in defining the states in a cache, so try to put one together for your own design, should you do one.

The columns in the table represent the state of the cache at the beginning of any cycle. Each row represents an external even which may have an impact on the way the cache operates or on a change of states within the cache. The tables in this book are not detailed enough to design from, and you will probably find yourself putting together several layers of similar tables to describe the actions of various portions of your own hardware.

4.3.1   The MESI Protocol

MESI is a write-once cache-based protocol, probably the one most often described in trade magazines. Why not? It has a catchy name. My wife (a student of theology, not engineering) is amused when I tell her that a computer can have a MESI protocol, use SCSI communications, and provide a GUI user interface. It seems somehow inconsistent with all this filthy language, then, that the MESI protocol rules out a cache's use of Dirty bits.

The acronym MESI stands for the four states of a typical indirect data intervention protocol which we described in Section 4.2.5, but uses other, less descriptive, but far simpler names for the same states: **Modified, Exclusive, Shared,** and **Invalid.** Here is how these four states correspond with those described in Section 4.2.5: Invalid is quite naturally the Invalid state; Shared is the state that we originally called Valid-and-never-written-to-by-any-CPU; Exclusive translates to the Valid-and-written-to-once-by-this-CPU state; and Modified is the name used in the MESI protocol for the state that we originally called Valid-and-written-to-more-than-once-by-this-CPU. As we shall see in the next section, these states are not exclusively applicable to indirect data intervention.

The names make a lot of sense. The Shared state is the only state which allows another copy of the same memory location to be stored within other caches. If one cache has an Exclusive or Modified line, all matching lines in other caches would have been marked Invalid (we'll go through this in more detail in Table 4.1). The Exclusive state signifies to the cache controller that the main memory location is current with the contents of the cache and that no other cache copies of the same main memory location exist; this is an exclusive cache copy of the main memory location (some refer to the Shared state as a **Nonexclusive** state). Finally, the Modified state indicates that the only current version of the address resides within this cache.

The MESI protocol was first developed to be used on the original version of multibus, a bus which does not already have any hooks to support coherency protocols. As a result, there is no write allocations or direct data in-

Table 4.1.   MESI

	Invalid	Shared	Exclusive	Modified
From CPU Bus				
Read Miss	Update line from main memory. Update status to Shared.	Update line from main memory. No status change.	Update line from main memory Update status to Shared.	Evict modified line to main memory. Update line from main memory. Update status to Shared.
Read Hit	Does not occur.	Read cache data. No status change.	Read cache data. No status change.	Read cache data. No status change.
Write Miss	Write to cache line. Write to system bus. Update status to Exclusive.	Write to cache line. Write to system bus. Update status to Exclusive.	Write to cache line. Write to system bus. No status change.	Evict modified line to main memory. Write to cache line. Write to system bus. Update status to Exclusive.
Write Hit	Does not occur.	Write to cache line. Write to system bus. Update status to Exclusive.	Write to cache line. Update status to Modified.	Write to cache line. No status change.
From System Bus				
Read Miss	No response. No status change.	No response. No status change.	No response. No status change.	No response. No status change.
Read Hit	Does not occur.	No response. No status change.	Update status to Shared.	Abort snooped cycle. Write modified line to main memory. Update status to Shared.
Write Miss	No response. No status change.	No response. No status change.	No response. No status change.	No response. No status change.
Write Hit	Does not occur.	Update status to Invalid.	Update status to Invalid.	Update status to Invalid.

tervention. All write cycles in an implementation of a MESI system on a simple bus are considered writes-for-invalidate, and will automatically invalidate any matching locations in other caches. This is shown in Table 4.1. Since the bus in such a system is not expected to support a Read-for-Invalidate state, write allocation is not used in the design of MESI caches.

Table 4.1 shows the four MESI states and the responses given in the event of processor and snoop read and write hits and misses in cacheable spaces. Most CPU cycles perform as would similar cycles in either a write-through or a copy-back cache, depending on the state the cache line was in before the transaction occurred. The two special cases are the write miss to a Modified line and a write hit to a line marked Exclusive. A write miss to a Modified line can either cause a main memory write cycle without updating the cache, or, as is shown in Table 4.1, the current contents of the line can be evicted followed by a write-through cycle which takes the line to the Exclusive state. A write hit to an Exclusive line will update the line to a Modified state without a bus transaction. Exclusive must be entered before going to Modified. No cache line is allowed to go directly from either of the other states to the Modified state.

There are always special cases. Intel's processors implement the MESI protocol using write allocation, to match the disparity between the processors' 16-byte internal cache line size and the processors' support of write cycles of between 1 and 4 bytes. This means that all write misses will appear as read misses on the processor bus. With this being the case, it helps performance if all read misses are first assumed by the system to be write allocation misses, and for the state of a newly fetched cache line automatically to be set to Exclusive, with all other cached copies to be automatically invalidated. This requires the cache/CPU combination to be supported with a main memory bus offering a Read-for-Invalidate mechanism, so that read cycles can cause invalidations in other caches, unless the designer is willing to suffer along with an occasional problem of pingponging, where two caches which share a piece of data continually invalidate the other's copy.

Snoop cycles in the MESI protocol are treated as you would pretty much expect a copy-back cache to perform on snoops. Snoop read and write misses are ignored, and read hits are only really noticed if the snooped cache line is either 1) in an Exclusive state, in which case, the exclusivity will be downgraded to the Shared state (a valid copy already exists in main memory), or 2) in the Modified state, where the other device's read request will need to be aborted, and the snooped cache must then be allowed to update main memory with the contents of the Dirty line before allowing the snooping processor to retry the aborted bus cycle. In either case, the line's status will be changed to the Shared state. All write snoop hits will invalidate the hit cache line, but a write hit to a Modified line is usually an indication of some very bad housekeeping on behalf of the software!

True minimalists will wonder if the Exclusive state can be done away with, and it can, but at a cost. The cache controller can easily enough determine that the cache is transitioning from a Shared state to a Modified state, and send out a bus write to invalidate any other cached copy, just as it would going from the Shared to the Exclusive state, but if the line were never again written to, the cache controller would not know and would evict the Modified line, whether or not it was still coherent with its main memory counterpart. This is not in keeping with the goal of reduced bus traffic, so it is rarely used, but a version of this will be discussed in Section 4.3.4.

4.3.2   Futurebus+

An open standard bus protocol, the IEEE Futurebus+ (the plus sign reminds me of a small letter t, but I doubt that it's any indication that this bus will meet with limited acceptance), takes advantage of a wealth of understanding and growth that bus experts have amassed since other, better established, open-standard buses were first conceived. Futurebus+ uses a split-transaction synchronous bus with its own voltage I/O levels called bus-transceiver logic (BTL) which, although they are incompatible with standard logic levels like ECL and TTL, make up for any difference by being blazingly fast.

Futurebus+ specifies a copy-back coherency protocol based on MESI, but far more bus support than the original MESI model is assumed, write allocation is used, and an additional mechanism is included which was given the hysterical name **snarf** or **write snarf.** When a processor is attempting to read data into a cache, but the bus is unavailable, the cache is capable of listening to the other transactions going on, and, if the requested address happens to be involved in a bus transaction, that processor's cache controller will grab a copy and will stop trying to arbitrate for control of the bus. The Futurebus+ specification is written to allow the designer to select from a broad menu of options, and an option exists which allows a cache to snarf a copy of a bus transaction whose address matches the address of an Invalid location, even if the processor is not requesting a copy of it. This looks a lot like reflection, doesn't it? It's almost zenlike in the way that the Futurebus+ committee decided to mimic the main memory technique of reflection, so that caches now capture data from a cache-to-main memory transfer, just as a reflecting memory captures data on a cache-to-cache transfer. It also makes a lot of sense to put reflection onto a processor as well as onto a memory card.

Some readers may disagree, and that's surely because you've considered that the odds of the exact address which the processor is requesting being on the bus while the processor is attempting to gain control of the bus are almost nil, and that the cache should be nearly completely filled with Valid locations. The counterarguments are twofold. First, any protocol which can reduce bus traffic will further increase the number of processors which can be tied to a bus, and, as the bus traffic is reduced, the likelihood of such interactions becomes a larger share of the overall chain of events. Second, those cache locations which are marked Invalid after the processor has been running long enough to fill its cache probably were Valid at one point, then got invalidated by another processor's taking the line into an Exclusive state. If the address again appears on the bus, this automatically implies that the line is being downgraded from its Exclusive state and is again ready to be replicated within other caches in the system.

Just because you use Futurebus+, you are not required to have copy-back caches on every processor board, nor even to have multiple processors, but since the bus contains all the protocols to support the most extensive implementations, it is straightforward to implement a mix-and-match system of write-through, copy-back, and noncache processor boards. As I said before, there is a vast menu of ways to implement your own board and still be assured of compatibility.

Futurebus+ differs from the MESI protocol upon which it is based in that it uses direct data intervention (the reading of cacheable locations from other caches, rather than from main memory) and write allocation, both of which are supported by a split-transaction bus protocol which has been specified around the cache implementation, rather than the other way around. There are three kinds of read cycles, two writes, and an invalidate, which is a faster way to invalidate a replica of a cache line in other caches than would be a Read-for-Invalidate or Write-for-Invalidate. Further, snoop hit acknowledgments are broadcast from the snooped caches onto the bus via a signal called tf*. This tf* or transaction flag is a bus signal whose definition depends upon the type of transaction which is occurring on the bus. For all of the cycles in this section, tf* signals a snoop hit. By monitoring the tf* signal, the requesting cache has the option of taking a line immediately into an Exclusive state, if that line is copied in no other cache. This makes Table 4.2 a bit more complex than Table 4.1 was for MESI, but it is worthwhile in keeping unnecessary write-once cycles off the main memory bus. Reflection is also required of the memory subsystems (if they exist), another bandwidth-saving measure, since high-speed direct data intervention cycles can be used without requiring followup cycles to update the main memory.

Wait a minute! What is this "if they exist" stuff about memory subsystems? Futurebus+ is defined in such a way as to allow the entire system to exist without a main memory, as long as any active main memory address is always accounted for in the system. For this they have the term **repository of last resort,** which is the place where that address eventually is brought to rest. In systems with main memories, this is the owner of the line, which is, more often than not, main memory. In a cache-only system, the repository of last resort is the current owner of the line, and the line is assured, through other parts of the bus protocol which we won't discuss here, to always be replicated somewhere within the system.

To understand the Futurebus+ bus commands using Table 4.2, the names of the four states should be defined. They are Exclusive Modified, which corresponds to the Modified state of the MESI protocol, Exclusive Unmodified (MESI's Exclusive), Shared Unmodified (Shared), and Invalid.

Two of the simplest bus commands to understand are those used by I/O bus masters, normally DMA devices. These are Read Invalid and Write Invalid. Although the Write Invalid command automatically invalidates all

Table 4.2.   Futurebus+

	Invalid	Shared Unmodified	Exclusive Unmodified	Exclusive Modified
From CPU Bus				
Read Miss	Update line from owner using Read Shared. Update status to Shared. Unmodified if another cache has asserted tf*, else may update status to Exclusive Unmodified.	Update line from owner using Read Shared. No status change if another cache has asserted tf*, else may update status to Exclusive Unmodified.	Update line from owner using Read Shared. Update status to Shared. Unmodified if another cache has asserted tf*, else no status change required.	Evict owned line to main memory using Copyback. Update line from owner using Read Shared. Update status to Shared Unmodified if another cache has asserted tf*, else may update status to Exclusive Unmodified.
Read Hit	Does not occur.	Read cache data. No status change.	Read cache data. No status change.	Read cache data. No status change.
Write Miss	Update line from owner using Read Modified. Merge write data with new line. Update status to Exclusive Modified.	Update line from owner using Read Modified. Merge write data with new line. Update status to Exclusive Modified.	Update line from owner using Read Modified. Merge write data with new line. Update status to Exclusive Modified.	Evict owned line to main memory using Copyback. Update line from owner using Read Modified. Merge write data with new line. No status change.
Write Hit	Does not occur.	Write to cache line. Issue Invalidate to system bus. Update status to Exclusive Modified.	Write to cache line. Update status to Exclusive Modified.	Write to cache line. No status change.
From System Bus				
Read Miss	No response. No status change.	No response. No status change.	No response. No status change.	No response. No status change.
Read Shared Hit	Does not occur.	Assert tf*. No status change.	Assert tf*. Update status to Shared Unmodified.	Disable main memory response. Output requested data. Assert tf*. Update status to Shared Unmodified.
Read Invalid Hit	Does not occur.	Assert tf*. No status change.	Assert tf*. Update status to Shared Unmodified.	Disable main memory response. Output requested data. Assert tf*. Update status to Shared Unmodified.

Table 4.2. (*continued*)

Read Modified Hit	Does not occur.	No bus response. Update status to Invalid.	No bus response. Update status to Invalid.	Disable main memory response. Output requested data. Update status to Invalid.
Write Miss	No response. No status change.	No response. No status change.	No response. No status change.	No response. No status change.
Write Invalid Hit	Does not occur.	Update status to Invalid.	Update status to Invalid.	Update status to Invalid.
Invalidate Hit	Does not occur.	Update status to Invalid.	Does not occur.	Does not occur.
Copyback Hit	Does not occur.	Does not occur.	Does not occur.	Does not occur.

cached copies in existence, the Read Invalid command does not, but rather downgrades copies to the Shared Unmodified state, and causes owners of Exclusive Modified copies to intervene in the case of a snoop read hit.

The Read Shared command is issued by a processor which has experienced a read miss cycle, and any snoop hit allows the data to come from either the main memory (if the snooped copy was Shared Unmodified or Exclusive Unmodified) or from the snooped cache in the event that the snoop hit was to an Exclusive Modified location. In all of these cases, the snooped cache will assert tf* and will come to rest in the Shared Unmodified state. (Being flexible, the Futurebus+ specification does allow a cache to invalidate its own copy of a line if it does not desire to assert tf*.) Since reflection is used in the main memory, the downgrade from Exclusive Modified to Shared causes no coherency problems. In every case, a valid copy of the line resides in main memory at the end of any Read Shared cycle. Now the requesting cache knows whether other cached copies of the line exist, since it will have received an asserted tf* if there were any other cached copies of the line, and a negated tf* if there were not. This being the case, the new cache line will be loaded as Shared Unmodified if there exist other cached copies, and will be immediately loaded into the Exclusive Unmodified state if no other cache has a copy. If the line which is loaded as Exclusive Unmodified is then the subject of a cache write hit, no write-first cycle needs to be invoked, thereby saving bus bandwidth over a standard MESI implementation.

The final Futurebus+ read cycle is a Read Modified, which is used by a cache to signal that it has suffered a write miss cycle, and must obtain an Exclusive copy of a line for its write allocation. When a Read Modified snoop hit occurs on a cache, that cache's copy of the line is invalidated. Since the line might be longer than the word which is being written (Futurebus+'s line length is 64 bytes), and since snooped Exclusive Modified copy may be modified in different bytes than would be modified by the requesting processor, the owner of a snooped Exclusive Modified line must perform a direct data intervention to hand the data to the new owner.

The two Futurebus+ write cycles are Write Invalidate, which has already been discussed, and Copyback. The Copyback cycle is used during evictions of Exclusive Modified lines. Since these lines are Exclusive, there can exist no replicas of them in other caches, so there will never be any snoop hits.

The only other Futurebus+ bus cycle which involves cache interaction is the Invalidate cycle. Invalidate is issued by a cache which owns a Shared copy of a line and wants to take that line into an Exclusive Modified state. Strangely enough, the Futurebus+ committee decided to call this a write miss cycle. In the name of consistency, I will follow a more general convention and call this a write hit to a Shared Unmodified location. Upon a snoop hit of an Invalidate command, any other cache which owns a Shared Unmodified copy of the line will have its copy Invalidated. It is impossible for a copy in another cache to have any other state, since a line which is in a Shared Unmodified state in one cache cannot be in either of the Exclusive states in any other cache.

In taking this relatively backward approach, we have discussed all of the snoop cycles at the bottom of Table 4.2 and have skipped the CPU cycles. Let's go over them. On a CPU read miss, if the line to be replaced is in an Exclusive Modified state, it must be evicted before the new data is read into the cache. This is done by writing the evicted line to main memory using the Copyback bus command. Then the same series of events is taken as during a CPU read miss to a line in any of the other states. A Read Shared command is placed on the bus, and the owner of the data responds, plus any snooped caches are given an opportunity to assert tf* to tell the requesting cache that the line is indeed Shared. The line is copied into the cache, and, if tf* is asserted, the line is marked Shared Unmodified, but, if tf* is not asserted, the line goes immediately to the Exclusive Unmodified state. Of course, the requesting cache does not absolutely have to put the line into an Exclusive Unmodified state, as Futurebus+ allows this as an option, but it's an option which is sure to add speed to the overall system's performance since it removes the need to perform a subsequent write-once cycle. Naturally, on read hits, the data goes straight from the cache to the CPU without any bus interaction or state changes.

On a write hit, an Exclusive Modified line will be written to without bus interaction or state change, while an Exclusive Unmodified line will be written to without bus interaction, but will undergo a state upgrade to Exclusive Modified. If the line started out in a Shared Unmodified state, other copies must be Invalidated, so the cache controller must issue an Invalidate command on the bus. This is a fast, abbreviated version of a write cycle, where data is never placed on the bus. The cache line can then be written to, and its status will be upgraded to the Exclusive Modified state.

Write miss cycles, like read misses, are all satisfied the same way, once any possible dirty line has been evicted. The eviction is handled the same as for a read miss: If the line is in an Exclusive Modified state, it is first written to main memory using the Copyback bus command. Then, for any line status, the line to be written to is read from its owner into the cache using the Read Modified command, invalidating all other cached copies, is written into, and is immediately put into the Exclusive Modified state. The status of tf* is ignored since the Read Modified command will invalidate any snooped copies.

Another unique facet of Futurebus+ is that it allows coherency to be maintained on hierarchical bus structures like the one shown in Figure 4.10. The key to this mind-bending problem is the use of two sorts of **agents**: **memory agents** and **cache agents**. A memory agent will receive read and write commands on one side of the bus and will respond to those commands with transactions which appear on that side of the bridge to be coming from

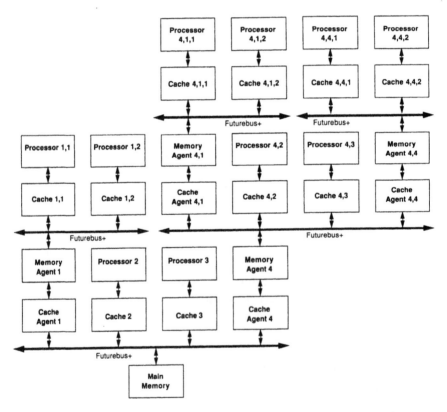

Figure 4.10. A large Futurebus+ system where five levels of the Futurebus+ are used. Coherency is maintained between all caches through the actions of the cache agents and the memory agents.

nothing but a simple main memory on the other side of the bridge. On the other side, the memory agent keeps track of caches and main memory locations, monitors the ownership of each line, and transacts with each line's owner on an individual basis. Since the memory agent must know whether to go to main memory or to a cache to get the current value of a piece of data, caches on the memory agent's side of the bridge cannot be allowed to use the Exclusive Unmodified state. The Exclusive Unmodified state allows a line to go into an Exclusive Modified state without bus interaction, so the memory agent would not discover when the ownership of the line transferred from the memory on that bus to the cache. If you look again at Table 4.2, you can see that the Exclusive Unmodified state is only entered if a read miss is serviced without the tf* line going active, and then only if the designer wishes to implement this. Otherwise, a read miss takes the new line into the Shared Unmodified state. If the cache resides on a side of a bridge which is monitored by a memory agent, then the response to the tf* on a memory read miss is simply disallowed.

A cache agent has only caches to worry about, so it is a bit simpler. Based on inclusion, the cache agent snoops the bus on the other side of the bridge from the side used by the caches it represents. The cache agent knows the addresses of every line which is cached on its own bus, and allows through to its own side of the bridge only those snoop cycles which are likely to cause snoop hits in the caches which it protects. This is a way of cutting down the bus traffic which flows across the bridge. By using cache agents and memory agents, snoops can be propagated up and down the hierarchy of Figure 4.10 without tying all the buses down in massive quantities of fruitless and irrelevant snoop traffic.

Another new multiple-processor bus specification is the Corollary C-bus II. This specification is very much like Futurebus+ since it uses a modified version of the MESI protocol with the additional support of write allocation, 32-byte lines, and direct data intervention. To support all of this, two special read-exclusive bus cycles are provided: Read Exclusive and Evict Exclusive. Both are used to support write allocation, with the Evict Exclusive command preceding its write allocation read cycle with the eviction of a Dirty line. Snooped hit copies of the line read into the cache using either of these cycles are invalidated by either of these commands in all other caches.

4.3.3 The MOESI Protocol

Although the **MOESI** acronym looks almost the same as MESI, it represents a very different protocol since it supports direct data intervention. The acronym stands for states with the same names as used in MESI, with the addition of the **Owned** state, but the meanings of the states are mostly different, and correspond to the long-named states used in Section 4.2.5 in the following manner: Invalid once again is the Invalid state; Shared likewise is the state originally called Valid; Exclusive, however, becomes Valid-and-written-to-once-by-this-CPU; Modified now becomes Valid-and-written-to-more-than-once-by-this-CPU-but-unsnooped; and Owned is added to mean Valid-and-written-to-more-than-once-by-this-CPU-and-snooped. The Modified, Owned, and Shared states show the difference between MESI and MOESI. If a processor in MESI has a Shared line, it means that main memory is current and that the line has not been written to in any cache. In the MOESI protocol, Shared means that this is just a copy of a location which may or may not be current in main memory, but is an exact copy of the owner's data. In MESI, the Modified state implicitly means that the location has not been snooped, whereas this needs to be spelled out in MOESI. Finally, the Owned state accounts for the difference between the direct data intervention of MOESI and the indirect data intervention supported by MESI. Owned locations may have replicas in other caches, similar to Shared lines, but main memory has never been updated, so it must be written to by the owning cache upon an eviction.

Table 4.3 shows the five MOESI states, and the responses given in the event of processor and snoop read and write hits and misses in cacheable spaces. Like MESI, the MOESI model assumes no special bus support. State transitions are described in detail in the following paragraphs.

On a CPU read miss, if the target line is Owned or Modified, it is evicted. The cache then updates the line either from main memory or from the owning cache, and the line will be loaded as Shared. If the line comes from an owning cache, that implies that this cached copy is either in the Owned or Modified state, and, if the state is Modified, it will be downgraded to Owned. During snoop read hits to Shared and Exclusive copies of a line, there will be no bus interaction, but, if an Exclusive copy receives a snoop hit, it will downgrade its own status to Shared.

As in the MESI protocol, all main memory write cycles are snooped for invalidation by all other caches. MESI and MOESI designs tend not to use write allocation, meaning that a CPU write miss must broadcast itself through the system as a bus write cycle. The write cycle then will be transmitted through the cache similarly to a write-through cache. In many designs, write misses are ignored by the cache. The assumption used to justify the cache's ignoring write misses is that anything which is not already in the cache when it is written is very possibly not going to be referred to in the future. This is indeed the case for such items as initialization values loaded into various areas, but is not the case for the first time a memory resident loop counter is set up, nor for the first time the stack reaches a certain depth. Still, these are the exception and not the rule, so write misses are usually ignored in MOESI caches.

Table 4.3. MOESI

	Invalid	Shared	Exclusive	Owned	Modified
From CPU Bus					
Read Miss	Update line from main memory. Update status to Shared.	Update line from main memory. No status change.	Update line from main memory. Update status to Shared.	Evict Owned line to main memory. Update line from main memory. Update status to Shared.	Evict Modified line to main memory. Update line from main memory. Update status to Shared.
Read Hit	Does not occur.	Read cache data. No status change.	Read cache data. No status change.	Read cache data. No status change.	Read cache data. No status change.
Write Miss	Write to cache line. Write to system bus. Update status to Exclusive.	Write to cache line. Write to system bus. Update status to Exclusive.	Write to cache line. Write to system bus. No status change.	Evict Owned line to main memory. Write to cache line. Write to system bus. Update status to Exclusive.	Evict Modified line to main memory. Write to cache line. Write to system bus. Update status to Exclusive.
Write Hit	Does not occur.	Write to cache line. Write to system bus. Update status to Exclusive.	Write to cache line. Update status to Modified.	Write to cache line. Write to system bus. Update status to Exclusive.	Write to cache line. No status change.
From System Bus					
Read Miss	No response. No status change.	No response. No status change.	No response. No status change.	No response. No status change.	No response. No status change.
Read Hit	Does not occur.	No response. No status change.	No response. Update status to Shared.	Disable main memory response. Output requested data. No status change.	Disable main memory response. Output requested data. Update status to Owned.
Write Miss	No response. No status change.	No response. No status change.	No response. No status change.	No response. No status change.	No response. No status change.
Write Hit	Does not occur.	Update status to Invalid.	Update status to Invalid.	Update status to Invalid.	Update status to Invalid.

In the example in Table 4.3, we have chosen to take the more complex route of updating the missed line. This can only be done if the cache line is the same size as the smallest write cycle supported by the CPU/software of the system (not all software uses byte write cycles when the CPU provides them). If smaller writes are allowed, and if a write miss is to be written into the cache, write allocation protocols should be considered. The table assumes that only word writes are supported by the cache. Since the design requires the replacement of a Modified line on a write miss, the bus subsequently must carry two cycles, an eviction followed by a write (for invalidation) of the replacement line.

Should write allocation be used, one of the several three-state and four-state protocols described in the following sections would probably be chosen over the five-state MOESI. In a MOESI system with write allocation, write misses to a Modified location would consume three bus cycles: first the eviction of the Modified line, then the read cycle to allow the allocation, then a write-once cycle to invalidate any other cached copies of the line. This can be a pretty heavy penalty!

On a CPU write hit, if the location is Modified, there is no bus activity, and the line is updated, remaining in the Modified state. Similarly, a CPU write hit to a line marked Exclusive will update the line without invoking any bus transactions, and the resultant line will end up in the Modified state. If the line is Shared or Owned, the line is updated, a write cycle to the bus is initiated to invalidate any other copies which may exist in other caches, and the state is updated to Exclusive. This is kind of weird when an Owned line is written to, since what appears to be a higher status, a Written-to-more-than-once status, is downgraded to Exclusive, a Written-to-once status, in response to a write hit. The rationale behind this is that an Owned line might be copied in another CPU's cache, so a bus cycle is absolutely necessary to invalidate any copies which could be stale in other caches. Since the main memory bus is assumed not to differentiate between different kinds of write cycles, an invalidation, rather than an update, must occur on a write snoop hit to assure that any cache wishing to take its copy to an Exclusive state through a main memory write cycle can do exactly that. Once this bus cycle has happened, the main memory is current, and there is no longer any need for the cache with the new Exclusive line to evict that line. Since both the Owned and Modified states require an eviction on a line replacement, they are inappropriate, and that leaves us with Exclusive as the only rational destination after a CPU write hit to an Owned line. Naturally, there is no such thing as a write hit to an Invalid location.

A write snoop hit always results in the snooped line being immediately invalidated, no matter what the original status was. This can signify software problems, just as it did in the MESI cache, if a dirty or Owned line gets invalidated. It might seem a waste that the eviction of an Owned copy will cause invalidation of coherent Shared copies of the same line in other caches. These caches will have to go back to main memory after the eviction to get the same data they had before. Further, this process will happen on every write hit cycle to an Owned location. This might rule out the use of MOESI in favor of other protocols in the design. The one beauty of MOESI which would offset this is that the alternatives require special bus architectures, whereas all MOESI needs is a prioritizing scheme to allow caches to turn off main memory in the event of a snoop write hit. This is quite a significant consideration in designs where the design team must fit a multiple-processor coherency protocol to an existing bus which was designed without coherency in mind.

On snoop read hits, Modified lines will supply their data directly to the requesting cache and will downgrade their status to Owned. Owned lines will respond to a snoop read hit in the same way, without any change to the responding cache's line status. Read snoop hits to Exclusive and Shared Locations cause no data to be supplied from the cache to the bus, since the data in that cache should be supplied by the owner, whether the owner is main memory, which is always the case with an Exclusive line but may or may not be the case with a Shared line. The owner may be a different cache. The Exclusive copy will, however, downgrade its status to Shared. If the snooped read hit is to an Owned or Modified line, data will be supplied by the cache to the bus, and the final state of the line will be Owned. Nope, there are no snoop read hits to Invalid lines.

The attraction to the MOESI protocol over MESI is that it uses direct data intervention. This speeds up interprocessor communication at a slight cost in cache complexity, since the cache must now track five states per line, rather than four. Either protocol uses standard main memory write cycles to invalidate matching locations in other caches, and neither uses write allocation, which is more complex, but actually helps to simplify some of the protocols to be discussed in the following sections.

4.3.4   N+1

A different protocol was developed by Synapse for their N+1 fault-tolerant computer (Table 4.4). This protocol uses a smart main memory (described in Section 4.2.5) with a single bit called a usage-mode bit maintained in main memory for each potential cache line, to indicate whether that line is owned by the main memory or by a cache. The usage-mode bit tells whether the line is Public or Private. This extra bit removes the need for caches to preempt main memory from responding to a system bus cycle since the main memory will disable itself from responding if the usage-mode bit is set, saving some time over daisy-chained or other less costly memory-disabling schemes. The main memory in the N+1 also accelerated its own performance through the use of a 15-entry queue on all memory boards.

Table 4.4.   N+1

	Invalid	Valid	Dirty
From CPU Bus			
Read Miss	Update line from main memory using Public Read. Update status to Valid.	Update line from main memory using Public Read. No status change.	Evict dirty line to main memory. Reset main memory Usage-Mode bit. Update line from main memory using Public Read. Update status to Valid.
Read Hit	Does not occur. No status change.	Read cache data. No status change.	Read cache data. No status change.
Write Miss	Update line from main memory using Private Read. Set main memory Usage-Mode bit. Write to cache line. Update status to Dirty.	Update line from main memory using Private Read. Set main memory Usage-Mode bit. Write to cache line. Update status to Dirty.	Evict dirty line to main memory. Reset main memory Usage-Mode bit. Update line from main memory using Private Read. Set main memory Usage-Mode bit. Write to cache line. No status change.
Write hit	Does not occur.	Update line from main memory using Private Read. Set main memory Usage-Mode bit. Write to cache line. Update status to Dirty.	Write to cache line. No status change.
From System Bus			
Read Miss	No response. No status change.	No response. No status change.	No response. No status change.
Public Read Hit	Does not occur.	No response. No status change.	Abort snooped cycle. Write dirty line to main memory. Reset main memory Usage-Mode bit. Update stats to Invalid.
Private Read Hit	Does not occur.	Update status to Invalid.	Abort snooped cycle. Write modified line to main memory. Reset main memory Usage-Mode bit. Update status to Invalid.
Write Miss	No response. No status change.	No response. No status change.	No response. No status change.
Write Hit	Does not occur.	Does not occur.	Does not occur.

Each CPU card in the N+1 contained a 16K-byte copy-back physical cache, each line of which had two status bits: Valid and Data-Modified. The Valid bit was used to assert the validity of the cache line (naturally), while the Data-Modified bit kept track of the coherency of the data in main memory. Synapse claimed to be able to support up to 28 processors on a system, each adding incrementally to the system's throughput.

This protocol only used three states: Invalid, Valid, and Dirty. The three states were effectively used to accomplish the same thing as other four-state coherency protocols (some call these states Invalid, Shared, and Modified, or **MSI**). Support for the three-state methodology came in two forms. First, write allocation was used for all write miss cycles as well as write hit cycles to Valid locations (write hits to Dirty locations required no bus interaction), so that the only bus writes to cacheable addresses were the result of evictions or read snoop hits. Second, the bus allowed two sorts of read cycles: Public Read and Private Read. Public Read cycles were used exclusively for read miss cycle line updates, where the main memory usage-mode bit remained reset (indicating that main memory continued to own the cache line), and other Valid copies were allowed to coexist in other caches. Private Read cycles were incurred for all write allocation cycles, those line update read cycles which were incurred specifically in support of write miss cycles or writes to Valid locations which were being taken to the Dirty state.

Something somewhat bizarre about this protocol is that a write hit to a location which was not already Dirty caused the cache to reread the location from main memory using a Private Read command. The line would have previously been read for a read miss with a Public Read command. The repeated read cycle both invalidated any other copies of the cache line before the missed write cycle occurs and set the main memory's usage-mode bit. The newly fetched line was loaded into the cache as Dirty. What is odd is that this process was not optimized for the way that most code performs write cycles. Writes are most often performed to locations which have been previously read. For the N+1 protocol, this meant that most write cycles caused two main memory read cycles: a Public Read cycle for the reading of the data and a Private Read cycle for the write. This was no larger a number of cycles than is required by MESI, since MESI performs a main memory read first, then the first write, but the N+1 caused more bus traffic than some of the following protocols which involve less main memory cycles.

In a step-by-step analysis of N+1, we see the familiar fact that all CPU read hits are serviced immediately from the cache, without bus interaction or state change. On a CPU read miss, if the target line is Dirty, it will be evicted, and in all cases a Public Read bus command will get the updated line from main memory. The new line is stored as Valid.

On a CPU write hit, if the line is Dirty, the data is overwritten without status change or bus interaction. If the line is Valid, however, it is reacquired from main memory, this time with a Private Read cycle, which will signify to snooped caches that they should invalidate their own copies of the line, and will set the main memory's usage-mode bit. The local cache will immediately place the line into a Dirty state, and the new data will overwrite the appropriate portion of the line. A similar cycle is used to support a CPU write miss cycle, since the N+1 protocol is based around write allocation. If the missed line is Dirty, it will be evicted. No matter what the state of the existing line, a Private Read will be used to perform the write allocation, and the line will come to rest in the Dirty state with the new data overwriting what was supplied by main memory. All Private Read cycles set the usage-mode bit in the main memory. There is one usage-mode bit per potential cache line, and this bit tells the main memory not to respond to a read cycle to that address, deferring to the cache which holds a Dirty copy. This extra bit allows the main memory to respond to read cycles much more quickly than it could if the more typical daisy-chained priority mechanism were used.

Snooping in the N+1 protocol is relatively simple. If the starting state of the snooped line is Invalid, no action will be taken. If the snooped line is marked as Valid, it will only respond to snoop hits which result from Private Reads, in which case, the line will simply be set to Invalid. On a snooped Public Read hit or Private Read hit to a Dirty line, indirect data intervention will be used. This means that the read cycle will be aborted, the cache with a Dirty copy will write its copy back to main memory and will clear the usage-mode bit, the read will be allowed to be retried, and the Dirty line will be invalidated (I'm not sure why, for a Public Read, the Dirty line won't simply be downgraded to Valid). This is where the balance becomes apparent in how the usage-mode bit is handled. When a Private Read moves a line into a cache, the line is set to Dirty, and the usage-mode bit is set. When the Dirty line is downgraded, main memory is updated, and the usage-mode bit is cleared.

You will notice in Table 4.4 that no allowance is made for the possibility of a write snoop hit, which is kind of odd. How come? Since the N+1 protocol calls for write allocates, all write cycles to Shared or other cache locations are initiated by either a read cycle or an invalidate. This means that the only write activity on the main memory bus will consist of evictions of Dirty locations (which necessarily will not result in snoop hits, since no other cache will contain a copy of a Dirty line) and writes to noncacheable areas. Ipso facto, there is absolutely no reason even to include logic to handle snoop write hits. It appears that this architecture does not use DMAs to handle any disk I/O.

4.3.5 Berkeley

The Berkeley protocol is detailed in Table 4.5. There are four states, as there are in the MESI protocol, named Invalid, Unowned, Owned Non-Exclu-

Table 4.5. Berkeley

	Invalid	Unowned	Owned Non-Exclusively	Owned Exclusively
From CPU Bus				
Read Miss	Update line from owner using Conventional Read. Update status to Unowned.	Update line from owner using Conventional Read. No status change.	Evict owned line to main memory using Write-without-Invalidation. Update line from owner using Conventional Read. Update status to Unowned.	Evict owned line to main memory using Write-without-Invalidation. Update line from owner using Conventional Read. Update status to Unowned.
Read Hit	Does not occur.	Read cache data. No status change.	Read cache data. No status change.	Read cache data. No status change.
Write Miss	Update line from owner using Read-for-Ownership. Merge write data with new line. Update status to Owned Exclusively.	Update line from owner using Read-for-Ownership. Merge write data with new line. Update status to Owned Exclusively.	Evict owned line to main memory using Write-without-Invalidation. Update line from owner using Read-for-Ownership. Merge write data with new line. Update status to Owned Exclusively.	Evict owned line to main memory using Write-without-Invalidation. Update line from owner using Read-for-Ownership. Merge write data with new line. No status change.
Write Hit	Does not occur.	Write to cache line. Write-for-Invalidation to system bus. Update status to Owned Exclusively.	Write to cache line. Write-for-Invalidation to system bus. Update status to Owned Exclusively.	Write to cache line. No status change.
From System Bus				
Read Miss	No response. No status change.	No response. No status change.	No response. No status change.	No response. No status change.
Conventional Read Hit	Does not occur.	No response. No status change.	Disable main memory response. Output requested data. No status change.	Disable main memory response. Output requested data. Update status to Owned Non-Exclusively.
Read-for-Ownership Hit	Does not occur.	No bus response. Update status to Invalid.	Disable main memory response. Output requested data. Update status to Invalid.	Disable main memory response. Output requested data. Update status to Invalid.
Write Miss	No response. No status change.	No response. No status change.	No response. No status change.	No response. No status change.

Table 4.5. (*continued*)

Conventional Write Hit	Does not occur.	No bus response. Update status to Invalid.	No bus response. Update status to Invalid.	No bus response. Update status to Invalid.
Write-for-Invalidation Hit	Does not occur.	No bus response. Update status to Invalid.	No bus response. Update status to Invalid.	Does not occur.
Write-without-Invalidation Hit	Does not occur.	No response. No status change.	Does not occur.	Does not occur.

sively, and Owned Exclusively. The states are relatively similar to the MESI states, with the exception that the Owned Non-Exclusively state is a Shared Modified state. The MESI Shared state maps closely into the Berkeley Unowned state (so we can assume that the Berkeley crew didn't embrace the idea that main memory is the owner if no cache owned a copy of a line), MESI's Modified state is akin to Berkeley's Owned Exclusively state, and there's never much difference between any two protocols' Invalid states. Invalid is Invalid. But the Owned Non-Exclusively state is a state where the main memory is not coherent with the cached copies of the data, yet more than one cached copy may exist.

Going through Table 4.5, a CPU read miss to a line which is either Invalid or Unowned will simply update the line using a conventional read cycle, but, if the line starts out as either Owned Non-Exclusively or Owned Exclusively, then the line is Dirty and must be evicted. The difference between these two states is that the Owned Non-Exclusively line might be replicated in another cache, even though it is not coherent with main memory. After the eviction, the line is updated the same as for the other two states, and, for all four cycles, the line comes to rest in an Unowned state. CPU read hits, as with the other cache protocols, are simply satisfied from the cache without status change.

The reader will note that the Berkeley protocol uses the terms Conventional Read and Conventional Write instead of the clearer Public Read and Public Write used in other protocols. The meaning is the same; only the terminology is different. Conventional Reads are read cycles owing to CPU read misses, reads to noncacheable addresses, or DMA activity. Conventional Writes only come from DMA activity or noncacheable write cycles.

CPU write misses cause write allocation cycles, where a Read-for-Ownership bus cycle must be used to invalidate any other cached copies of the same line. As we saw in the Futurebus+ and the N+1 protocols, the use of write allocation requires special bus cycles to be used to support some sort of invalidating read cycle. The replaced line will first need to be evicted if it starts out as either Owned Non-Exclusively or Owned Exclusively, the same as in the case of CPU read misses, but the state of the line after the CPU write miss has been serviced is Owned Exclusively.

CPU write hits are handled differently than the other protocols we have examined. If the line starts the cycle out as Unowned or Owned Non-Exclusively, other copies will have to be invalidated, so the cache sends a Write-for-Invalidation cycle to the bus, just as would happen with MESI or MOESI write-once cycles. A Write-for-Invalidation cycle is a fast write which does not update main memory, but does invalidate matching lines in other caches, just like the Invalidate signal in Futurebus+. The line's state is then changed to Owned Exclusively. If the line started out as Owned Exclusively, then it is simply updated without any bus interaction. If the line started out as Invalid, there can be no CPU write hit cycles.

Other than the special reads and writes, the Berkeley protocol requires the support of two bus mechanisms: write allocation and direct data intervention. As we have seen in other protocols, write allocation requires two sorts of read cycles: Conventional Read and Read-for-Ownership. Read-for-Ownership is issued when a write allocation cycle is in process, that is, the cache is updating a line into which data from a write miss cycle will be merged. Direct data intervention is used to allow the owning cache to supply a replacement line to the requesting cache for either type of read cycle.

Since there are two types of read cycle and three writes, snooping in the Berkeley protocol involves a lot of possibilities. The two reads are Conventional Read, used to replace lines during CPU read misses and for DMA read cycles; and Read-for-Ownership, which is used to support the read portion of write allocation, and must cause invalidation of other cached copies of the requested line. The three write cycles are Conventional Write, used by CPUs to write to noncacheable addresses and by DMA devices; Write-for-Invalidation, which is used to take a line from a nonexclusive state to an exclusive state by invalidating any other cached copies in the system (on a CPU write hit to an Unowned or Owned Non-Exclusively line) and, as was mentioned before, does not require the main memory to record the written data; and Write-without-Invalidation, which is used during evictions to move a Dirty line which needs to be replaced back into main memory.

Snoop hits of Conventional Read cycles only cause responses from lines which are owned by the snooped cache. This means that a response will come from a cache with a copy of the line either in the Owned Non-Exclusively or the Owned Exclusively state. The data is supplied from the cache to the reading device after the cache has disabled main memory from responding, and the final state of the line is Owned Non-Exclusively. Main memory is not updated during these intervention cycles. This allows fast cache-to-cache transfers to occur when necessary, but reduces the number of slow main memory writes to the absolute minimum required. The same process occurs with a snooped Read-for-Invalidation cycle, except that the final status of the line is Invalid, even if the line starts out in the Unowned state.

Snooped Conventional Writes and Write-for-Invalidation cycles both cause a line starting in any state to become Invalid. No data is lost as a result, even though the system supports lines which are longer than the CPU's shortest write cycle, since Write-for-Invalidation cycles will only cause a hit to a line which is exactly copied in the cache which issues the Write-for-Invalidation command. A Write-for-Invalidation snoop hit can only be encountered by lines in either nonexclusive state (Unowned and Owned Non-Exclusively), since they are only issued upon CPU write hits to cache lines in the originating cache. If the line exists, then it cannot exist in an Owned Exclusively state in any other cache. The difference between Conventional Write and Write-for-Invalidation cycles, then, is only in the way that main memory responds to them. The Write-for-Invalidation cycle does not need main memory to update itself, since this write cycle terminates with the line being owned by a cache, so the only write cycle which needs to last long enough for main memory to be able to absorb a copy is the Conventional Write.

A Write-without-Invalidation cycle can only be snooped by a cache with a matching line in the Unowned state, since the issuing cache has the line in either the Owned Non-Exclusively or the Owned Exclusively state. The end result of a snoop hit during a Write-without-Invalidation cycle is simply that the cached line's ownership will move from the owning cache to main memory, so the cache with the Unowned line doesn't really need to care about this transaction. As a result, there is no response to snooped Write-without-Invalidation cycles.

Two of the three write cycles, Write-for-Invalidation and Write-without-Invalidation, are used in cache data transfers. Write-for-Invalidation is used during a write hit cycle to an Unowned or Owned Non-Exclusively line and allows all snooped caches' matching lines to be invalidated as the writing processor takes its own copy of the cache line to the Owned Exclusively state. Write-without-Invalidation is used in the eviction of either an Owned Exclusively or an Owned Non-Exclusively line during replacement for either a read or write miss cycle. The Write-without-Invalidation cycle takes advantage of the fact that the writing cache knows full well that no other cached copies exist, so it doesn't interrupt the other caches with snoop cycles which it knows in advance will have absolutely no effect other than to slow down the other processors. This is important if the Berkeley protocol is implemented in a multiplexed cache-tag RAM design, and the processor is halted every time the cache-tag RAM is to be snooped.

Here's an example of how two Berkeley protocol caches might play against one another. Say there were only two CPU/cache subsystems on a system built around the Berkeley protocol. The same line could reside in a Valid state in the two caches only as either Unowned/Unowned or as Unowned/Owned Non-Exclusively. In the first case, the main memory would contain the most current version of the cache line, but in the second case, both caches would contain data which was more current than that in the main memory. It would be up to the cache which contained the Owned Non-Exclusively copy to update main memory when that line was replaced.

So, to sum up, a CPU write miss causes a Read-for-Invalidation. A CPU write hit causes a Write-with-Invalidation when the hit line is not in an Owned Exclusively state, and it causes no bus cycle if the line is Owned Exclusively. Read misses cause Conventional Read cycles and are directly intervened, if possible. Evictions are handled via Write-without-Invalidations. Snooped Conventional Read hits to an Owned Exclusively line result in intervention and that line's being downgraded to an Owned Non-Exclusively, but if the line has an Unowned or Owned Non-Exclusively state, data is supplied by main memory and the state is unchanged. Read-for-Invalidation snoop hits cause invalidation. Conventional Write and Write-for-Invalidation snoop hits cause invalidations, and Write-without-Invalidations are ignored if they cause snoop hits to Unowned lines, the only type of snoop hit that such a cycle can invoke. Whew!

4.3.6   University of Illinois

The University of Illinois protocol (Table 4.6) supports direct data intervention similarly to Futurebus+, Berkeley, and the MOESI protocol. Like Berkeley, the N+1, and Futurebus+, this requires more bus support than MOESI, in that the Illinois protocol has a Read-for-Ownership cycle, a conventional Read cycle, and an invalidate cycle, as well as a signal which indicates to the reading cache whether the line which it is reading has been supplied from another cache or from main memory (very much like the tf* signal in Futurebus+). Main memory in this system is designed to respond to simultaneous read and write commands as it would to a simple write cycle, since this is what is intended during intervention, which the Illinois protocol supports by placing both cycles simultaneously on the bus. In addition, write allocation is used as it is in the N+1 to remove the need for individual caches to snoop bus write traffic. The four states used in the Illinois protocol are Invalid, Shared, Valid-Exclusive, and Dirty, all of which bear a strong similarity to their counterparts in the MESI protocol. The only state which supports copies of the same line in multiple caches is Shared.

Starting off in an Invalid state, assume we get a CPU read miss cycle. The cache issues a standard Read cycle to all other caches and the main memory.

Table 4.6.   University of Illinois

	Invalid	Shared	Valid-Exclusively	Dirty
From CPU Bus				
Read Miss	Update line from owner. If from another cache, update status to Shared. If from main memory, update status to Valid-Exclusive.	Update line from owner. If from another cache, no status change. If from main memory, update status to Valid-Exclusive.	Update line from owner. If from another cache, update status to Shared. If from main memory, no status change.	Evict dirty line to main memory. Update line from owner. If from another cache, update status to Shared. If from main memory, update status to Valid-Exclusive.
Read Hit	Does not occur.	Read cache data. No status change.	Read cache data. No status change.	Read cache data. No status change.
Write Miss	Update line from owner, using read-for-ownership. Write to cache line. Update status to Dirty.	Update line from owner, using read-for-ownership. Write to cache line. Update status to Dirty.	Update line from owner, using read-for-ownership. Write to cache line. Update status to Dirty.	Evict dirty line to main memory. Update line from owner, using read-for-ownership. Write to cache line. No status change.
Write Hit	Does not occur.	Send invalidation signal to system bus. Write to cache line. Update status to Dirty.	Write to cache line. Update status to Dirty.	Write to cache line. No status change.
From System Bus				
Read Miss	No response. No status change.	No response. No status change.	No response. No status change.	No response. No status change.
Read Hit	Does not occur.	Supply cache line to bus, if highest priority of caches snooped. No status change.	Supply cache line to bus. Update status to Shared.	Supply Dirty line to bus and write to main memory. Update status to Shared.
Read-for-Ownership Hit	Does not occur.	Supply cache line to bus, if highest priority of caches snooped. Update status to Invalid.	Supply cache line to bus. Update status to Invalid.	Supply Dirty line to bus. Update status to Invalid.
Invalidate Hit	Does not occur.	Update status to Invalid.	Does not occur.	Does not occur.

Table 4.6. (*continued*)

Write Miss	No response. No status change.	No response. No status change.	No response. No status change.	No response. No status change.
Write Hit	Does not occur.	Does not occur.	Does not occur.	Does not occur.

The memory is given lowest priority to respond, and the highest priority device which receives a snoop hit will feed the data to the requesting cache even if the line is only in a Shared state. If that device has a Valid-Exclusive or Dirty copy, it downgrades that line's status to Shared. Also, if the snooped copy was Dirty, the responding cache intervenes directly, using a main memory write cycle to copy the line back into main memory simultaneously with the read cycle which caused the snoop hit. The initiating cache will see that the data did not come from main memory and will set the line's status to Shared. If no other caches respond, the main memory supplies the data to the requesting cache, which sees the signal indicating that the copy came from main memory, and sets the state of its line to Valid-Exclusive. As in Futurebus+, the notification of snoop hits can remove the need for a write-once cycle to be performed for certain lines, thus reducing the bus traffic.

A CPU read miss to a Shared or a Valid-Exclusive location is treated the same as the CPU read miss just described. If the missed line is Dirty, however, an eviction is instigated, but then is followed by the same CPU read miss cycle. Read hits, as in any other cache, cause no bus activity whatsoever, and the hit line's status is not changed. One slightly unusual possibility is that a Shared line can be overwritten without other processors noticing that one less copy of the cached line exists. This means that there will be times when a processor will have the only copy of a cache line and will have that line marked in a Shared state, even though it could rightfully have that copy of the line in a Valid-Exclusive state, which would allow it one faster write cycle should the processor ever want to write to that line. Although this might cause an extremely minor performance impact, it will not make the coherency protocol any less bulletproof.

Since the cache is implemented using a write allocation strategy, all CPU write miss cycles begin similarly to their equivalent read miss cycles, with the exception that a Read-for-Ownership cycle is used to indicate that the requesting cache intends to take the line immediately into a Dirty state. If the line is cached, the highest priority cache which contains a copy of this line will supply it to the requesting cache, and all caches which experience snoop hits will immediately invalidate their own copies. As opposed to most of the other coherency protocols reviewed here, the transition of a cache line from a Dirty state in one cache to a Dirty state in another cache is not a sign of sick software. Write allocation schemes are typically used if the shortest CPU write cycle is less than the line length, so one cache/CPU could have only written to the least significant byte or word of a line, while the next cache/CPU would write to a more significant byte or word. Something else which is pretty unique about the Dirty-to-Dirty transition is that main memory does not need to be updated in this case. If reflection is not built into main memory, there is no reason to expect main memory to grasp a copy of the interim version of this line.

Only one type of CPU write hit cycle will produce any bus activity, and that is a CPU write hit to a Shared location. When a processor writes to a line which is already in the Shared state, the cache controller sends an invalidate cycle out on the main memory bus, causing all other Shared copies of the same cache line to immediately invalidate themselves. By the nature of the Illinois protocol, there can be no matching lines in any other states except the Shared state. The cache which sent the invalidation signal can now take its line into the Dirty state. A CPU write hit to a Valid-Exclusive or a Dirty location results in an immediate write cycle, and the line ends the cycle in the Dirty case.

Snoop write hits just plain don't happen since write allocation is used. Anything that is written is either in a noncacheable space or is written because a Dirty line was evicted, and a Dirty line will only be copied in a single cache, so no snoop hit can occur.

4.3.7   Firefly

The DEC Firefly was an unusual implementation in that it never used an Invalid state. As Table 4.7 shows, there are only three states: Shared, Valid Exclusive, and Dirty. How does the cache work without an Invalid state? It's something like the cache we looked over in Section 2.1.3, which used no status bits whatsoever, but assured that all locations were valid after a cold start by disabling the cache until a start-up routine had given all cache lines a chance to be replaced. Unlike MESI and MOESI, write cycles from one CPU/cache don't cause invalidations of matching addresses in other caches. Instead, the Firefly protocol requires snooped caches to update their contents during snoop write hit cycles. All CPU write cycles to cached locations which are not in an Exclusive state are propagated to the main memory bus. Thus, CPU write cycles to cache lines which are not in an Exclusive state in the local cache update both main memory and all snooped cache locations. This is broadcasting and was described in Section 4.2.5.

This special protocol requires a bus signal to indicate that a snoop hit has occurred in another processor's cache (as do Futurebus+ and the University of Illinois protocol), and, as with Futurebus+, the University of Illinois pro-

Table 4.7.   Firefly

	Shared	Valid Exclusive	Dirty
From CPU Bus			
Read Miss	Update line from owner. If from another cache, no status change. If from main memory, update status to Valid-Exclusive.	Update line from owner. If from another cache, update status to Shared. If from main memory, no status change.	Evict Dirty line to main memory. Update line from owner. If from another cache, update status to Shared. If from main memory, update status to Valid Exclusive.
Read Hit	Read cache data. No status change.	Read cache data. No status change.	Read cache data. No status change.
Write Miss	Update line from owner. If from another cache, write-through to cache and main memory. No status change. If from main memory, write to cache only. Update status to Dirty.	Update line from owner. If from another cache, write-through to cache and main memory. Update status to Shared. If from main memory, write to cache only. Update status to Dirty.	Evict Dirty line to main memory. Update line from owner. If from another cache, write-through to cache and main memory. Update status to Shared. If from main memory, write to cache only. No status change.
Write Hit	Write data to system bus. Write to cache line. If other caches respond to write, no status change. If no other caches respond to write, update status to Valid-Exclusive.	Write to cache line. Update status to Dirty.	Write to cache line. No status change.
From System Bus			
Read Miss	No response. No status change.	No response. No status change.	No response. No status change.
Read Hit	Supply cache line to bus, indicating shared data. No status change.	Supply cache line to bus, indicating shared data. Update status to Shared.	Supply Dirty line to bus and write to main memory, indicating shared data. Update status to Shared.
Write Miss	No response. No status change.	No response. No status change.	No response. No status change.
Write Hit	Update contents of line. Indicate shared data.	Does not occur.	Does not occur.

tocol, Berkeley, and N+1, Firefly uses write allocation to reduce the complexity of having to deal with write snoop hits. All bus write cycles fall into one of three categories: 1) They are not in cacheable areas, so coherency is not an issue, 2) they are to a Shared cache line, so they are observed by the other caches which have a Shared copy of the same cache line, or 3) they have come from the eviction of a Dirty line, and, therefore, no other cache can own a copy. Any cache which observes a snoop hit will not only tell its own cache controller of this occurrence, but will signal the fact to the entire bus, similarly to the tf* signal in the Futurebus+. This allows the CPU/cache which instigated the transaction to figure out how to handle the cache line. As opposed to most of the coherency protocols discussed in this chapter, only one type of read and write cycle is used, with the entire protocol being handled via the single snoop hit signal.

You by now have noticed that this cache, like many of the other protocols, behaves as if it were two different kinds of cache with two different kinds of write policies, depending on the current state of the line being written. Lines which are marked as Shared are treated as write-through, unless no other cache responds (with a snoop hit) to a main memory write cycle to one of these locations. Any line marked as Valid Exclusive or Dirty is treated as if it were in a single-processor copy-back cache until a read snoop hit is encountered. This ties neatly into the discussion in Section 4.2.3 about the ease of assuring coherency through a write-through strategy versus the improved use of bus bandwidth afforded by a copy-back cache. Only those cache lines which are truly Shared will use up precious bus bandwidth.

As with the Illinois protocol, an attempted main memory read cycle which is intervened because of a read snoop hit immediately causes the evicting cache to initiate a write command during the same memory cycle. This means that the main memory must respond to a combined read and write command as if it were simply a write cycle.

In summary, the cache behaves as if it were write-through for lines which are copied in other caches. If there is no other cached copy of a cached line, the cache uses a copy-back write strategy. All snoop hits are responded to by the snooped cache flagging the hit via and main memory bus. All snooped caches supply the line simultaneously. Bus crashes are not a problem since the snooped caches all respond during the same bus cycle.

Snoop hits to a Shared location do not change the status of the location. Snoop hits to Valid Exclusive or Dirty locations downgrade those locations to a Shared status. Lines can be upgraded to Valid Exclusive through an absence of a snoop hit during any shared read or write activity and are automatically loaded as Dirty during the read cycle of a write allocation. CPU write hit cycles to Valid Exclusive lines upgrade those lines' status to Dirty without bus interaction.

4.3.8 Dragon

Xerox PARC (Palo Alto Research Center, in California, the same people who brought us the graphic user interface of the Apple Macintosh) devised a multiprocessing protocol called the Dragon (Table 4.8). The protocol is another four-state version (Shared Clean, Shared Dirty, Valid Exclusive, and Dirty), yet it is similar to the Firefly and Futurebus+ in using a signal to indicate snoop hits on the bus, and, like the Firefly, it does not have an Invalid state. Unlike both the Firefly and the University of Illinois protocols, system bus read cycles don't suddenly convert to main memory write cycles. The only memory write cycles which appear on the system bus are noncacheable writes and evictions. Two states can result in evictions: Shared Dirty and Dirty. These are indeed ownership states, but the word "owned" appears to have been carefully avoided in the development of this terminology.

Table 4.8. Dragon

	Shared Clean	Shared Dirty	Valid Exclusive	Dirty
From CPU Bus				
Read Miss	Update line from owner. If from another cache, no status change. If from main memory, update status to Valid-Exclusive.	Evict dirty line to main memory. Update line from owner. If from another cache, update status to Shared-Clean. If from main memory, update status to Valid-Exclusive.	Update line from owner. If from another cache, update status to Shared-Clean. If from main memory, no status change.	Evict dirty line to main memory. Update line from owner. If from another cache, update status to Shared-Clean. If from main memory, update status to Valid-Exclusive.
Read Hit	Read cache data. No status change.	Read cache data. No status change.	Read cache data. No status change.	Read cache data. No status change.
Write Miss	Update line from owner. If from another cache, write-through to local and remote caches. Update status to Shared-Dirty. If from main memory, write to cache only. Update status to Dirty.	Update line from owner. If from another cache, write-through to local and remote caches. No status change. If from main memory, write to cache only. Update status to Dirty.	Update line from owner. If from another cache, write-through to local and remote caches. Update status to Shared-Dirty. If from main memory, write to cache only. Update status to dirty.	Evict dirty line to main memory. Update line from owner. If from another cache, write-through to local and remote caches. Update status to Shared-Dirty. If from main memory, write to cache only. No status change.

Table 4.8. (*continued*)

Write Hit	Write data to other caches, but not main memory. Write to cache line. If other caches respond to write, update status to Shared-Dirty. If no other caches respond to write, update status to Dirty.	Write data to other caches, but not main memory. Write to cache line. If other caches respond to write, no status change. If no other caches respond to write, update status to Dirty.	Write to cache line. Update status to Dirty.	Write to cache line. No status change.
From System Bus				
Read Miss	No response. No status change.	No response. No status change.	No response. No status change.	No response. No status change.
Read Hit	Indicate shared data on bus. Do not sent bus data. No status change.	Supply cache line to bus, indicating shared data. No status change.	Indicate shared data on bus. Do not send bus data. Update status to Shared-Clean.	Supply Dirty line to bus, indicating shared data. Update status to Shared-Dirty.
Write Miss	No response. No status change.	No response. No status change.	No response. No status change.	No response. No status change.
Cache Write Hit	Update contents of line. Indicate shared data on bus.	Update contents of line. Indicate shared data on bus.	Does not occur.	Does not occur.
Memory	No response. No status change.	Does not occur.	Does not occur.	Does not occur.

The bus does need to support a third kind of write cycle, one which updates other caches, but not main memory. By using this sort of write cycle (which is designed to be much faster than a main memory write cycle), the owner of a cache line can use a broadcast to update all other copies of the same cache line, as occurs in the Firefly. Like the Firefly and Futurebus+, snoop hits are signaled on the bus, and each line is set up to use either a write-through or a copy-back protocol during subsequent CPU write hit cycles, depending on the status of this signal during a bus transaction.

Going through the protocol step by step, cache read misses which do not generate snoop hits in other caches are loaded into the cache as Valid Exclusive lines. If they do generate snoop hits, the lines are loaded as Shared Clean (i.e., unowned). The responding caches take their lines from the Valid Exclusive state to the Shared Clean state, or from the Dirty state to the Shared Dirty state, but if the snooped lines were already Shared Clean or Shared Dirty, their status does not change. If the snooped line is in either

Dirty state, the read cycle is satisfied from the snooped cache. If the snooped line started out as either Valid Exclusive or Shared Clean, then the snooped cache does not place data on the bus, but leaves this task up to main memory. Naturally, the bus has been designed to allow the snooped cache to disallow a main memory response. Finally, if a CPU read miss is aimed at a Dirty or Shared Dirty line in the local cache, that line must be evicted. Read hits, quite naturally, generate no bus traffic and are satisfied from the local cache without incurring a state change.

On a CPU write miss, since a write allocation scheme is used, the same process is followed as was detailed for a read miss in the preceding paragraph, except that the line is loaded as Dirty if no other cache responds. If other caches respond, the requesting cache sets its line as Shared Dirty, and broadcasts a Cache Write cycle to the other caches. This is a special bus cycle which writes a line to other caches, but not to main memory. In response to this write cycle, any other Shared Dirty copy will change its status to Shared Clean. During the reading portion of this allocation, any Valid Exclusive snooped copy of this line would have changed states to Shared Clean already, and a Dirty snooped copy would have changed its status to Shared Dirty, so the Valid Exclusive and Dirty states will not be encountered during a Cache Write snoop hit.

If you look at this closely, you'll see that a CPU write miss to a location which is snooped as Dirty in another cache will first result in the Dirty copy being converted to Shared Dirty during the read portion of the allocation, then will be changed from Shared Dirty to Shared Clean during the Cache Write portion of the cycle. This is a pretty involved little two-step! In the case where the missed line in the requesting cache is also Dirty, it also amounts to a heavy overhead of bus traffic. A CPU write miss to a Dirty or Shared Dirty line which is replaced with a Dirty or Shared Dirty line read from another cache will require three bus cycles. First, an eviction must be performed to make room for the new line. Second, the requesting CPU/cache performs a read cycle, and the requested data is read into the requesting cache from the intervening cache. Last, the requesting cache performs a Cache Write to update the line in the intervening cache which satisfied the request in the first place!

Two kinds of write hit cycles emulate either a write-through or a copy-back protocol. If the line is already either Dirty or Valid Exclusive, the cache behaves as if it were a copy-back cache in a single-processor system and writes only to the cache, without causing any bus traffic. At the end of either cycle, the status of the line will be Dirty. If the line is Shared Clean or Shared Dirty, the write cycle is broadcast to all other caches, but not to main memory, via a Cache Write cycle. At the end of either of these cycles, the line's status will be Shared Dirty, unless no other cache responds, in which case, the line can start to act as if it uses a copy-back strategy, and the status goes immediately to Dirty. Main memory is not updated until the Dirty line is evicted from the owning cache, the one which has a Dirty or Shared Dirty copy of the line. This is performed using a Memory Write cycle. Since the Memory Write cycle only occurs during an eviction or a write to a non-cacheable address, the reaction which it causes in a snooped cache is straightforward. The only possible status of such a cycle in another cache is Shared Clean, which only happens if the line being evicted is Shared Dirty. In this case, the eviction has no effect, since the evicted line already matches the contents of the same line in the other cache. The Shared Clean line need not be invalidated as it would in a bus which did not have as much coherency support. A Dirty line cannot have a counterpart in another cache, since Dirty is an Exclusive state.

4.3.9   Others

There are several good design examples which you can research to see ways in which the problem of coherency can be addressed in copy-back multiprocessor systems. These include commercial microprocessors which are all well documented and use their own solutions for these exact problems, cache controllers, as well as the several minicomputer and mainframe architectures which can be researched in professional journals like the Association of Computing Machinery's *Transactions on Computer Systems* or even *Electronic Design Magazine.*

I have attempted to show enough alternatives here to get you thinking, but have not given any concrete numbers for one system's performance against another's for the same very good reasons I have shied away from statistics throughout this book. First, your software is different from any that has been used to run any cache statistics to date. This means that you would be leading yourself astray if you were to use another person's statistics. Second, your system is different from others, so the amount of gain in reducing main memory reads and writes will be important to your selection of read and write policies, line size, and even coherency protocol. By all means, do whatever you can to measure real statistics on a real system before committing to a cache design. Any other method would be a crap shoot.

CHAPTER **5**

INTERESTING CACHE TRICKS

At some time or another every cache designer runs into difficulties caused by the approach of the cache design. It could be that the cache couldn't include all of the most elegant goals specified in the original design, or maybe there were practical constraints that warranted the use of an off-beat tactic in one area, and now there are logical consequences in another. Whatever the reason, all designers know that an answer to nearly every quandary of this sort is possible, but finding that answer usually requires a different way of thinking about the problem.

This chapter is devoted to some tricks used by various processor designers to improve system performance in certain situations. In some of these cases designers take advantage of system partitioning, and in others, they solve problems caused by another approach they decided upon for other reasons. All of the tricks shown here are a little off the beaten track, and for this reason I have decided that they are worth an extra look.

5.1   EFFICIENTLY FEEDING A SUPERSCALAR MACHINE

Perhaps one of the most interesting caches the author has run across was designed by IBM for an implementation of an early version of the Power processor—the RS/6000. This superscalar CPU has four processors which can each be fed from one of four instruction caches. As shown in Figure 5.1, the instruction cache line is fetched four words at a time from four caches, each cache containing every fourth word from main memory. These four words would be fed into a sort of crosspoint matrix (the instruction buffer/multiplexer network) which would route each instruction to the appropriate processor.

The optimizing compiler plays an important role in getting the appropriate data into the cache, with four adjacent words being loaded with useful instructions for each of the four processors; however, it is clear that once the compiler runs into an area where less than all four processors can be kept busy at once, no instruction will be needed by a certain processor, and this would result in cache locations not being used at all. This cannot be an optimum situation. As a matter of fact, if this were the case, the processors could be decoupled a little more than they are, each having its own cache

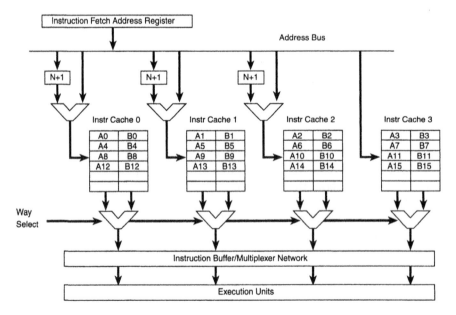

Figure 5.1.   The instruction cache of the RS/6000 architecture. Four separate caches can feed instructions to any of four execution units through the instruction buffer/multiplexer network.

and its own instruction fetch address register and processing instructions somewhat independently of the others. One of the beauties of superscalar architectures is that they are always well synchronized, and the more loosely coupled system described here would lose that benefit.

Instead, the architects at IBM decided to load the four caches, and have them feed the separate processors on a round-robin basis through the cross-point switch. This still makes each processor appear to have its own instruction cache, although a more efficient shared-cache approach is actually used.

Now, how could they assure that they were not constrained to having to waste valuable cache locations on missing instructions? First of all, the compiler was given the freedom to pack instructions into memory as densely as possible. If only three processors are needed for the next step, then only three instructions are inserted into the memory space in three adjacent locations. The next instruction set would then be loaded starting at the fourth, rather than the fifth location. The same case was taken for times when the compiler generates only one or two instructions.

Unfortunately, the instruction fetch address register moves in increments of four, representing the four caches. How do we synchronize the instruction fetch address register to the instruction boundaries? This is the interesting part of the design.

The answer lies in the incrementers placed between the instruction fetch address register and each cache's address inputs. These are the little boxes labeled "N+1" and the downstream multiplexers in Figure 5.1. With these incrementers the output of the instruction fetch address register can be seen as pointing to either the line it is actually pointing to, or to the next line after that. For example, let's say that the instructions happen to have come in groups of three, as is shown in Figure 5.2 (we'll call them triplets). "Xn" is an instruction aimed at processor X, "Yn" at processor Y, and so forth. For simplicity's sake, we will assume that processor W is to be left idle for several instructions in a row, although X, Y, and Z are being fed a new instruction every cycle. We will also leave out any issue of using multiple Ways in the cache, and only look at the left one for this example. Figure 5.2a shows how main memory would store these instructions, then Figure 5.2b shows how they would be loaded into the caches. Now the trick is to get the instructions out of the caches and into the four processors in a way that makes sense.

First, the instruction fetch address register points at set address zero of each of the caches. The first three caches supply these instructions, which are then routed by the crosspoint switch to the appropriate processors: instruction cache 0 to processor X and so on. After this instruction is fetched, the instruction fetch address register is *not* updated, but the instruction from instruction cache 3's set address zero is fed through the crosspoint

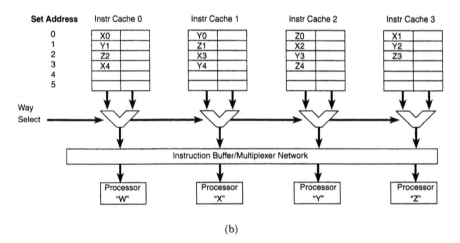

Address   Contents

Address	Contents
0	X0
1	Y0
2	Z0
3	X1
4	Y1
5	Z1
6	X2
7	Y2
8	Z2
9	X3
A	Y3
B	Z3
C	X4
D	Y4
E	Z4
F	

(a)

(b)

Figure 5.2. (a) Triplets of instructions as the compiler would load them into main memory. (b) How the instructions get loaded into the RS/6000's instruction cache.

switch to processor X, and all three of the incrementers are directed to route the incremented output of the instruction fetch address register so that the cache from set address one of instruction caches 0, 1, and 2 is output to the crosspoint switch, allowing instruction cache 0 to feed processor Y and instruction cache 1 to feed Processor Z. This way, the triplets don't have to be aligned to four-instruction boundaries, and the cache memory locations are efficiently used.

And if you wonder about how complex the data cache is for the RS/6000, don't. It's a simple four-Way set-associative virtual copy-back cache with 128-byte lines. Concurrent line write-back is managed by both read and write buffers.

Although the cache is deeper than the virtual address page length, data cache alias issues are avoided by the use of a rule that the two virtual address bits that would normally be translated to a different physical address must instead exactly match the physical address bits. The overlapping set addresses and page bits are always kept the same as each other. This is managed by software, one of those niceties that comes with having control of both the hardware and the software in your system design.

5.2 PRIMARY AND SECONDARY CACHES ON THE SAME CHIP

Many system designers think that primary cache necessarily means "on chip" and secondary cache necessarily means "off chip." This could not be farther from the truth. One good reason for the processor chip to sport two levels of caches was given in Chapter 2—that a small cache needs less complex address decoding logic, and this may make the use of a small primary cache help increase the chip's overall operating frequency. Another reason designers now give is that today's large die sizes take a lot of time to cross, so several small caches peppered around the design may perform at higher clock frequencies than could be reached in a similar design using one large centralized cache.

Two more good reasons have been given recently by Exponential Technology in their higher speed version of the Power PC processor. Exponential's architects point out that the more complex a cache controller is, the slower it operates, yet such complexity is desirable. Their approach is to put all of the complexity into the secondary cache, and make the primary cache simple, yet designed for the fastest clock rate possible. In the design current at the writing of this manuscript, the primary cache had an access time of 0.8ns, while the secondary cache's access time was 1.3ns. One factor that helped cause this difference was that the primary caches were designed with a high power budget and a fast access, whereas the secondary cache was designed to consume lower power at the expense that it would run more slowly.

Second, since the chip must be interrupted to perform snoop cycles, it makes sense to perform these snoops on the secondary cache while leaving the primary cache/CPU complex alone until there is reason to suspect that a primary invalidation is required (see the bit about inclusion in Section 4.1.1). If the secondary cache is inside the same chip as the processor and primary cache, primary cache invalidations can be forced to occur at the smallest possible time penalty after secondary cache snooping has determined that such an invalidation cycle is required. Other approaches the designers evaluated included one using dual-ported cache-tag RAMs on the primary cache, but this consumed too much die area and increased the complexity of the tags, slowing down the design, and another using a larger primary cache with a snoop tag, an approach which cost too much in die area to be worthwhile.

Hitachi demonstrated an approach to increase memory speed within a SRAM on processor IC which the company dubbed *separated bit-line memory hierarchy architecture* or SBMHA, but we will not refer to it by this unwieldy name. What the memory designers on this project did was to realize that a big portion of the delays in getting data into and out of an SRAM stem from the need to drive long lines within the memory array. Typically the array is laid out in address order, the lower addresses being at one end of the array, and the higher addresses at the other end. One of these ends will be closer to the read/write amplifiers than will be the other, and this end of the array always has a performance advantage over the other. Hitachi split the bit lines (see Figure 5.3) lengthwise and made the faster end be a smaller primary cache, with the farther end acting as the secondary cache. Fancy mapping had to be used to rearrange the addresses so that they would make sense, but this can be done without too much trouble. When data needs to be

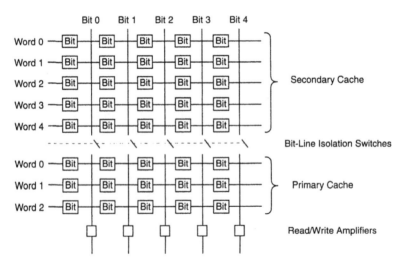

Figure 5.3. Hitachi's separated bit-line cache. Long bit lines are switched out of the circuit to reduce capacitive loading.

moved between primary and secondary caches, the bit lines are rejoined, and the transaction is completed at the slower cache's speed.

Since long bit lines behave as capacitive loads, the longer the bit lines are, the more power is consumed. One advantage of Hitachi's approach is that the array consumes significantly lower power whenever there is a primary hit, since the effective bit lines are shorter. In Hitachi's chip, there was an order of magnitude difference between the length of the primary array's bit lines and those of the secondary array.

5.3 CONTROLLING THE CACHE'S CONSISTENCY WITH ITS WRITE BUFFERS

Since the i486 was developed, Intel has had a cache and a write buffer in its IntelArchitecture chips. The write buffer runs the risk of holding updated data which may be needed later by the processor. The two cases where this could cause problems are these:

1. The data which is in the write buffer data is not copied in the cache (there was a cache miss during the write cycle) and the processor wants to read back the buffered memory location before the buffer has been able to update main memory.
2. The data which is in the write buffer data does reside in the cache (there was a cache hit during the write cycle), and the processor can get a copy of the required line directly from the cache itself. If the cache line is not updated, then stale data will be fetched.

There are several possible approaches to this dilemma. One quite simple one is to allow every single write cycle to clobber the contents of the matching cache line (the line whose set bits match). Although this would work in a direct-mapped implementation, since there is only one Way which would need to get updated, in Intel's four-Way design it becomes impossible, since all four Ways would have to be changed to become the same line, unless the designer wanted to incur wait states to check each of the four lines for a match first. Another more dramatic approach would be to invalidate lines with matching set addresses. This means that every single write cycle would invalidate four lines of cache data—not a good way to assure that useful data would stay within the cache to service the processor. Instead, during a write miss, subsequent reads or cache updates are not satisfied until the write buffer is empty.

In the second case, we have the cache hit during a write cycle. The problem mentioned above seems like it should not be a big difficulty, since the data to be written to the cache should be able to go right into the cache line. Since the tag lookup takes some time, though, this messes up the timing. Also, if the write is for a piece of data that is smaller than the entire cache line (and these caches use multiple word lines, while the processor supports writes as small as a single byte) then the complexity of the cache SRAM must be increased to support these short write cycles to arbitrary parts of the line. The more complex an SRAM is, the slower it performs.

Intel's simple approach to this problem is to invalidate matching cache lines whenever there is a write hit. This seems to be a solution that would slow things down, and it does a little, but it makes up for problems in other places.

The last question is what to do with the data in the write buffer if there is a read for data that is not in the cache because the cache line got overwritten? Some caches use a special sort of write buffer that intercepts read cycles and satisfies those whose contents are held in the write buffer. This requires that the write buffers contain a comparator for each address written in the buffer itself, making the write buffer far larger than it would be without this comparator. Also, the write buffer might only hold a portion of the requested line (for example, the Intel write buffer holds individual bytes). Because of this, the write buffer is left simple, and the subsequent read miss, like the one mentioned above, is forced to wait until the write buffer has been conveyed to main memory before this read cycle is allowed to progress.

5.4   ACHIEVING A TRUE LRU BY USING A STACK

IBM has implemented a clever cache chip based upon a very high-speed DRAM. This chip has both a high-speed fully associative SRAM primary cache, which IBM chooses to call a line buffer, and a larger, slower two-Way DRAM secondary cache all on the same chip. Although most of the chip's design (other than the use of the DRAM) is relatively straightforward, the designers used a novel approach to generate a true LRU replacement mechanism for the fully associative primary cache.

As you recall from Chapter 2, one of the more trying aspects of designing more highly associative caches is assuring that the line replaced is the one least useful to the processor. The ideal cache is fully associative and uses a true least recently used algorithm to determine which line is to be replaced. As we reviewed, this can take an enormous number of bits to implement. IBM's approach works, but must have taken a lot of work to meet the speed requirements of the processor.

Figure 5.4 shows only the primary part of the cache, or the line buffer. There are 32 lines, each of which is 32 bytes long. Each of these lines is rep-

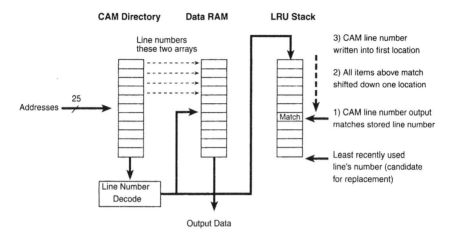

Figure 5.4.   This true LRU algorithm keeps a stack of addresses ranging from most recently used at one end, to least recently used at the other end.

resented by an entry in a 32×25-bit address translation CAM, which translates the 25-bit processor address into the 5-bit line address required.

The LRU stack is also a small CAM (32×5) and the output of the address translation CAM is sent to the LRU stack, which determines which LRU stack location contains a duplicate line number. Once this line address is located within the LRU stack, all line addresses in stack locations above the location where the address was found are shifted down into that address, marking them as less recently used than the current line address. The current line address is then loaded onto the first entry in this stack, so that the line addresses in the stack are listed in true order of use. This requires a shift operation to be performed within a single cache access cycle, which is a relatively power-hungry approach. Fortunately, there are only 32 locations, each shifting only five bits, so the power consumption is not overwhelming. Now the best line address for replacement will fall to the bottom of the stack every time.

In comparison to the associativity discussion of Section 2.2.2, where we showed that each cache line would require $N!$ bits to store a true LRU, this approach uses 32×5 bits, or 160 bits. Since there is only the equivalent of one line in this cache, and this line has 32 ways of associativity, the traditional approach would need to represent 32! states, which could be encoded in $\log_2(32!)$ bits, or 118 bits. The 26% difference in the number of bits used is small enough that we should warmly welcome the use of a much more intuitive stack-based approach than to use a more arcane minimized coding technique.

5.5   A "SEMIASSOCIATIVE" CACHE

This is a relatively difficult hybrid IBM conceived of: a fully associative cache
and an eight-Way set-associative cache. It shows what happens if you apply
nearly unlimited mental horsepower to a limited transistor count.

The basis of the cache is an eight-Way set-associative physical cache with
single-word lines. Nothing special here. The catch comes with the addition
of an extra directory based upon a CAM design. This is shown in the relatively complex diagram of Figure 5.5. By adding the CAM the access time of
the cache does not suffer from delays in the Way selection mechanism as do
most multiway caches.

The CAM looks at an eight-bit subset of the virtual address bits before
they have a chance to be translated into their real address counterparts by
the memory management unit (MMU). Contents of the cache's CAM are
similar to the contents of the MMU's page table CAM. By looking up the virtual address in the extra CAM directory before the address is translated by
the MMU, the Way selection of the cache data RAM can occur early, allowing a data path to be set up which should be expected to be correct in most
instances (after all, we *are* dealing with statistics here).

One advantage of using a CAM instead of a cache-tag memory in this application is that the search on the CAM commences as soon as the virtual ad-

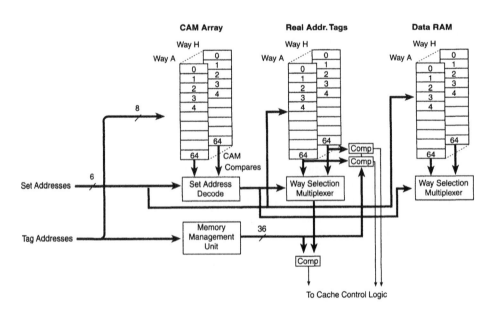

Figure 5.5.   IBM's semiassociative cache.

dress is presented to the array, not having to wait for set address decoding to occur. Every tag for every line looks at the virtual tag bits simultaneously with all the rest. Of course, one Way of each of several lines may hold matching virtual address bits, so the six set addresses are decoded, and only the CAM virtual address match which is from a matching set address is allowed to route to the data RAM's Way-selection multiplexer.

Six set address bits are also decoded by the cache-tag RAM and the cache data RAM while the CAM's compares are going on. By the time the data is ready from all eight Ways of the cache data RAM, the CAM search has enabled the multiplexer to route the appropriate Way's data onto the processor's data input pins. If for any reason there is no match in any of the Ways, the CAM's downstream logic tells the processor that a cache miss has resulted.

Meanwhile, the address is being translated from virtual to physical in the MMU, and the 36-bit output of the MMU is compared against the 36 tag bits held by the corresponding Way in the cache tag RAM. This is the acid test as to whether or not the CAM chose the correct Way in the cache data RAM, or even if a hit was identified correctly in the first place. Just in case there was a false hit to an alias in the wrong Way, the directory goes ahead and performs compares of the MMU output on all eight directory Ways during a subsequent cycle. By doing this, the cache can speedily recover from a false hit generated by the CAM.

The net of all of this is that the long delay path of Figure 2.11 is avoided, and a faster path like that in Figure 2.10 is realized even though the cache is truly an eight-Way set-associative design. In this design IBM constructed the cache using 11-transistor CAM cells, so the die area cost of the CAM was about twice that of the 6-transistor cell-based cache data RAM array. It is believable that an eight-Way set-associative cache of a certain size operating with no wait states would outperform one three times the size operating with one wait state. On the other hand, it is interesting to guess what would have happened if the eight-Way design (which is what would have forced the use of a wait state without the CAM) gave way to a direct-mapped zero-wait design. Could IBM have simplified by using a much larger zero-wait direct-mapped design? It probably depends on the software the system is running.

5.6 CONTROLLING ALIASES BY USING EIGHT COMPARATORS

AMD has used a logical instruction cache in one of their processors, and has taken a real brute-force approach to the problem of aliases. The number of set bits in the cache is two address bits larger than the number of index address bits within the page. This means that there is a real problem with the possibility of aliases, as was described in Section 2.2.1.

The cache tag stores the physical address of the cached location. When a page index address is fed into the cache, it could be mapped into any of the four locations indicated by the four possible states of the overlapping bits. For this reason, either the processor will have to wait for the MMU to translate the address before identifying if the cycle was a cache hit or a cache miss, or all four of the set addresses' tags which relate to the index address must be evaluated before the MMU translation occurs.

AMD decided to take the second route, and to examine every possible cache line which could represent a given set address, all at the same time. On each processor cycle, the tag bits for all four possible hit locations (as determined by the two overlapped bits) is compared for each of the two ways of the cache, a total of eight compares all at the same time. Snoop cycles are treated the same way, requiring eight snoops to be completed at once. This approach took a lot of logic, but really solved the problem of aliases without forcing the cache to have to slow down to the speed required by the MMU.

5.7   WRITE BUFFERING VS. MULTIPROCESSING

The IntelArchitecture specification encompasses all versions of the x86 architecture since the 8086, and works to make sense of the several upgrades that have been made since this architecture was originated. It is no mean feat that the architects of the Pentium Pro processor and subsequent devices have had to worry about the combined effects of multiprocessing, cacheing, multiprogramming, and write buffering. The following notes will illustrate some of the approaches taken by Intel to maintain some modicum of sanity in the conflicting requirements of all of these needs.

Something that has not been addressed in this text so far, mainly because it is a subject which rarely is solved within the cache's design, is the means by which processors in a multiprocessing system determine which is which after a power-up reset. In some systems each processor is defined by solid hardware, so that, perhaps, the first processor on the bus is the scheduler, and each position away from this processor is assigned a number according to its physical location. In other systems, processors share dedicated communications channels, so that processor 1 can communicate with processor 2, 2 with 3, and so on. The most puzzling approach (yet one that is well thought out in published papers) is where all processors have equal opportunities to be the scheduler or one of the subservient processors. Intel has decided to implement support for this last, most difficult approach, although they also support a less symmetrical approach, in which a processor can be hard-wired to be the "boot processor" at power-on. This simplifies software development.

The support for this type of multiprocessing is simple enough. The bus must be "locked" to disable other processors from accessing a shared location whenever one processor is modifying that location. This way the first processor to hit this location can say "I am #1," the second can then observe this and say "Then I am #2," and so forth. To accomplish this, there needs to be a mechanism whereby the processor can examine a location and determine its contents, then modify them without the possibility that the contents will be read or altered by another processor at the same time. This is handled by a "locked" cycle. Locked cycles involve a read followed by a write, or in some cases, a write followed by a read. The most typical locked cycles are increment or decrement instructions (read, increment, and write). These instructions would not work if the communications location were replicated only in a copyback cache but not in the main memory.

When there are these locked cycles Intel has provided a means for having the processor *not* tell the other processors that this is happening. This may seem odd until the reader reflects that there may be certain cases where communication between processors would take advantage of read/modify/write cycles, but that the communicated address would only sporadically be read by other processors. Since there may be a reason to accelerate performance by taking such locations to a modified state in a MESI cache (which is the approach favored in the IntelArchitecture), Intel has added the necessary hardware to support locked cycles to the copyback cache. They call this **Cache locking**.

This gets even more complex when there are write buffers. In most buffered caches the write buffer doesn't have to worry too much about what is where. If a cached location is updated, it is usually updated in the cache (in the case of a copyback cache), or is simply invalidated (in a write-through cache) as the data is being written to the write buffer. In an allocated cache, the data is read first, then the write buffered data and the cache line are updated. This gets tricky if the location happens to be one in which the processor communicates, and in a processor where certain pages are designated write-through while others are designated copy-back. In the IntelArchitecture, lines in the write buffer represent cache lines that have been invalidated if there is a write hit and the line is in a page that is designated as write-through. Since the architecture allows virtual memory pages to be overlapped, and allows individual pages to be declared to be write-through, copy-back, or uncacheable, the cache controller selects the least sophisticated cache selection for the overlapped range.

The Pentium II processor has 16 load buffers and 12 store buffers, each of which can contain data which might conflict with the contents of the cache, unless properly managed. Read cycles snoop the write (store) buffers, so this simplifies certain cycles. Some of the read buffers are often used for reading speculated branch cycles, and need to be purged whenever there is any doubt that the branch target may have been modified by a write cycle. All write buffers are written to main memory in certain cases, including any time that an I/O cycle is performed (just in case the I/O cycle initiates a DMA that would need for main memory to be current). There is a "write combined" cycle, which assembles write cycles into a single cache line write. This is often used in uncached spaces to write to screen memories. Byte gathering is not used in order to keep from further complications in the processor's ordering. Write allocation is used to replace lines in the case of a write-miss cycle.

When an address is not cached and a locked cycle is performed on that address, the buffers are cleared out so that there is no ambiguity about when the read and write cycles occur with respect to each other in the read/modify/write cycle. In other words, the processor moves from a weak ordering to a strong ordering in this case. When the address is cached as write-through, or if the cache line is copy-back but is in a shared state, the cached copy is marked invalid. If the line is in a copy-back location and is marked as exclusive, it is taken to the modified state, and the write is not buffered.

If this seems difficult, consider the fact that the author has elected to not even attempt to diagram the complexities of the process. It would not fit into one of the type of diagrams that are found in Chapter 4. Although determining the ins and outs of this can be a mind-numbing puzzle, it boils down to considering each and every case, determining the appropriate response of each of these cases, and then implementing the state machine (which is invariably smaller than the challenge would indicate) to make these states fall together.

Another odd case that Intel has decided to allow is the case of self-modifying code. Although the instruction cache does not need a write protocol, the data cache has the potential of containing an update to the code in the instruction cache. For this reason alone, the IntelArchitecture has hooks that help the instruction cache to snoop the data cache, and to reflect any changes that the program may want to inflict on the code.

GLOSSARY

Aborting A fetch strategy for caches with identical line and wrapping fetch sizes, where the CPU is allowed to proceed as soon as the missed data is obtained from main memory, and any subsequent miss will abort a continuing line refill midstream. The opposite of **nonblocking.** (Section 2.2.6)

Address comparator Also called **cache address comparator.** See **cache-tag.** (Section 1.5)

Agent The device in a bus bridge which allows the bridge to assure that coherency problems do not arise across the bridge. See **memory agent** and **cache agent.** (Section 4.3.2)

Alias Virtual addresses which are mapped to the same physical address location. This is a problem with logical caches but does not occur in physical caches. Also called **synonyms.** (Section 2.2.1)

Allocation See **write allocation.** (Section 2.2.5)

Associativity A measure of the number of locations into which a single main memory address can be placed within a cache. A fully associative (all-Way set-associative) cache can put any main memory address into any cache address. A direct-mapped (single-Way set-associative) cache has only one location into which any main memory address can be replicated. Increasing associativity increases cache cost in discrete cache designs, since each Way of associativity is implemented as a separate cache, and faster parts are required to meet the same access time in a cache which is not direct mapped. (Section 2.2.2)

Background write-back   Another term for **concurrent line write-back.** A means of reducing CPU delays when hiding evictions of dirty lines from a copy-back cache. (Section 2.2.6)

Backing store   Another term for main memory. (Section 1.1)

Back-invalidate   An invalidation owing to a snoop read or write hit, depending on the cache's snooping policies. (Section 4.1.1)

Backoff   A bus command which causes the current cycle to abort. (Section 4.2.5)

Bandwidth   See **bus bandwidth.** (Section 1.8)

Bank   Another word for **Way.** Not commonly used. (Section 2.2.2)

Block   The size of a section of main memory which can be mapped into cache. Although some designers interchange the terms **block** and **line,** others interchange the words **sector** and **block.** (Section 2.2.5)

Block fill   The replacement of a cache block in response to a miss. The same as a **line fill** to those who use the term **block** instead of **line.** (Section 2.2.5)

Broadcasting   A method used by copy-back caches in multiple-processor systems that allows a CPU to invalidate or update all matching lines in other caches once the CPU has determined that it will be performing a write cycle to a cached location. (Section 4.2.5)

Buffered line fill   A policy which allows a cache line to be updated after data has been passed from main memory to the processor. Line buffers are used to support concurrent line write-back. (Section 2.2.6)

Buffered write   Write cycles are not run at the system bus rate, but are put into a register or FIFO, which can absorb CPU write cycles or evicted cache lines at zero wait states, then can write the write data or cache lines to the main memory at the bus' speed. Also called **posted write.** (Section 2.2.6)

Burst   A higher speed method of fetching a cache line over a slow bus. In normal bus transactions, one address output is required for every read cycle. In a bursting bus protocol, one address is output, and several pieces of read data are expected in return. (Section 2.2.5)

Burst refill   Line replacement using a burst read mechanism, but not necessarily burst writes. See **burst.** (Section 2.2.5)

Bus bandwidth   Measure of the utilization of system buses in bytes/second that can be transferred. Caches help reduce bandwidth problems because most memory cycles do not use the system bus (data reads and writes occur just between CPU and cache). A system with a cache and a low bus bandwidth can often outperform a system with no cache and a high bus bandwidth, at a much lower cost. (Section 1.8)

Bus concurrency   An architecture where the CPU/cache interface is on a bus which is isolated from the system or main memory bus. The possibility of both of these buses doing something useful at the same time. (Section 2.2.6)

Bus master   See **master.** (Section 4.1)

Bus traffic   See **bus bandwidth.** (Section 1.8)

Bus utilization   The portion of the available bus bandwidth which is used by the system. (Section 1.8)

Bus watch   A technique for constantly monitoring the system bus. In a write-through cache, bus watch is used to assure that any data written to main memory (from a CPU or any DMA device) is accurately reflected in any matching cached copies. Techniques used include invalidating or updating the cached copy of the matching address. Bus watch mechanisms in copy-back caches are considerably more complex. Also called **snooping.** (Section 4.1.1)

Bypass   A line replacement method in which the first main memory read cycle is immediately passed to the CPU, allowing processing to continue while the remainder of the cache line is being updated. There are several other names for bypass, including **streaming** and **early continuation.** (Section 2.2.6)

Byte gathering   Some write buffers provide a feature where successive byte writes to the same main memory location are collapsed into a single main memory write cycle. The process of collapsing these byte write cycles into a single word-write cycle is called **byte gathering.** (Section 2.2.6)

Cache   See **cache memory.** (Section 1.3.2)

Cache agent   A device within a bus bridge which keeps track of all of the addresses for which there are cache copies on the far side of that bridge. (Section 4.3.2)

Cache bandwidth   The speed at which a cache memory can supply data to or accept data from the CPU. (Section 1.8)

Cache-based   A copy-back bus protocol in which all caches in a multiple processor system are required to snoop the bus to determine the validity of their contents. Also, all caches are required to broadcast their intentions of removing cached items from general circulation. (Section 4.2.5)

Cache coherency   See **coherency.** (Chapter 4 Introduction)

Cache comparator   Also called cache address comparator. See **cache-tag.** (Section 1.5)

Cache consistency   See **coherency.** (Chapter 4 Introduction)

Cache controller   Logic used to control a cache composed of external cache-tag and cache data RAM chips. The cache controller contains the logic necessary to carry out a fixed set of cache policies. (Section 1.4)

Cache data RAM   The fast static RAM where replicas of often-used main memory locations are stored. (Section 1.4)

Cache directory   Storage for the addresses represented in the cache data memory. See **cache-tag** and **CAM.** (Section 1.4)

Cache hit   See **hit/miss.** (Section 1.4)

Cache locking   Assigning an Exclusive cache location to be inaccessible to other processors. (Section 5.7)

Cache management logic   See **cache controller.** (Section 1.4)

Cache memory   A high-speed memory array which acts as a buffer between the CPU and main memory. Cache works because most software repeatedly executes the same instructions or manipulates data in the same location (spatial locality). By assuring that slower main memory is only accessed once to fetch that instruction or data, and all subsequent executions operate from the faster cache memory, effective memory speed is greatly increased. Cache consists of a controller, directory, and data memory. (Section 1.3.2)

Cache miss   See **hit/miss.** (Section 1.4)

Cache policies   See **policies.** (Section 1.4)

Cache size   Usually expressed in bytes (8 bits), cache size is the number of entries held within a cache. A 64K cache is equivalent to 16K 32-bit words. (Section 1.4)

Cache-tag   The memory used to store the address tags of corresponding lines currently held in the cache data RAM and then compare the stored tags to the current address to determine a cache hit or miss. Most discrete cache implementations store status bits within the tag RAM. Used as a part or all of a cache directory. (Section 1.5)

Cache-to-cache transfer   See **direct data intervention.** (Section 4.2.5)

CAM   Content addressable memory. This device, once popular in mainframe caches, was used to store the cache directory. It appears to be an array of single-word cache-tag RAMs. When an address is presented to a CAM, a table is interrogated, and, if a matching entry is found, another address is output, showing where a matching cache entry exists. (Section 1.5)

Class 1, Class 2   Two prefetch algorithms used on caches which fetch portions of data which are greater than their line size. In a class 1, or **fetch on fault** cache, fetch cycles are only started on a line miss/replacement cycle. In a class 2 or **fetch always** design, a fetch may be initiated whether or not a cache miss occurred. (Section 2.2.6)

Coherency   Agreement between data stored in cache and in main memory (or other caches on the same bus). Coherent caches all contain the same data for all replicas of the same main memory location. (Chapter 4 Introduction)

Coherency domain   The portion of the memory hierarchy which is kept coherent. Usually does not include mass storage or caches for mass storage, but can extend onto multiple buses connected via bus bridges. (Section 4.2)

Color   A logical direct-mapped cache can run the risk of containing two copies of the same physical memory location if the cache uses as set bits some of the page bits, or those bits which are translated from logical to physical address values in the MMU. The set bits which comprise a portion of the page number are also known as color bits, with their value being the color of the cache line. (Section 4.2.2)

Comparator   Also called **cache address comparator.** See **cache-tag.** (Section 1.5)

Compulsory line fill   A line fill which would happen no matter how a cache was designed. A line fill caused by a compulsory miss. (Section 2.1.3)

Compulsory miss   A cache miss cycle which could not be avoided by any cache strategy. Often it is the miss which results from the first access of a main memory address after a restart or a cache flush. Also referred to as **nonconflict miss,** or **stationary miss.** (Section 1.6)

Concurrency   The capability of a cache to perform more than one function at a time. Caches which use write buffers or certain sorts of snoop mechanisms which operate independently of the CPU are said to be concurrent. Concurrent designs tend to scramble the order of the processor's read and write cycles before they reach the main memory bus, or to affect the **write ordering, read ordering,** or **sequential consistency.** (Section 2.2.6)

Concurrent line write-back   In a copy-back cache, during a read miss line update, the dirty cache line can be written back to main memory, and the cache line can be updated through the use of one or more write buffers without requiring the processor to wait for more than the main memory's normal latency. This is done by updating the cache while concurrently feeding the processor the requested line. (Section 2.2.6)

Consistency   See **coherency.** (Chapter 4 Introduction)

Control domain identifier   Also called CDID. A term used within IBM for the status bits within a cached line which identify the user level of the memory location which the line represents. (Section 2.2.9)

Copy-in   See **Line Fill.** (Section 2.1.3)

Copy-back   Data written into cache by the CPU is not written into main memory until that data line in cache is to be replaced. A Dirty bit is set in the cache when a location has been written into. If the Dirty bit is not set, the contents of that cache location can be destroyed. Also called **write-back, store-in cache** (or **SIC**), and **nonwrite-through.** Also, as an alternative to **eviction,** the name for the cycle used to move dirty data back to main memory when a line is to be replaced. (Section 2.2.4)

Copy-out   See **Eviction.** (Section 2.2.4)

Critical word first   Another term for **data requested first.** (Section 2.2.6)

Critical word last   Another term for **data requested last.** (Section 2.2.6)

Cross-interrogate   The terminology used within IBM for what is commonly called **snooping** or **bus watch.** Also referred to as XI. The act of a bus master looking in another master's cache for a piece of data. (Section 4.1.1)

Currency   See **coherency.** (Chapter 4 Introduction)

Data (or instruction) cache   A cache scheme where two separate caches are used, one for data and one for instructions (common in RISC systems). One of the caches in a **split-cache** architecture. (Section 2.2.3)

Data path   The critical path between the cache data RAM I/O, the system bus, and the processor bus, sometimes implemented as separate buses. (Section 1.4)

Data RAM   A memory used to store replicas of main memory locations which can be either instructions or data in cache. This is opposed to the addresses of those replicas which are stored in the cache's tag RAM or directory. (Section 1.4)

Data requested first   A line fill order in which the word which caused a cache miss is the first to be obtained from the main memory during a line replacement cycle. See **wrapping fetch, line fill order.** (Section 2.2.6)

Data requested last   A line fill order in which the word which caused a cache miss is the last to be obtained from the main memory during a line replacement cycle. See **line fill order.** (Section 2.2.6)

Deallocation   See **eviction.** (Section 2.2.4)

Deferred write   Another term for a **copy-back** write strategy. (Section 2.2.4)

Desired word first   A line fill order in which the word which caused a cache miss is the first to be obtained from the main memory during a line replacement cycle. See **wrapping fetch, line fill order.** (Section 2.2.6)

Desired word last   See **desired word first, wrapping fetch, line fill order.** (Section 2.2.6)

Direct data intervention   A bus cycle in a multiple-processor system during which one processor's bus read is satisfied by data supplied from another processor's cache. As in other types of intervention, direct data intervention helps maintain coherency, but it also serves a useful purpose by allowing one processor to supply modified or unmodified data to another processor faster than that processor would be able to get that same data from main memory. (Section 4.2.5)

Direct mapped   A cache where there is only one possible location for each data entry. (Section 2.2.2)

Direct memory access (DMA)   A high-speed data transfer method which lets data be written to or read from main memory without CPU intervention. During DMA the CPU relinquishes main memory bus control, but can still execute from a cache. (No definition in the text. You should already know this if you're reading this book.)

Directory   See **cache-tag** and **CAM.** (Section 1.4)

Directory-based   See **memory-based.** (Section 4.2.5)

Dirty   The state of a line in a copy-back cache which has been written to in cache, but not yet in main memory. (Section 2.2.4)

Dirty bit   Used only in copy-back caches, this bit identifies a location which has been modified (by the CPU) within the cache, and has yet to be updated in main memory. (Section 2.2.4)

Dirty inclusion   A superset of inclusion for multilevel copy-back caches. If a line exists in a Dirty state in primary cache, then it is also in a Dirty state in secondary cache; however, not all Dirty lines in secondary cache must be maintained as Dirty in primary cache. (Section 4.1.1)

Distributed memory multiprocessor (DMM)   See **loosely coupled.** (Section 1.8)

DMA through cache   A coherency mechanism in which the CPU/cache interface is taken over by the DMA device, and the CPU is shut down for the duration of the DMA cycle. (Section 4.1.1)

Downstream cache   See **successor cache.** (Section 2.2.10)

Drain   To force write buffer data to be written to main memory. (Section 2.2.6)

Dual directory   A cache coherency implementation which uses two distinct directories of the same size and organization and whose contents are always identical to the cache directory and the snoop directory. (Section 4.1.1)

Dual-ported directory   Coherency hardware which snoops the bus through a mechanism which shares the data in the cache directory with both the CPU/cache bus and the main memory bus. (Section 4.1.1)

Dual-ported tag   See **dual-ported directory.** (Section 4.1.1)

Dual tag   See **dual directory.** (Section 4.1.1)

Dumb   A main memory controller in a cached multiprocessing system which doesn't fit the definition of **smart** falls into the dumb category. A dumb main memory controller will respond to any system bus read request until it is preempted by a cache which owns the address being read. (Section 4.2.5)

Early continuation   A fetch strategy which allows a processor to continue operation once the requested data has been loaded into the cache, even though the cache line replacement has not been fully completed. Also known as **early restart.** Often provided through the use of a **line buffer.** (Section 2.2.6)

Early restart   See **early continuation.** (Section 2.2.6)

Entry   A term sometimes used instead of the word **line,** and sometimes used instead of **sector.** Usually the smallest portion of a cache to which the CPU can write data. (Section 2.2.5)

Eviction   In copy-back caches, when a dirty line must be replaced with data which is currently needed by the processor, the dirty line must be copied back into main memory. The removal of the dirty line from the cache is known as eviction or **copy out.** (Section 2.2.4)

Exclusive   One of the four states in the MESI and other copy-back concurrency protocols. An Exclusive cache line is valid only in one cache within the system. The processor can take an Exclusive line to a Modified state without an intervening bus cycle. (Section 4.3.1)

Export   The process in a copy-back cache wherein a dirty line is moved from the cache into the main memory without being replaced or invalidated. After an export, the original line remains in the cache as a valid, unmodified value. Used in **indirect data intervention** cycles. (Section 4.2.5)

Fault   See **miss.** (Section 1.4)

Fetch   The cycle used by the cache to obtain data with which to replace a cache line. See **line fill.** (Section 2.1.3)

Fetch always   See **class 1, class 2.** (Section 2.2.6)

Fetch on demand   The fetching algorithm used by caches which update no lines which the processor has not already requested. The opposite of **prefetch.** See **class 1, class 2.** (Section 2.2.6)

Fetch on fault   Another term for **fetch on demand.** See **class 1, class 2.** (Section 2.2.6)

First-level cache   See **primary cache.** (Section 2.2.10)

Flush   The act of instantly invalidating at least one, but usually all cache lines. (Section 4.1.1)

Fly-by write-back   See **concurrent line write-back.** (Section 2.2.6)

Full backoff   A protocol used in multiple copy-back cache implementations where delays are allowed in the servicing of a snoop hit to a dirty line. Opposite of **restricted backoff.** (Section 4.2.5)

Fully associative   A cache policy which allows any main memory location to be mapped to any cache line. A fully associative cache must use a content addressable memory (CAM) to translate processor addresses into cache data RAM addresses. (Section 1.5)

Global directory   A directory maintained on the main memory bus, which replicates each of the CPU-local directories in a multiple-processor system. The global directory is not always an exact replica of the individual cache directories, but may be a superset of all the directories' contents (see **inclusion**). (Section 4.2.5)

Hashing   Algorithms used to map the processor address into the cache address. Hashing refers to the short cuts used to reduce cost or increase throughput. Dividing an address into set bits and tag bits is the most often used form of hashing in today's caches. (Section 1.5)

Hierarchy   Levels of a memory system distinguished by access times and cost/density trade-offs. Common levels of memory hierarchy in present systems are registers, cache, main memory, hard disk, and tape (in descending order). (Section 1.7)

Hit/miss   A cache hit occurs when the data which the CPU wants is located in cache. A miss occurs when the data is not in cache and must be fetched from main memory. (Section 1.4)

Hit rate   The number of times that data is found in cache, expressed as a percent of the total number of data it accesses. Modern primary CPU caches usually have hit rates in the range of 90% or more. See **miss rate.** (Section 1.4)

Inclusion   A method of using a larger secondary cache's directory to prescreen invalidation cycles before they are passed to a smaller (possibly more associative) primary cache. The primary cache's contents are always forced to be a subset of the contents of the secondary cache. (Section 4.1.1)

Index   A term sometimes used instead of **set** for the subset of the CPU address bits used to get to a specific location within the cache memory. (Section 1.5)

Indirect data intervention   In a multiple-processor system, a bus read cycle from one processor is aborted by another processor if the other processor encounters a read snoop hit to a dirty cache location. The second processor then updates the main memory before allowing the first processor to retry the bus read cycle. This is an indirect way of assuring that coherency is maintained between the second processor's previously dirty cache data and the newly fetched data added to the second (and subsequent) processor's cache. (Section 4.2.5)

In-line cache   An IBM term meaning the same as **look through.** (Section 2.1.3)

Inquire   See **snoop.** (Section 4.1.1)

Instruction cache   See **data cache.** (Section 2.2.3)

Interrogate   Another word for **snoop.** (Section 4.1.1)

Intervention   An action taken during a snoop cycle, where dirty data within a processor's cache is offered in place of stale main memory data in response to another processor's read cycle on the system bus. Intervention cycles are used to maintain coherence between caches, and sometimes to provide faster data access than is possible through main memory. There are two types of intervention: direct (see **direct data intervention**) and indirect (see **indirect data intervention**). (Section 4.2.5)

Invalid The state of a cache line which is not usable by the processor. Also one of the states in the MESI and MOESI protocols. In most cache designs, all cache lines are marked invalid after a power-on reset. Most snooping algorithms invalidate cache entries of the current bus operation would cause the matching cache entry to become incoherent. (Section 4.3.1)

L1, L2 Level 1 and Level 2 caches. Alternative nomenclature for **primary cache** and **secondary cache,** respectively. (Section 2.2.10)

Least frequently used (FRQ) A method of using a pointer to show which Way of a multiway cache was not used recently. A pointer on every line is made to point away from the Way that was just hit on that line. After a while it is hoped that the pointer will settle to an address that has stopped being used. (Section 2.2.2)

Least recently used (LRU) One of many techniques used to determine which Way (of an N-Way set-associative cache) is to be used to store a new data word. The Way which has lately received the least amount of attention from the processor is chosen for replacement. (Section 2.2.2)

Level 1, 2 Another name for **primary cache** or **secondary cache.** (Section 2.2.10)

Line The smallest division of a cache memory for which there is a distinct tag. A line may consist of one or more words of cache memory. Sometimes referred to as a sector. (Section 2.2.5)

Line buffer A buffer used to temporarily store data as it is being received from main memory, before it is written into a cache during a cache line update cycle. The processor can access data from the line buffer before it is written into the cache. (Section 2.2.6)

Line fill Updating a cache line with data from main memory (or a successor cache) in response to a cache miss. Also known as **copy-in.** Called **block fill** by those who refer to lines as blocks. (Section 2.1.3)

Line fill order The sequence in which elements of a line are moved from main memory into the cache in response to a line update main memory read cycle. Two orders are data requested first and data requested last. See **wrapping fetch.** (Section 2.2.6)

Line replacement The act of replacing existing valid cache data with data which is immediately required by the processor. Also called a **line update.** The replacement of a dirty line in a copy-back cache is called **eviction.** (Section 2.1.3)

Line size   The basic amount of data transferred between the cache and main memory. An 8-byte line consists of 64 bits of information. It is also the amount of cache data corresponding to a single cache-tag entry. (Section 2.2.5)

Line update   See **line replacement.** (Section 2.1.3)

Load forwarding   The act of starting a multiple-word line replacement with the word which the processor requested when a cache miss was detected. (Section 2.2.6)

Locality   The principle under which caches operate. Most code is found to operate frequently within very small address spaces. The two types of locality are locality of reference (spatial locality) and locality of time (temporal locality, or time of reference). (Section 1.3)

Lock   A line which is locked into a cache cannot be removed until it is unlocked under software control. Locking is used to keep a very frequently used word from being temporarily removed from the cache to be replaced by a line which for a very short period might be heavily used. (Section 2.2.9)

Logical cache   A cache which is attached to the logical address outputs of the processor. An advantage to tying the cache to the logical address bus rather than the physical address bus is that delays from the MMU no longer factor into the cache's critical timing path. Two disadvantages are that single-entry invalidation from the physical address bus becomes extremely difficult and that several copies of the same data may concurrently reside in different parts of the cache simultaneously, wasting valuable cache space. Also called **virtual cache.** Opposite of **physical cache.** (Section 2.2.1)

Look aside   A cache strategy which allows a cache to be inobtrusively removed or inserted into a system, with the only difference being the system's performance. Main memory transactions are initiated before a cache hit or miss is detected, and are aborted if a cache hit occurs. Look aside caches do little to reduce main memory bus traffic. (Section 2.1.3)

Look through   A cache strategy in which the cache fits between the processor and main memory. The cache becomes an integral part of the processor-to-main-memory interface. Main memory transactions are not initiated until a cache miss is detected. (Section 2.1.3) Also called **In-line cache.**

Look up penalty   The time lost during a cache miss cycle in a look through cache due to the cache needing to determine that a miss took place before a main memory cycle can be started. (Section 2.1.3)

Loosely coupled   Multiple processors which do not communicate through a shared main memory are said to be loosely coupled or **distributed memory multiprocessors (DMM).** Opposite of **tightly coupled.** (Section 1.8)

LRU   See **least recently used.** (Section 2.2.2)

Mapping   The process by which a main memory address is translated into a cache address. The mapping of a cache is determined by the cache depth, associativity, and whether the cache is tied to the processor's logical or physical address bus. Mapping is also used in the processor to convert a virtual (logical) address into a physical address. (Section 1.5)

Master   Any device which can send read or write commands to main memory. In a single-processor system, the processor and DMA devices (i.e., disk drives) would be the only masters. In a multiple-processor system, each processor can be a master. (Section 4.1)

MCM   See **multichip module.** (Section 2.5.1)

Memory agent   A device within a bus bridge which helps maintain coherency across the bridge by causing both snoop responses and memory responses on one side of the bridge to appear as relatively homogeneous main memory responses on the other side. (Section 4.3.2)

Memory-based   One protocol for assuring coherency in a cached multiprocessor system. Under a memory-based protocol, extra bits are stored with each word or cache line in main memory. These bits are used to indicate which cache is currently using that word. Also called **memory tagging,** and less often **directory-based.** (Section 4.2.5)

Memory tagging   See **memory-based.** (Section 4.2.5)

Merge   Alternate name for **write allocation.** (Section 2.2.5)

MESI   A protocol to assure coherency in multiple cached processor systems with copy-back caches. This acronym stands for modified, exclusive, shared, and invalid. (Section 4.3.1)

Miss   See **hit/miss.** (Section 1.4)

Miss rate   See **hit rate.** (Section 1.4)

Modified   Also known as **dirty.** A modified cache line has been written to without writing to the main memory. A line with the Modified status must be copied back into main memory at some time to assure that any copy stored on disk contains the most current data. This state is the M in the MESI and MOESI protocols. (Section 4.3.1)

MOESI   A protocol to assure coherency in multiple copy-back cached processor systems. This acronym stands for modified, owned, exclusive, shared, and invalid.

MOESI differs from MESI in that the MOESI cache can supply modified (dirty) data to another processor's cache. See **intervention.** (Section 4.3.3)

Most recently used (MRU)   The inverse of the LRU bit in a two-way cache. Taken as a default means to enable data onto a bus before a hit has been detected. (Section 2.5.2)

MSI   The three states of the modified, shared, invalid copy-back cache coherency protocol. (Section 4.3.4)

Multichip module   A hybrid circuit used to reduce the interchip delays in the operating environment of the high-speed chips on the CPU bus of a high-performance computer. Also called an **MCM.** (Section 2.5.1)

Naive   A naive ownership protocol is an ownership coherency protocol based on write allocation which uses a Dirty bit to indicate whether a cache line must be copied back into main memory, and which reads lines which are to be owned using the same read command as would be used for a line which will not be owned. All owned lines must eventually be copied back to main memory. Requires no compiler support. Opposite of a **sophisticated** protocol. (Section 4.2)

NLU   See **not last used.** (Section 2.2.2)

Nonblocking   A fetch strategy for caches with identical line and wrapping fetch sizes, where the CPU is allowed to proceed as soon as the missed data is obtained from main memory, and any subsequent miss will wait upon a continuing line refill if the line fill is not yet complete. The opposite of **aborting.** (Section 2.2.6)

Noncacheable address (NCA)   See **uncached address.** (Section 2.2.7)

Nonconflict miss   See **compulsory miss.** (Section 1.6)

Nonexclusive   An ownership state in multiple-processor systems in which a dirty copy of a main memory location is allowed to reside in more than a single processor's cache. (Section 4.3.1)

Nonuniform memory architecture   See **NUMA.** (Section 4.2.5)

Nonwrite-through   See **copy-back.** (Section 2.2.4)

Not last used (NLU)   An alternative to an LRU in multiway caches, where the most recently used Way is the only one which is ineligible for replacement. (Section 2.2.2)

NUMA   Nonuniform memory access architecture, a means of constructing a multiprocessor system where main memory is physically split between different CPU cards. Although the address space will appear uniform, main memory access times will depend upon the physical location of the memory with respect to the requesting processor. This is the opposite of the **UMA** (uniform memory access) architecture. (Section 4.2.5)

N-Way set-associative   Set associativity is a hashing algorithm where a number (N) of possible locations exist in the cache memory for each cache line. If $N = 1$, the cache is called **direct mapped.** A two-Way set-associative cache can be thought of as two separate caches, either of which can generate a cache hit, thus decreasing the probability of a miss. (Section 2.2.2)

Owned   A state in the MOESI and other ownership protocols. (Section 4.3.3)

Ownership   A set of protocols in multiprocessor systems' copy-back caches where the cache with an owned line realizes that other processors may have cached copies of that line, and the main memory may not be coherent with that cached location. (Section 4.2.5)

Page   Most commonly used to describe the minimum size of a portion of main memory which is mappable from logical to physical address space, but sometimes used to describe a Way in a multiway cache, or even as an alternative to the word **line.** (Section 2.2.2)

Physical cache   A cache which is connected in the physical address space of the processor, downstream of the MMU. This cache has tighter timing than a logical cache, since the MMU delay is now in the critical address-to-data path. (Section 2.2.1)

Pingponging   1) The effect where a cache line in a copy-back cache is taken to an Exclusive state, then is immediately put into a Shared state by bus snooping, then taken Exclusive again, and so on. Since these state changes require write cycles to the main memory, this has the potential to double bus traffic for the line in question. 2) Same as thrashing. The same cache line is needed to represent two locations in main memory, both of which are to be used by the CPU at the same time. This effectively disallows cache benefits from being realized for either main memory location. (Section 4.2.5)

Placement   Another seldom-used name for **replacement algorithm.** (Section 2.2.2)

Policies   The rules chosen to implement a cache. This includes direct-mapped vs. N-Way, write-through vs. copy-back, line size, snooping, etc. (Section 1.4)

Pollution control caching   A special case of the **victim cache.** (Section 2.2.6)

Posted write   See **buffered write.** (Section 2.2.6)

Posted write buffer   A device used to temporarily store write data, usually in a write-through cache, to disencumber the CPU from main memory write cycle latencies. See **buffered write.** (Section 2.2.6)

Predecessor cache   A cache in a multiple-cache hierarchy which is more intimately tied to the CPU than other caches which service the same CPU. Also known as an **upstream** cache. Opposite of **successor** or **downstream** cache. (Section 2.2.10)

Prefetch   The act of reading things into the cache which have not yet been requested by the processor, with the expectation that the processor will be better able to use the new data than the line the new data just replaced. The opposite of **fetch on demand.** See **class 1, class 2.** (Section 2.2.6)

Primary cache   In a system which has more than a single cache cascaded between the processor and main memory, the primary cache is the cache which satisfies the majority of the processor's read, and possibly write, cycles. A cache which connects directly to the processor and is accessed for every memory read and write cycle. (Section 2.2.10)

Private   A state in certain write-back coherency protocols corresponding to the Exclusive state. See **exclusive.** (Section 4.2.5)

Private read   Bus support for certain multiprocessor copy-back cache coherency protocols can take advantage of special main memory bus cycles to simultaneously both read data and invalidate possible copies in other caches. A private read is one such cycle. Sometimes called **Read-for-Ownership.** (Section 4.2.5)

Processor ordering   Data appears on the bus in the exact sequence as it does at the processor. See **write ordering.** (Section 2.2.6)

Protocol   The method in which the cache interacts with the system bus and tells other caches what it is doing. Popular protocols are write-once, which includes MESI and MOESI, write-through and memory-based. (Section 4.1)

Public read   In a multiple-processor system with a private read cycle, there is often a read shared or public read cycle to support reads without invalidates. (Section 4.2.5)

Purge   The act of copying-back all dirty or modified lines from the cache into main memory as a single event. Purges are most useful in logical caches, where coherency is difficult to maintain across context switches. (Section 4.2.5)

Random replacement   An alternative replacement algorithm in multiway caches, where the Way whose line is to be replaced is chosen at random. (Section 2.2.2)

Read-for-Ownership   See **private read.** (Section 4.2.5)

Read only   See **write protect.** (Section 2.2.8)

Read ordering   The degree to which main memory read cycles follow the read cycle sequence of the CPU. Similar to **write ordering** and a part of **sequential consistency.** (Section 2.2.6)

Read shared   See **public read.** (Section 4.2.5)

Read through   See **DMA through cache.** (Section 4.1.1)

Reader's/writer's lock   An extra status bit which can prohibit unauthorized processes or processors from performing illicit write cycles to a cache entry. (Section 2.2.9)

Reflection   In multiple-processor systems which support intervention, two or more caches may contain coherent copies of an updated main memory location without ever having updated the main memory's corresponding contents. More adept main memories can be designed to snoop the bus just as a cache would, and to update their contents automatically where appropriate. This is called reflection. (Section 4.2.5)

Replacement algorithm   The replacement algorithm chosen for a cache determines which line is removed from the cache in response to a read miss cycle. In multiway caches, the choices for replacement include least recently used, random, pseudo-least recently used, and others. In direct-mapped caches, the unlocked line which has a matching set address is replaced. Also sometimes called **placement.** (Section 2.2.2)

Repository of last resort   The owner of the only, or last, remaining copy of a sharable line. Although this is usually main memory, in a cache-only system which has no main memory, safeguards must be in place to assure that at least one copy of any active memory address continues to survive somewhere within the system. (Section 4.3.2)

Restricted backoff   A protocol used in multiple copy-back cache implementations where a snoop hit to a dirty line must be immediately serviced with an intervention cycle. Opposite of **full backoff.** (Section 4.2.5)

Secondary cache   Also referred to as a second-level cache or L2 cache. A cache which is placed between the primary cache and either the main memory or a third-level cache. (Section 2.2.10)

Second-level cache   See **secondary cache.** (Section 2.2.10)

Sector   See **sectoring.** (Section 2.2.5)

Sectoring Some caches economize by using a single tag for every two, four, or more words stored in the cache, yet each word has its own valid bit. Each of these words is called a sector of the line pointed to by the tag. Sectors may also be longer than a single word, and each sector has a single valid bit. A sectored cache line does not need to be pulled into the cache all at once, but can be updated a sector at a time. All sectors within a line share the same tag. Occasionally used interchangeably with "line," but, fortunately, this usage is as rare as it is confusing. (Section 2.2.5)

Sequential consistency The relationship between read and write cycles on the CPU/cache bus and their counterparts on the main memory bus. If the sequence of reads and writes on the main memory is closely related to the events occurring on the main memory bus, a high degree of sequential consistency is then said to exist. The more effective the cache, the lower the expected sequential consistency. Systems with high concurrency tend to exhibit low sequential consistency, and vice versa. Also known as **read ordering** and **write ordering.** (Section 2.2.6)

Set The set is the address used to find a line within a cache. If the cache contains 1,024 lines, then ten set bits are required to find a line within the cache. (Section 1.5)

Set-associative A hashing algorithm used in most cache designs. In a set-associative cache, the lower bits of the address normally sent to main memory are used to address cache lines within one or more cache Ways. The opposite of **fully associative.** (Section 1.5)

Shared The Shared line status is a part of the MESI and MOESI copy-back coherency protocols. A Shared cache line is valid within the cache, and may exist within the caches of other processors. Shared lines need not match the contents of main memory in some protocols. (Section 4.3.1)

Shared memory machine (SMM) A **tightly coupled** architecture computer. (Section 1.8)

SIC See **store-in cache.** (Section 2.2.4)

Smart A type of main memory controller in a cached multiple-processor system which keeps track of the addresses which it does not own and automatically suppresses responses to bus read requests for those addresses. The opposite of dumb. (Section 4.2.5)

Snarf The Futurebus+ protocol allows a processor which is trying to access a certain address to monitor the system bus and to update the contents of its own cache line based on another processor's main memory or interprocessor transaction using the same address. (Section 4.3.2)

Snoop   Monitoring bus traffic to maintain coherency. When a main memory bus transaction occurs to an address which is replicated in the cache, a snoop hit is detected, and appropriate actions are taken, according both to the write strategy of the cache and to the coherency protocol being used by the system Snoop misses are ignored in all protocols. Also called **bus watch.** (Section 4.1.1)

Software transparent   Caches which are designed to be retrofitted into an existing software base must accommodate all the quirks of the existing software. If they do accomplish this feat, they are called software-transparent caches. (Section 1.3.2)

Sophisticated   A sophisticated coherency protocol is an ownership protocol for processors using write allocation which does not require a Dirty bit to mark whether or not a line needs to be copied back to main memory, since this is known before the line is even read from main memory. Requires compiler to give information to the cache controller about the likelihood that a line will become owned by the processor. Opposite of a **naive** protocol. (Section 4.2)

Spatial locality   The concept that most software accesses data within a given region repetitively before moving to a new region. Also known as **locality of reference.** (Section 1.3.1)

Split cache   An organization of cache where certain cached data is kept in different cache banks. Two examples are instruction/data caches and user/supervisor caches. Opposite of **unified cache.** (Section 2.2.3)

Split transaction   A bus structure which more easily supports intervention. Split transactions allow a processor to dispatch a read or write cycle, then to get off the bus immediately. The responding device arbitrates for the bus, then responds with the requested transaction response in a cycle very similar to the requesting cycle. (Section 2.1.2)

Stale data   Data which is less current than another copy of the same address within the same system. If a DMA access updates a main memory address without updating a cached copy of the same address, the cached copy is now stale and must not be used by the processor. (Chapter 4 Introduction)

Stationary miss   See **compulsory miss.** (Section 1.6)

Status bits   Bits which are used to tell the cache controller the status of a line in cache, or a segment within that cache line. Example status bits are Valid, write protect, Dirty, locked, or encoded bits used for the MESI, MOESI, or similar protocols. (Section 2.2.9)

Storage control element (SCE)   A name used within IBM for the bus interface side of a cache controller. (Section 1.4)

Storage hierarchy The difference between small high-bandwidth storage, and large low-bandwidth storage. Typical stages, in order of speed/size, would be CPU registers, primary cache, secondary cache, main memory, magnetic hard disk, optical disk, and/or tape. (Section 1.7)

Store-in cache A name used within IBM for a copy-back cache. Also referred to as **SIC.** (Section 2.2.4)

Store-through A name used within IBM for a write-through cache. Also referred to as ST or STC. (Section 2.2.4)

Strategy The algorithm used to set the cache policies. The strategy is determined by the hit rate of the cache, as well as the cost of implementation. (Section 1.4)

Streaming Certain caches will update a line or several lines while feeding a stream of instructions to the processor. Processor execution can occur simultaneously with line updates. This can be simplified by harnessing certain DRAM techniques, which allow several adjacent addresses to be quickly accessed as long as their more significant address bits remain unchanged. (Section 2.2.6)

Strong See **write ordering.** (Section 2.2.6)

Sub-block See **sector.** (Section 2.2.5)

Successor cache A cache in a multiple-cache hierarchy which is less intimately tied to the CPU than the primary cache. Also known as a **downstream** cache. Opposite of **predecessor** or **upstream** cache. (Section 2.2.10)

Synonyms Locations within a virtual or logical cache which, due to mapping anomalies in the MMU, can be confused with relation to their physical address locations. An example would be the mapping of two different logical spaces to the same physical space, and another would be the mapping of a logical space to a new physical space after a context switch. In either case, the logical cache representation may not contain the actual data of its corresponding physical memory location. Also known as **aliases.** (Section 2.2.1)

Tag The remainder of the address generated by the processor (and used by the system) after the set bits have been removed. The tag bits of the address are compared with the tag bits of the cache directory which are stored at the same set address. If matching contents are found, then the data within the cache data RAM at the same set address represents the contents of the main memory location being accessed. (Section 1.5)

Tag RAM See **cache-tag.** (Section 1.5)

Temporal locality The concept that repetitive accesses to a region in memory usually occur at around the same time and are not usually spread evenly across the execution time of the program. Also called **locality of time,** and sometimes **time of reference.** (Section 1.3.2)

Thrashing   A difficulty caused by the same data being repeatedly inserted and removed from the cache. This signifies a discrepancy between the cache's mapping algorithm and the code being run out of the cache, where two frequently used words share the same set address and therefore must be mapped into the same cache address. A thrashed cache location performs no better than an uncached location. Thrashing can be reduced by increasing the cache's degree of associativity. (Section 1.6)

Tightly coupled   Two or more processors which share a common main memory are called tightly coupled processors. Also called a **shared memory machine (SMM).** Caches in tightly coupled systems must take measures to assure cache coherency, and caching strategies often involve the reduction of bus traffic. A loosely coupled multiple-processor system uses separate main memories for each processor. Interprocessor communication in a tightly coupled system is through main memory, whereas loosely coupled systems usually communicate via serial channels, FIFOs, or dedicated communication buffers. (Section 1.8)

Time of reference   See **temporal locality.** (Section 1.3.2)

Traffic   See **bus bandwidth.** (Section 1.8)

Transaction   Another term for a CPU-to-main-memory cycle. If a 32-bit processor communicates with main memory via a 16-bit bus, two bus cycles will be required per transaction. (Section 1.8)

UMA   Uniform memory access architecture, a method of multiprocessor system construction where no main memory is physically located upon any CPU cards. The access time for any address is the same for all CPUs. This is the opposite of **NUMA** (nonuniform memory access). (Section 4.2.5)

Uncached address   Certain memory addresses which are never written into cache. Some types of memory-mapped I/O devices, for example, require memory which would not be allowed to be cached. (Section 2.2.7)

Unified cache   Some cache implementations (split caches) use separate caches for separate software spaces, typically instructions and data. A unified cache does not distinguish between different software spaces, but will map anything anywhere it fits. (Section 2.2.3)

Uniform memory architecture   See **UMA.** (Section 4.2.5)

Unowned   The status of a cache line in a multiprocessor system which is known to either be coherent with main memory or not to have been updated by the local CPU. (Section 4.2.5)

Update   See **line replacement.** (Section 2.1.3)

Upstream cache   See **predecessor cache.** (Section 2.2.10)

Utilization   Percent of available bus bandwidth actually employed by a processor. (Section 1.8)

Valid bit   A status bit stored in cache used to identify cache addresses with currently valid data. (Section 2.1.3)

Victim   The cache line which is to be evicted in a copy-back cache design. (Section 2.2.4)

Victim cache   A term for a tiny, fully associative cache which handles individual lines which the normal cache would ordinarily thrash. (Section 2.2.6) Some victim caches are called **pollution control** caches.

Victim write   An alternative to **eviction,** the name for the cycle in a copy-back cache design used to move dirty data back to main memory when a line is to be replaced. (Section 2.2.4)

Virtual cache   Most commonly a term used as an alternative to **logical cache** to describe a cache addressed by the CPU's virtual address bus. (Section 2.2.1) Used by Headland Technologies to describe a **byte-gathering write buffer.** (Section 2.2.6)

Way   The degree of associativity of a cache. An N-Way cache can store data from a main memory location into any of N cache locations. A direct-mapped cache is a one-Way cache, since any main memory location can only be mapped into the single cache location which has matching set bits. Also refers to the **bank** of cache used to implement one of the degrees of associativity of the cache (i.e., a two-Way cache would have two banks, which might be referred to as Way A and Way B). (Section 2.2.2)

Weak   See **write ordering.** (Section 2.2.6)

Wrapping fetch   During a line replacement of a multiword line, the desired word is the first one fetched from main memory; then the other words in the same line are fetched in some predetermined order, wrapping around until the first address is again encountered. Also called a **desired word first** fetch. See **line fill order.** (Section 2.2.6)

Write allocation   The policy of updating cache lines in copy-back caches, even though the write cycle resulted in a cache miss. This implies that the write cycle was first treated as a read miss, then the new entry was modified. (Section 2.2.5)

Write back   See **copy-back, eviction.** (Section 2.2.4)

Write broadcast   A multiprocessor coherency protocol similar to **write-first,** in which all caches which detect snoop write hits automatically update, rather than invalidate, their copies of the cached line. See **broadcasting.** (Section 4.2.5)

Write buffer   A small memory that temporarily holds data later to be written to main memory. (Section 2.2.6)

Write combining   Similar to byte gathering, but refers to the process of gathering words into a full-length cache line or burst sequence. (Section 2.2.6)

Write-first   Another name for **write-once** coherency protocols. (Section 4.2.5)

Write-for-Invalidate   Bus support cycle for certain kinds of multiple-processor cache coherency protocols. This write cycle both writes the data to main memory, and simultaneously invalidates all copies of the same line which may exist within other caches. (Section 4.2.5)

Write invalidate   Not to be confused with Write-*for*-Invalidate, a write invalidate cache is one which responds to write miss cycles by invalidating cache lines. An alternative approach is **write update.** (Section 2.2.4)

Write-once   This refers to any of a number of coherency protocols used in copy-back caches in multiprocessor systems. The processor must write to a main memory location once before it can maintain exclusive use of that location. During this write cycle, that address is invalidated in all other caches on the bus. Exclusive use is lost when another processor tries to read that location from main memory. MESI is a write-once protocol. Also called **write-first.** (Section 4.2.5)

Write ordering   The relationship between the cache-to-main-memory write cycles and the write cycles as commanded by the processor. In a system with a copy-back cache, the write ordering becomes **weak,** or poorly related to the sequence which originally emanated from the CPU. **Strong** write ordering implies that the cache-to-main-memory interaction closely replicates the way the write cycles emanated from the CPU. (Section 2.2.6)

Write policy   The method used by the cache controller to handle processor write cycles. Two common write policies are **write-through** and **copy-back.** (Section 2.2.4)

Write protect   A line status bit used by some caches to indicate that the cache line is not to be updated in the event of a write hit to a valid location. This is useful if the system has I/O ports mapped into the same addresses as ROM code. Cached copies of the ROM code will not be overwritten by commands to the I/O port. Some memory management units also keep track of write-protected memory addresses on a page-by-page basis. (Section 2.2.8)

Write side effects   Circumstances caused by overlaying read-only memory with a write-only register. This is sometimes done to save memory addresses when used in a memory-mapped I/O system. (Section 2.2.8)

Write snarf   See **snarf.** (Section 4.3.2)

Write strategy   The way the cache designer determines that the cache should handle CPU write cycles. Two strategies are in general use: **write-through,** of which there are buffered and unbuffered categories, and **copy-back.** Write strategies are implemented via **write policies.** (Section 2.2.4)

Write-through   A technique for writing data from the CPU simultaneously into cache and into main memory to assure coherency. This is one of the simplest methods of implementing a cache memory, but requires a slow main memory access cycle for every write cycle the CPU initiates, unless a write buffer is used. Write-through caches also consume far more main memory bus bandwidth than do copy-back caches. (Section 2.2.4)

Write update   During a write miss cycle, if the cache's response is to update the missed line, the cycle is called a write update. Two other alternatives are **write invalidate** and to ignore the write cycle on a miss. (Section 2.2.4)

Write-without-Invalidation   The counterpart to a Write-for-Invalidate cycle in certain multiprocessor buses, which supports write cycles which need not invalidate copies of the same memory address within other caches. (Section 4.2.5)

XI castout   The IBM term for a cross-interrogate castout, when a line of dirty data in a copy-back cache is copied back into main memory in response to an attempted read of the same data by another bus master. Also known as **indirect data intervention.** (Section 4.2.5)

INDEX

Printed and bound by CPI Group (UK) Ltd, Croydon, CR0 4YY

03/10/2024

01040414-0002